The Price of Middle East Oil:

An Essay in Political Economy

The Price of
Middle East Oil:

An Essay in Political Economy

Wayne A. Leeman

Professor of Economics, University of Missouri

Cornell University Press

ITHACA, NEW YORK

This work has been brought to
publication with the assistance of
a grant from the Ford Foundation.

Library of Congress Catalog Card Number: 62-8486

PRINTED IN THE UNITED STATES OF AMERICA
BY VAIL-BALLOU PRESS, INC.

To
My Mother and Father

Preface

THE price of oil in the Middle East has been a subject of much controversy. Europeans have said that it is too high because the American oil companies have kept it up to protect the value of their investments in the Western Hemisphere; a staff report of the Federal Trade Commission in the United States suggested that it is a cartel price rather than a competitive price; the ECA (Economic Co-operation Administration) in using Marshall Plan funds to buy oil for Europe argued that the companies were discriminating against Europeans; congressmen frequently aver that Middle East prices are "tied" to prices at the U.S. Gulf Coast and suggest that the cord be severed; most of the time the Arabs and Iranians contend that the price is too low, though the contrary charge that the price is too high (and the volume too small) also has been heard in the Middle East. This book is an attempt to analyze all of these controversies, to apply to them existing economic theory presented in a nontechnical way, and to strike a balance between the opposing views.

By the uninitiated, study of a price may be thought a barren activity, concerned with the petty higgling of the market and the baser passions of men, and limited to a narrow review of the current and immediate factors of supply and demand. But properly conceived such a study goes much beyond this. For a price mirrors the whole world: the dreams of men and their greed, geography, technology, past history, and the long shadow of future revolution. Certainly the price of Middle East oil reflects all these, and more. Hence, along with a strictly economic treatment of the subject, I have sought to deal more broadly with the matter in hand; I have tried to write, without sacrificing the rigor of serious economic analysis, a political economy of Middle East oil.

This book will, of course, be of most interest to oil men and to government people who deal with oil. I hope, however, that others will find it of value: economists interested in the application of economic theory to practical affairs, international businessmen in lines other than oil who must live in a world of rising nationalism, and all those who seek rational solutions for the perplexing problems of the Middle East. (The nonspecialist may want to skip, or skim over lightly, Chapter V, dealing with geographical price discrimination.)

The reader should be careful not to judge the book alone by the critical, skeptical tone of the early chapters. Human institutions are imperfect, and it is comparatively easy to find imperfections in the way men conduct their affairs. Toward the end of the book I attempt the more difficult task of proposing alternatives, and then my approach becomes rather conservative. In a multinational industry the problems of industrial organization are formidable, and it behooves the outsider to step lightly.

Any study of oil prices must begin at the point to which two noted thinkers have carried this subject. Dr. P. H. Frankel of London and Mr. Walter Levy of New York (together, of course, with a number of thoughtful men, mostly anonymous, in oil companies) have developed a comprehensive and elegant theoretical structure to explain the pattern of world oil prices.

Readers of my book will observe the great extent to which I have drawn upon the work of these two men.

I would like to thank Dr. Frankel for the personal help he has given me and to thank the many oil men, petroleum reporters, and government officials—persons of several nationalities—who patiently sought to teach me something of the realities of the oil industry. In addition, I owe a great deal to the people who have read part or all of my manuscript. Most of them are oil company executives and prefer to remain anonymous. Mr. Zuhayr Mikdashi of the American University of Beirut read Chapter IX, and his comments were most helpful. Despite so much careful and patient instruction by so many people, errors of fact and interpretation no doubt remain; for these I accept full responsibility.

I wish to thank the Research Council of the University of Missouri for grants which enabled me to travel to New York, London, and the various countries of the Middle East, and which covered part of the costs of typing; I owe thanks also to the Alumni Achievement Fund of the University for a typing grant. My study was pursued independently and not financed by any of the parties (companies or governments) interested in oil.

While sympathetic to the desires and goals of practically everyone involved in Middle East oil, I have sought to remain detached and to provide an objective analysis. There remains one problem: What are the duties of a scholar as citizen of a particular nation? May he write freely and frankly when his country and countrymen are involved? I have taken the position that the long-run interests of one's country will be served by the truth, that the duties of a scholar, therefore, are carefully and conscientiously to explore his subject and then to speak the truth as he sees it.

WAYNE A. LEEMAN

Columbia, Missouri
July 1961

ix

Contents

xi

xiii

Text Tables

xv

Figures

xvi

The Price of Middle East Oil:

An Essay in Political Economy

I

Introduction

THE discovery in the Middle East of a vast reserve of oil is one of the great ironies of history. Far from the large and concentrated oil markets of the world, located near one of the vital strategic points of the Eastern Hemisphere—the land route to Africa and the water route to Asia—in a region where originated three of the important religions of man, Judaism, Christianity, and Islam, at a time of rising nationalism in the area, the oil found here seems like a deliberate attempt on the part of the gods to confound the thoughts of men with all the emotions of which they are capable.

1. The Importance of Middle East Oil

Although at the end of 1958 the Middle East had about 70 percent of the proved crude oil reserves of the non-Communist world, it produced during 1958 only about 27 percent of the non-Communist world crude oil production.[1] These figures suggest that Middle East oil is likely to become increasingly important in the years to come. The United States is a long way

[1] *World Oil*, August 15, 1959, p. 109.

from the Middle East and obtains only about 3 percent of its supplies from this area,[2] but it is expected to draw more heavily on distant supplies as time passes. The interest of the United States in Middle East oil is mostly indirect: its allies in Europe get the largest part of their oil from the Middle East. Europe is expected to become increasingly dependent on petroleum as a source of energy for the next decade or so. In 1959 the Energy Advisory Commission of the Organization for European Economic Co-operation forecast that the contribution of oil to the total energy supply of the OEEC countries would increase from 25 percent in 1958 to something like 37 percent in 1975.[3] Most of the oil consumed in Europe will be imported, much of it from the Middle East. With the rise of the Sahara as an oil-producing area, Europe probably will not continue to get 86 percent of its crude oil from the Middle East, as it did in 1958.[4] But almost certainly it will continue to obtain a relatively high proportion of its oil from this part of the world. Oil flowing from the Middle East, while no longer the jugular vein of Europe, will remain a large and important artery of the European economic body.

Middle East oil is, of course, tremendously important to the Arabs and the Iranians. Oil revenues constitute about 45 percent of total government receipts in Iran, about 60 percent in Iraq, 83 percent in Saudi Arabia, and 98 percent in Kuwait.[5] In addition, Arabs and Iranians receive large sums in wages

[2] Calculated from data in *Petroleum Press Service*, April, 1959, p. 127; *World Oil*, August 15, 1959, p. 107; Petroleum Industry Research Foundation, *United States Oil Imports: A Case Study in International Trade* (New York, 1958), p. 95.

[3] *Petroleum Press Service*, February, 1960, pp. 43–47; *Petroleum Week*, February 5, 1960, pp. 37–38.

[4] *Petroleum Press Service*, October, 1959, p. 374.

[5] The figures for Iran and Iraq are from the Statistical Office of the United Nations, *Statistical Yearbook* (New York, 1958), pp. 485, 486; the figures for Saudi Arabia and Kuwait are from the Economics Division, Shell International Petroleum Company, Ltd., *The Economic Impact of Oil Operations in Producing Countries*, August, 1959, p. 22.

2

from the oil industry and sell materials and merchandise to it. Middle East oil, then, is important to both Europe and the Middle East. The mutual interest which Europeans, Arabs, and Iranians have in a continuous flow of Middle East oil to market makes agreement possible, though sufficient conflicts in interest remain to make the road to agreement a stony one.

2. The Meaning of Posted Prices

Oil companies in the Middle East "post," or publish, prices for both crude oil and oil products. Of what significance are these posted prices? Who pays them? What proportion of Middle East oil is traded at prices which are published?

We know that oil is often sold at a discount off the posted price. *Petroleum Week* reports discounts on Middle East oil frequently; on oil which was posted at $1.80 to $2.00 per barrel, it reported on various dates between October, 1956, and February, 1960, cash discounts ranging from 10 to 35 cents. And it told of numerous nonprice devices which effectively lower the terms of sale: unusually favorable tanker rates, special refinery processing deals, easy credit terms, and so forth. Laurent Wolters, managing director of Petrofina, a large, nonaffiliated Belgian firm, has asserted that "no independent would dream of contracting for crude at the posted price." [6] One sometimes hears the statement that "only fools and affiliates pay posted prices." And apart from an occasional independent which purchases a single cargo at the posted price, it is apparently only affiliates which pay these prices.

But discounts in themselves do not deprive published prices of significance. Discounts for quantity or for long-term commitments on the part of the buyer are common and are often justified; large orders may be handled at a lower cost and the risks carried by a supplier are reduced when he sells under long-term contracts. Even when discounts are not related to

[6] Quoted in Gilbert Burck, "World Oil: The Game Gets Rough," *Fortune*, May, 1958, p. 125.

3

quantity purchases or long-term commitments, they may be quite defensible. For discounted prices may reflect short-run, temporary forces in the market place, whereas published prices reflect conditions of long-run supply and demand. Sellers in dealing with short-run situations prefer to grant temporary discounts rather than lower posted prices; they find it easier to withdraw discounts when they are no longer justified. And both sellers and buyers can plan more effectively when they have in relatively stable posted prices an estimate of fundamental, long-run conditions of supply and demand.

Still there is reason to doubt the significance of posted prices in Middle East oil. It is true that affiliates pay these prices and that, indeed, affiliates purchase about 90 percent of the oil produced in the Middle East.[7] It is doubtful, however, that posted prices in the Middle East actually reflect fundamental market forces in view of the fact that they are not established by arm's length bargaining in the open market; affiliated buyers and sellers are not free to take their trade elsewhere, to go to competitors, if they are unhappy about the price. Hence one can speak of an arbitrary element in Middle East postings; when a seller and a buyer must trade with one another, the market is classed as bilateral monopoly and the price is indeterminate. In fact we have evidence which suggests that posted prices for crude oil have been maintained unrealistically high, so high that in the second half of the fifties there has been little or no profit in the transportation, refining, and marketing of Middle East oil.[8] It seems unlikely that postings as high as these would have been paid by refiners who were free to change suppliers.

One ends up doubting that posted prices of Middle East oil

[7] A more exact percentage figure than this would require a precise definition of "affiliate" and a careful study; no study of this sort has been published, but the oil trade generally agrees that 90 percent is about right. See *Petroleum Week*, October 18, 1957, p. 21; *Petroleum Press Service*, July, 1958, p. 246.

[8] We discuss the evidence and the reasons for this situation in Chapter III, Section 3.

are very meaningful, since they are established without arm's length bargaining, hence are noncompetitive and indeterminate, and since they leave for affiliates exceedingly small profits in transportation, refining, and marketing. Nevertheless, posted prices, in all probability, can be used to show the large postwar decline of Middle East prices relative to prices at the U.S. Gulf Coast. In Chapter IV we shall use them in this way in the belief that Middle East discounts generally have been as great or greater than discounts at the U.S. Gulf Coast.

II

Structure of the Market
in Middle East Oil

IN attempting to decide whether or not the price of oil in the Middle East is satisfactory, we will find it our most promising line of inquiry to examine such matters as the number of firms in the market, their size and their relationships to one another, the ease or difficulty of entry by other firms into the area, and the availability of substitute products. The problem of norms immediately arises: What constitutes a normal or ideal market structure against which we can measure the institutions of the real world?

1. Competition or Monopoly: Quest for a Norm

One norm often employed by economists is the model of perfect competition: a market containing a large number of relatively small sellers, so many and so small that no one of them believes he can influence the price by varying the quantity which he offers for sale. All of the firms sell the same standardized product, and entry into the market is perfectly free. Economists demonstrate that these circumstances will result in an optimum pattern of output in the economy, an optimum scale of plant and equipment with utilization at an optimum rate, a selection of the most economical operations, and prices which are flexible as well as just high enough, over the long run, to cover costs, including in costs necessary profits.

It is doubtful that truly *perfect* competition, unlimited competition in the short as well as the long run, is desirable. Perfectly free entry would produce a great deal of insecurity; accumulated wealth, through a sudden obsolescence of acquired skills or fixed plant and equipment, could become valueless overnight. There is much to be said in support of short-run restraints on entry as a means of providing a certain measure of stability in a world quite possibly otherwise one of overwhelming change. Indeed, Schumpeter has pointed out that some check on entry is necessary if change is to occur at all. A firm would not undertake the risks of entering a new field if it knew that imitators could rush in immediately and eliminate the gains of innovation.

Largest-scale plans could in many cases not materialize at all if it were not known from the outset that competition will be discouraged by heavy capital requirements or lack of experience, or that means are available to discourage or checkmate it so as to gain the time and space for further developments. . . .

Perfectly free entry into a *new* field may make it impossible to enter at all.[1]

In asserting that some restrictions on entry will hasten economic change, Schumpeter states that "there is no more of a paradox in this than there is in saying that motorcars are traveling faster than they otherwise would *because* they are provided with brakes." [2] Society recognizes in its patent laws that restraints on entry may stimulate progress.

However, to depart from the model of perfect competition

[1] Joseph A. Schumpeter, *Capitalism, Socialism, and Democracy*, 3d ed. (New York: Harper and Brothers, 1950), pp. 89, 104.
[2] *Ibid.*, p. 88.

7

in the interest of orderly advance entails dangers. Stability with its attendant security may produce lethargy and sloth, and short-run restraints on entry may turn into long-run monopoly.

In our search for a normal or ideal market structure we need to look at some situations which are imperfectly competitive. But pure monopoly is too wide a departure from the ideal to be useful here. So we turn to oligopoly: market of a few sellers, each supplying a large part of total output, each believing that it is large enough to influence price by an increase or decrease in the amount of goods it offers for sale. An oligopoly price generally is a rigid or "sticky" price. An oligopolist hesitates to raise price because he will lose business if his rivals do not follow, and he hesitates to reduce price because his rivals probably will match the cut, with the result that he and the others end up selling only a small additional volume at the lower price. More-over, since any price reduction is sure to hurt other firms when there are only a few sellers, a company which cuts prices is running the risk that its competitors will retaliate and that it will have set off a chain reaction of serious price rivalry. The tendency is to remain quiet, to settle for existing prices, to initiate changes only when prices clearly are out of line with conditions of long-run supply and demand. Furthermore, it is likely that the stable, rigid prices of oligopoly will be higher than prices under conditions of competition, that output will be lower, and that ex-cess profits, oligopoly profits, will be secured. The several oligop-olists will tend to exploit the market position in which they find themselves, tacitly following a leader toward relatively high prices and "comfortable" profit margins or otherwise obtaining concurrence in policies of restraint on output and avoidance of price competition.

But oligopolists vary considerably in the success with which they maintain a (shared) "monopoly" position and maximize aggregate profits. The threat of entry by outsiders or even by firms not yet in existence, the competition of substitutes, Schumpeter's "perennial gale of creative destruction" (innova-

8

tion), or the difficulty of acting in concert may check severely the inclination or the ability of firms in an oligopoly to restrict output and raise price. On the other hand, a small group of firms may be well protected against the incursions of new rivals and thoroughly capable of acting as a group to maximize aggregate profits.

To be sure, there is one set of circumstances in which oligopolists definitely will be more competitive than is generally recognized, and that is in their bidding on contracts for the sale of large quantities of their product. The usual hesitation about cutting price, the danger that rivals will match the cut, and the fear that all will end up selling the same volume at a lower price probably will not prevail. A low bidder is certain to obtain a large volume of business, and there will be no opportunity for competitors, seeking to defend their positions, to meet the price reduction. Hence even a very few sellers are likely to compete vigorously for contracts to supply large volumes of a product. Of course the possibility of a conspiracy exists: the several sellers may agree to take turns at being low bidder, thereby dividing up the business over a period of time while eliminating serious competition. But a successful conspiracy is more difficult to maintain than most people realize. The more persons knowing a secret and the longer the period of time over which it is to be kept, the smaller the chances of effective concealment. An oil company executive has pointed in conversation to an interesting analogy in the common business problem of internal accounting control. In order to prevent internal theft of corporate funds, public accountants seek to have at least two people know of every transaction, the principle being that the wider the knowledge of a transaction, the more difficult it is to obscure it. A conspiracy in restraint of trade, an attempt to pattern bids and divide up contract business over a period of time, would be exceedingly difficult to conceal if, as is likely, a number of people knew about it.

Where there exists a strongly entrenched oligopoly in which

stability has become rigidity, the resulting state of affairs will be a most unsatisfactory one, with outputs tending to be low and prices high and with excess, oligopolistic, profits being secured. On the other hand, perfect competition is not, for the short run, an ideal market structure: with a complete absence of restraint on entry, the risks of innovation could be so heavy as to inhibit progress, or insecurity might become overwhelmingly great as values in acquired skills and invested capital were subject to sudden destruction. The market structure representing a norm or ideal acceptable to most people (at least to most people in the West) would serve the goal of orderly advance, though some would value order more highly while others would place a greater value on advance. What we want, apparently, are islands of stability thrown up temporarily by a river relentlessly progressive: short-run restraint on entry, long-run freedom to enter; short-run stability in price, long-run flexibility.

Imperfect competition, then, has its advantages in the short run, but for the long run the competitive model, with its numerous sellers, approaches the ideal.

2. Sellers in the Middle East

About twenty firms have crude oil or the refined products of crude oil for sale in the Persian Gulf, and seven of these firms also sell crude oil on the Eastern Mediterranean at the terminals of the cross-desert pipelines. But these observations do not provide a proper indication of the degree of competition in Middle East oil. Many of the companies in the Persian Gulf have only a small share in the production of the area, a share not large enough to exert a noticeable influence on price. And the large companies in the Middle East are engaged in a number of interlocking joint ventures which almost certainly limit, in some degree at least, their inclination or ability to act independently in the market place.

The principal firms with production in the Middle East are shown in Table I, along with their ownerships. The operating companies rarely sell oil in the open market, the main exception being the American Independent Oil Company ("Aminoil"). Most of the oil produced and refined in the Middle East is turned over to the parent companies or, rather, to affiliates under their

TABLE I

MIDDLE EAST OIL: STATES, COMPANIES, AND OWNERSHIPS
(Excluding Egypt, Israel, and Turkey, countries which have oil only in relatively small quantities, and excluding companies which have not found oil)

State	Kuwait	
Operating company	Kuwait Oil Company	
Ownership	British Petroleum Company ("BP") (in which the British government has a controlling interest)	50%
	Gulf Oil Corporation *	50%

State	Saudi Arabia	
Operating company	Arabian American Oil Company ("Aramco") *	
Ownership	Standard Oil Company (New Jersey) *	30%
	Standard Oil Company of California *	30%
	Texaco Inc.*	30%
	Socony Mobil Oil Company *	10%

State	Iraq	
Operating company	Iraq Petroleum Company and associated companies ("IPC")	
Ownership	British Petroleum	23.75%
	Royal Dutch–Shell (shareholders 60% Dutch, 40% British)	23.75%
	Compagnie Française des Pétroles (in which the French government has 40% of the voting rights)	23.75%
	Near East Development Corporation * (50% Jersey Standard * and 50% Socony *)	23.75%
	Gulbenkian Foundation	5 %

* Asterisks indicate American companies.

11

TABLE I (continued)

State	Iran	
Operating companies	Iranian Oil Exploration and Producing Company Iranian Oil Refining Company	
Ownership	Iranian Oil Participants, Ltd.— the "Consortium" (installations leased from National Iranian Oil Company and operated on its behalf)	
	British Petroleum	40%
	Royal Dutch–Shell	14%
	Compagnie Française	6%
	Jersey Standard *	7%
	Socony Mobil *	7%
	Standard of California *	7%
	Texaco *	7%
	Gulf Oil *	7%
	Iricon Agency, Ltd. (9 U.S. companies)	5%
State	Qatar	
Operating company	Qatar Petroleum Company	
Ownership	Same as IPC	
State	Bahrein	
Operating company	Bahrein Petroleum Company *	
Ownership	Standard of California *	50%
	Texaco *	50%
State	Neutral Zone (between Kuwait and Saudi Arabia)	
Operating companies	American Independent Oil Company ("Aminoil") * Getty Oil Company * Arabian Oil Company	
Ownership	Aminoil: 10 U.S. companies Getty Oil: Mr. Getty and other U.S. interests Arabian Oil: about 60 Japanese companies	

* Asterisks indicate American companies.

control. Crude oil production, reserves, and refinery capacity in the different Middle Eastern states are shown in Table II.

TABLE II

MIDDLE EAST OIL: PRODUCTION, RESERVES, REFINERY CAPACITY
(Excluding small refineries which supply mostly domestic markets)

State	Crude oil production, 1959 (avg. bbls./day)	Proved crude oil reserves, end of 1958 (thousand barrels)	Refining capacity, 1958 (bbls./day)
Kuwait	1,390,000	60,000,000	170,000
Saudi Arabia	1,095,399	45,000,000	189,000
Iraq	837,000	21,800,000	48,000
Iran	925,000	32,000,000	412,000
Qatar	171,590	1,650,000	
Bahrein	45,133	170,000	187,000
Neutral Zone (between Kuwait and Saudi Arabia)	113,819	2,500,000	80,000
Aden			120,000
Middle East totals	4,587,108	163,120,000	
World totals	19,456,173	232,076,075 (non-Communist countries)	

Sources: Production: World Oil, February 15, 1960, p. 95. Reserves: ibid., August 15, 1959, p. 109. Refining capacity: ibid., August 15, 1959, pp. 184, 198; Aramco, Middle East Petroleum Data (n.p., 1957), pp. 11–12.

Many of the parent companies, as we noted, own only a small share in the output of the Middle East and are of little significance in the establishment of Middle East prices. Although each of the nine companies in the Iricon Agency of the Iranian Consortium posts prices and presumably has oil to sell, the entire Iricon share of Iranian production in 1959 probably amounted to about 1 percent of Middle East crude output. In Iraq the oil

13

of Participations and Explorations Corporation (the Gulbenkian share) is sold to the other partners in the Iraq Petroleum Company at a mutually agreed price, an arrangement which eliminates this oil as an independent factor in the market. Getty Oil Company and Aminoil, both in the Neutral Zone, produced in 1959 only 113,819 barrels a day or 2.5 percent of Middle East crude oil. After the numerous small interests in Middle East oil are set aside, relatively few sellers remain in the picture. In the Persian Gulf the suppliers of crude oil and products are the following:

> Standard Oil Company (New Jersey)
> Socony Mobil Oil Company
> Texaco Inc.
> Standard Oil Company of California
> Gulf Oil Corporation
> British Petroleum Company
> Royal Dutch–Shell
> Compagnie Française des Pétroles

Seven of these firms, all but Gulf Oil Corporation, also sell crude oil on the eastern Mediterranean. Excluding Compagnie Française des Pétroles, the listed firms are known as the "international majors."

Some of the governments in the Middle East are entitled, under agreements, to receive "royalty oil" as payments in kind, and this is oil which they might market themselves,[3] but they seldom avail themselves of the opportunity to do so and are not likely to change their policies soon. The price of Middle East oil is not appreciably influenced by royalty oil independently marketed.

We find, then, eight large companies with Middle East oil for sale (mostly through affiliates), all of them selling crude

[3] See pages 190–194 for a more detailed description and analysis of these arrangements.

oil and products f.o.b. Persian Gulf and seven of them selling crude f.o.b. eastern Mediterranean. Together these firms controlled about 96 percent of Middle East production in 1959.[4]

This is oligopoly, market of a few sellers. But the picture is still far from complete. Later we shall discuss factors which widen the market, rendering it less oligopolistic, or which might do so in the future: the potentially larger role of the "independent," nonaffiliated companies in the Middle East; the possibility of a more active participation by Arab and Iranian governments in the marketing of Middle East oil; and the competition, actual or potential, of alternative sources of power and heat. Now, however, we want to look at factors which tend to narrow the market and strengthen its oligopolistic character, factors which make the eight large sellers of Middle East oil less independent of one another. I am referring, of course, to the various joint operations, many of which interlock. We will consider joint production first, then in due course joint marketing, joint refining, and the joint use of pipelines and terminals.

The pattern of joint production in the Middle East can best be seen in Table I on page 11. Each of the large producing companies—Arabian American Oil Company, Iraq Petroleum Company, Kuwait Oil Company, and the operating companies of the Consortium—is owned by two or more major firms, and all of the majors have a share in more than one of these producing operations. But before discussing the actual lifting arrangements in each of the concessions (the arrangements for producing oil on behalf of the various owners), we will find it useful to consider the fundamental economics of joint production.

3. Joint Production in Theory and Practice

The oil companies frequently contend that the large scale and great risks of operation in the Middle East require more than

[4] Calculated from data provided in *World Oil*, February 15, 1960, p. 95.

one firm, often require several firms, to join in partnership in the production of oil. At the same time they allege that such joint operations in no way act to check competition in the marketing of the oil produced. It seems likely, however, that the degree of competition in jointly produced oil is frequently less than it would be were each of the companies producing separately.

In the first place, a jointly held concession not infrequently will be developed more slowly, and as a consequence its owners will have less oil to push into the market. The less dynamic owners will tend to hold development back; they will be reluctant to invest in capacity which they may not use, in capacity, indeed, which is more likely to be used by the other parent companies. At the same time, of course, the less aggressive sellers will not be inclined to allow the others to go off without them, invest more than their ownership shares, and acquire larger claims on the oil underground. Investment in a joint operation will be in proportion to ownership. A dynamic firm which is producing on its own will be more often in a position to invest in a rapid development of its oil and, competitively, to thrust its way into new markets.

To be sure, where a concession encompasses but one oil field, the production of individual firms probably will be controlled by the state in the interest of conservation, and the concession probably will be developed no more rapidly with individual production than under joint operations. But where a concession includes a number of fields which might be produced separately, a joint operation is likely to develop the area more slowly than separate and independent enterprises. A crowd in oil, like crowds elsewhere, tends to move slowly.

Moreover, the degree of competition in jointly produced oil may be reduced by concerted action: the common costs of joint operations may lead oligopolists to act in concert on price, explicitly or tacitly, and (the possibility cannot be ruled out) the

16

necessarily frequent consultation with each other may prove to be the means whereby they concert their responses.

It might be argued that the "crowd" in joint activities will move as slowly in contracting output as they move in expanding it, that over the long run production in jointly operated concessions will be as large, and the degree of competition as great, as if the properties were developed by separate firms. But it seems probable that a group in control of a joint enterprise will more readily contract than expand output. Those inclined to move slowly will be prodded more effectively by the pain of losses than by the hope of gain. Over a period of time, then, one would expect jointly operated concessions to develop more slowly than those operated by individual firms.

It is true that during the late fifties, in the large concessions of the Middle East, certain factors tipped the balance toward the owners who wanted a rapid expansion in capacity. The Suez interruption of supply along with memories of Iranian efforts to nationalize its oil made a margin of excess productive capacity in each of the major concessions seem very attractive. Possibly the governments of consuming countries put pressure on the international oil companies to establish excess capacity in each concession as protection against interrupted supplies elsewhere. At the same time, most of the governments in producing countries have wanted a rapid development of their oil. (Some excess capacity simply reflects the fact that certain investment programs are indivisible. "We cannot build a deepwater pier one pile at a time," say oil men.)

Although special factors in the late fifties tended to promote expansion, we must recognize that these factors might have led to a still more rapid expansion had the concessions been controlled by individual companies; there would have been no chance for conservative firms to slow up the others. Moreover, these special expansionary factors may lose their force as time passes. Once excess capacity is created, there is a strong inclination to produce with it; the consequent price declines may make less attractive the notion of securing oil supplies through the establishment of excess capacity in each of the concessions. Any preferences for excess capacity expressed by governments in consuming countries are more likely to be ignored, and the governments of producing countries, hurt by price reductions, will not push so hard for expansion.

Over the long run it is probable that the degree of competition in jointly produced oil will be lower than if the oil could be produced by separate companies. The rate of expansion will be slower, while common costs will provide oligopolists with a basis for possible concerted action on prices, tacit or explicit, and frequent consultation will provide them with the means.

We shall find it useful to examine the actual arrangements for development and production in various Middle East concessions. Three of the four principal concessions will be considered in some detail, those in Iraq, Saudi Arabia, and Kuwait. (The agreement between the companies in the Iranian Consortium, which is the group controlling operations in the fourth of the major producing areas in the Middle East, has never been published.)

In IRAQ the concession is held by the Iraq Petroleum Company (strictly speaking by IPC and certain associated companies). IPC in turn is owned by five firms; four of these— British Petroleum, Royal Dutch–Shell, Compagnie Française des Pétroles, and the Near East Development Corporation— each own a share amounting to 23.75 percent, and the fifth one, Participations and Explorations Corporation (the Gulbenkian Foundation), owns the 5 percent interest which completes the total. Near East Development is owned in equal shares by Jersey Standard and Socony Mobil. A parent firm purchases at cost its ownership share of the oil produced (actually at cost plus one shilling), and it buys the oil it acquires above its ownership share at a so-called "halfway price," a price midway between cost and market value. Market value here is the posted

18

price less certain small discounts, such as a marketing allowance of 1 percent. In reality what occurs is that an overlifting firm, that is, one which obtains more than its ownership share, purchases the excess from an underlifting company at the halfway price, and of course the underlifting firm acquires this oil at cost. The underlifter and the overlifter, then, each receive half the profits on oil sold by the one to the other.[5] Half of the profits reward the firm lifting the extra oil, while the other half go to the firm which in effect owns the oil.

Until the late fifties IPC was developed slowly. One check on development may have been the "five-sevenths rule." In establishing a production plan, each owner in IPC nominates its requirements independently, and the nominations are then added up to obtain an IPC program for a particular period of time. Once the production program is established, a program of investment is set up to enable IPC to meet it, and the parent companies are expected to invest the necessary capital in proportion to their ownership shares. But when the production program is put together, the highest nomination is not allowed to exceed five-sevenths of the sum of the two lowest nominations. For example, if the two low firms propose to lift six and eight respectively, the high firm cannot expect to lift more than ten. Now it must be admitted that although the five-sevenths rule could slow up a dynamic firm it is not exceedingly restrictive. But there is another rule which probably has done more to check the development of the Iraq concession. This rule obliges the owners to nominate their oil requirements for five-year periods, with the nominations being submitted five years before the beginning of the period.[6] The program for the years 1962–1967 had to be prepared in 1957. Since the owners commit themselves,

[5] Staff Report to the Federal Trade Commission, *The International Petroleum Cartel* (Washington, D.C., August 22, 1952), p. 106. The report was submitted to the Subcommittee on Monopoly of the Select Committee on Small Business, U.S. Senate. Henceforth it will be cited as the "FTC Report."

[6] *Ibid.*

under these arrangements, to lift oil a long time in advance, they have tended to nominate conservatively. This tendency toward conservative nominations in IPC is reinforced by the greater flexibility of two of the other Middle East concessions in their provisions for development and production, the result being that companies with holdings in these concessions tend to request smaller amounts from IPC, with the intention of obtaining extra quantities, if they are needed later, from one of the other concessions. An owner may also hesitate to lift large quantities simply because of the moral obliquity attached to being greedy; a firm may feel that the generous provisions for lifting were put into the agreement in order to obtain flexibility and that immoderate lifting would constitute an abuse of these provisions.[7]

It seems probable that competition in Iraq oil has been less intense than if the owners of IPC had been able to produce separately and operate independently. The necessity of nominating for five or ten years in advance, along with the five-sevenths rule, probably has checked the inclinations of dynamic firms to seek enlarged output and greater markets. And the costs common to all the owners of concession oil may have provided a basis for, tacit or explicit, concerted action on price.

Along with the other big producing companies in the Middle East, IPC in the late fifties entered into a large program of expansion: productive capacity was to reach 1,140,000 barrels per day by the end of 1961, and then perhaps it would be pushed on up to 1,400,000 barrels daily.[8] (Iraq production in 1959 averaged 837,000 barrels a day.) Considerable competition in Iraq oil may occur for a time.

[7] Until the oil of the Sahara appeared on the horizon, Compagnie Française apparently nominated large quantities from IPC; it lacked substantial alternative sources of oil (Michel Laudrain, *Le Prix du pétrole brut: Structures d'un marché* [Paris: Éditions Génin, n.d.], p. 230). But it is extremely doubtful that Compagnie Française represents a competitive force in Middle East oil. Most of its oil is carried to France and sold there in a market which is tightly controlled by the government, largely through import quotas.

[8] *Petroleum Week*, March 27, 1959, p. 46.

In SAUDI ARABIA the large producing company is the Arabian American Oil Company. "Aramco" is owned by four firms; each of three of them—Jersey Standard, Standard of California, and Texaco—holds 30 percent of the total, while the remaining 10 percent is held by Socony Mobil. The present lifting arrangements in Aramco have not (or had not at the time of writing) been published. My description of these arrangements is based on information acquired in interviews with executives of the oil companies involved. The information that I received is undoubtedly accurate.

Compared with other concessions in the Middle East, Aramco is organized in an unusual way. Unlike the other major producing companies in the area, it is operated for a profit. The four owners buy their oil from Aramco not at cost but at posted prices, or if they resell the oil to a nonaffiliated customer at a discount, they buy at their discounted resale price. The owners then receive profits on production in the form of dividends from Aramco. These profits are distributed as follows: A notional profit figure is calculated—equal to posted price less cost, the difference multiplied by Aramco volume. Fifty percent of these notional profits are distributed in accordance with ownership—30 : 30 : 30 : 10. The profits remaining, that is the remainder of actual profits, are distributed in accordance with the contributions of each of the owners to the gross receipts of Aramco—with contribution measured, approximately, by posted price less actual discounts granted by an owner on its sales, times the quantity an owner lifts. Since the distribution in proportion to ownership is based on posted price whereas the distribution in proportion to contribution is based on realization prices, which are often below postings, the ownership distribution frequently exceeds 50 percent of the total of actual profits and the contribution distribution often is less than half of the total. It is of interest to note that when all the owners are posting the same price and none is selling at a discount the Aramco distribution is the same as would occur under an IPC-type system, in which the parent companies buy their ownership shares at cost and buy overlifted quantities at a halfway price.

In the later fifties the owners of Aramco agreed to provide it regularly with a capital budget which would enable it to maintain a margin of excess productive capacity, a margin in any one year of 250,000 to 300,000 barrels a day above the actual offlift of the previous year. (Aramco crude oil production in 1959 averaged 1,095,399 barrels a day.) When stating their anticipated needs of Aramco crude, the parent companies almost always nominate for their entire share of the announced capacity of Aramco, since no penalty is attached to not lifting oil which has been nominated.

It is clear that the regular provision of excess capacity in Aramco provides a dynamic owner with oil which it can use in expanding its markets; it is likely to lead to a good deal of competition in Saudi Arabian oil. Moreover, a system of "entitlement" gives an aggressive marketer assurance of future supplies. If one owner lifts less than its ownership share of capacity, the others can lift more than their shares; the overlifters can lift all the oil the underlifters do not take, up to the limit of Aramco's capacity. Once an owner lifts above its share, it is *entitled* to lift the higher percentage of capacity the next year. And this entitlement percentage continues in subsequent years as long as the larger share of capacity is lifted without interruption. Suppose that Aramco has an announced capacity of 100 and suppose that the nominations of the four owners along with the actual quantities lifted are as shown in columns two and three of the table below; then the entitlement for the following year will be as indicated in the fourth column of the table.

Owner	Nominations	Actual offtake	Entitlement for next year
A	30	35	35%
B	30	25	25%
C	30	30	30%
D	10	10	10%
	100	100	100%

If capacity the next year is 130, then A is entitled to lift 35 percent of 130, or 45.5.

Entitlement applies to all grades of crude oil. Since an owner is in a better competitive position if it has a variety of crudes available for its customers, it tries to obtain and protect a position on each grade of crude that Aramco has for sale. Early in 1960 when Aramco made crude oil from a new field available along with additional quantities of crude oil from an old field, it witnessed a mad scramble for position on each of these two crudes.

The system of entitlement clearly increases the degree of competition in Saudi Arabian oil. A dynamic firm enlarges present profits and may increase its percentage claim on future large supplies. It may obtain a growing share, and conceivably end up with a very large percentage share, of an increasing capacity. At the same time a conservative firm may be forced to compete in order to prevent its share of Aramco oil from shrinking. Of course the owners of Aramco will not forget that they are oligopolists and that price cuts will be matched by rivals, and they may remember their common costs (which might be used as a basis for tacit or explicit concerted action on price), but, even so, behavior in Aramco will be more competitive than our earlier analysis of joint production led us to expect. As a consequence, one wonders how long so large an excess capacity will be established in Aramco and how long such generous entitlements will be permitted. Perhaps the most dynamic firms will take it easy, perhaps they will act less competitively, in order to keep the less dynamic owners from insisting that excess capacity be reduced and that the system of entitlements be eliminated.

In KUWAIT the concession is held in equal shares by "BP (Kuwait) Company" and "Gulf Kuwait Company," fully owned subsidiaries of British Petroleum Company ("BP") and Gulf Oil Corporation respectively. On behalf of British Petroleum and Gulf Oil the concession is operated by the Kuwait Oil Company. According to their agreement, Gulf and BP may each require

Kuwait Oil Company "to produce such quantity of crude oil as may be decided by the party making the request," and the lifting company acquires all oil at cost (actually at cost plus one shilling).[9] The only limit on lifting is occasioned by the unavailability of physical facilities, and in practice both owners have proved willing to invest in a truly rapid development of Kuwait oil.

With each company free to lift virtually unlimited quantities of oil at cost, it is clear that these arrangements could be highly competitive. Each parent firm, being inclined to continue lifting as long as its marginal revenue exceeds its marginal cost, would have almost as much incentive to compete with the other parent in the sale of Kuwait oil as it would have to compete with any supplier in the Middle East. How does it happen that BP and Gulf have agreed on so much freedom in lifting Kuwait oil, that both of them indeed, although potential underlifters, have been prepared to invest in part simply for the benefit of the other, the overlifter? Oil company executives have explained to the writer that these arrangements are possible, and rational, because oil in Kuwait, for all practical purposes, is unlimited. The underlifter need not worry about the quantity taken by the overlifter, since the concession (the scheduled year of termination of which is 2026) will have expired long before the oil is depleted, or the oil will have been expropriated or nationalized, or alternative sources of power and heat will have been developed. In the language of economic analysis, the abundant oil of Kuwait is to its two owners a "free good," and neither values it in the ground. Moreover, an underlifter receives interest on that part of its invested capital which in effect is being used by an overlifter, and it recovers this capital as depreciation occurs; for the cost paid by a lifting firm includes depreciation, amortization, and interest on capital at agreed rates [10] (and extra charges of this sort when paid by an overlifting firm increase the assets of

9 FTC Report, p. 133.   10 Ibid., p. 133n.

Kuwait Oil Company, giving the underlifter an appropriate increase in its equity).

The explanation offered by oil company officials of the provisions for unlimited lifting of Kuwait oil at cost does, however, leave some questions unanswered. The agreement embodying these provisions was concluded in 1933, whereas oil was not discovered until 1938. Gulf Oil and British Petroleum could not have known that oil would be found in so large a quantity that its value to them in the ground would be virtually nil; hence the oil men's explanation of unlimited lifting at cost in the Kuwait agreement can be held at most to explain the continuation of these arrangements when the agreement was renegotiated in 1951. It seems a more likely explanation of the original agreement that each company at the outset was thoroughly confident of its ability to obtain markets for half of any oil which it might discover. Does this mean that the contracting parties were prepared to compete with each other for markets, whatever magnitude of oil would be found, that each of them was prepared to lose customers to the other, and that each was ready to lose the entire profit on the oil involved? For at least one of the two firms, the answer to these questions was negative, as is evidenced by provisions restricting competition which were written into the original (1933) agreement.

In that agreement the parties assured one another that neither would use Kuwait oil to "upset or injure" the other's "trade or marketing position directly or indirectly at any time or place." And they undertook "to confer from time to time as either party may desire and mutually settle . . . any question that may arise between them regarding the marketing of Kuwait oil and products therefrom." [11] Gulf Oil declared in 1946, in an application to the Securities and Exchange Commission, that these restrictive marketing provisions were repugnant to it, and it stated that efforts had been made through the British government (which

[11] *Ibid.*, p. 131.

25

has a controlling interest in BP) to have them modified or re-moved. In 1951 Gulf Oil and BP canceled the 1933 agreement and negotiated a new one which apparently is without restrictions on marketing.[12]

With some justification, however, the authors of the FTC Report contend that restrictions on competition between Gulf and BP are maintained through another agreement, one which was concluded not between these two companies but between Gulf and another firm. This is the Gulf-Shell contract of 1947 (discussed in detail in Chapter VI, Section 5), under which Gulf agreed to sell huge quantities of Kuwait crude oil over a period of years to Shell Petroleum Company, Ltd. Originally, deliveries were to be made through 1956, but later the agreement was extended indefinitely beyond that year. Rather than sell the crude outright to Shell at a stated price, Gulf agreed to share equally with Shell the total profits on production, transportation, refining, and marketing. In effect, Gulf and Shell in this agreement became partners in the production and distribution of oil covered by the contract, with Gulf, through its holding in Kuwait Oil Company, taking responsibility for production of the oil and Shell undertaking to refine it and carry it to market over a large part of the Eastern Hemisphere. The terms of the Gulf-Shell agreement almost certainly reduce the inclination of Gulf to compete with Shell, in numerous territories, for Gulf's half-share of the profits earned under the agreement will decline if Gulf invades areas in which Shell is marketing the Kuwait oil. Only if Gulf feels that over the long run it can produce and market more economically on its own, rather than in partnership with Shell, will it enter territories where Shell is distributing Kuwait oil, and even then fear of short-run losses through depressed prices should Shell choose not to give way will cause it to hesitate. The same contract which has the tendency to reduce the competition of Gulf with Shell is likely to reduce

[12] *Ibid.*, pp. 132, 144n.

Gulf competition in some areas with BP, since Shell and BP market jointly in numerous countries of the Eastern Hemisphere. Therefore, though the restrictive marketing provisions of the 1933 Gulf-BP concession agreement apparently were canceled in 1951, it may be that in many areas Gulf still is not competing with BP because of the numerous joint-marketing arrangements which BP maintains with Shell, the profit-sharing "partner" of Gulf in the production and distribution of Kuwait oil.

But we can proceed beyond examination of restrictive provisions in the early concession agreement or observation of later inhibitions on competition between Gulf Oil and BP which seem likely to have been introduced by the Gulf-Shell contract. We can look at actual marketing practices of Gulf and BP in Kuwait oil to learn that competition between the two concessionaires has been markedly circumscribed until recent years, that arrangements permitting each of them virtually unlimited lifting at cost have been slow to produce serious competition.

In practice, BP has distributed almost entirely in the Eastern Hemisphere, while Gulf has marketed for the most part on the other side of the world. Only in a few countries have they met in competition. In the Western Hemisphere BP has established a marketing subsidiary in Canada, it has sold oil in Argentina and Brazil, and it sells crude to a few companies on the eastern seaboard of the United States. Late in 1958 BP entered into an agreement with Sinclair Oil Corporation, a large U.S. firm, to market jointly in the Western Hemisphere its Middle East oil and Sinclair's Venezuelan oil and to explore and produce jointly in Latin America. In considering actual or potential competition between BP and Gulf Oil, we observe that under the new agreement BP will supply all the needs of Sinclair for Middle East crude after Sinclair's older contract with Gulf Oil expires in three years! [13] This is competition with a vengeance. In the

[13] *Petroleum Week*, November 7, 1958, p. 19; *Economist*, November 1, 1958, p. 448.

Eastern Hemisphere, Gulf and BP both have marketing organizations in Sweden and Switzerland, Gulf is in Japan while BP is becoming active there, and in addition Gulf sells crude in India, Australia, New Zealand, and possibly some other countries where BP is established. It is worth noting that the few Eastern Hemisphere markets listed here as having been entered by Gulf Oil are all markets in which BP distributes independently of Shell, allowing one to infer that the Gulf-Shell contract may indeed have checked Gulf's inclination to enter and to compete against BP when the latter is associated with Shell in marketing. Gulf sells oil also in Formosa and the Philippines, but BP is not represented in these countries. The feeling in the industry is that sales by Gulf Oil in the Eastern Hemisphere, apart from those taking place under the Gulf-Shell contract, are relatively small.

For the next few years, however, competition in Kuwait oil between Gulf and BP may grow more intense. Programs set up in the United States to limit oil imports may force Gulf to find new outlets abroad for its Kuwait oil, perhaps in Eastern Hemisphere markets now being supplied by BP. And we have already mentioned the new arrangements under which BP is to market jointly with Sinclair in the Western Hemisphere.

Apart from the possibility of competition between the owners of a single joint concession, there is a possibility of competition between owners in separate and distinct joint enterprises. Interlocking ownership in the Middle East, however, among firms which control the various producing companies probably tends to check competition in oil lifted from separate concessions. When directors from parent companies sit on the boards of two or three joint ventures, regularly meeting directors from the other international majors, information concerning output and price is bound to travel among them more freely than it would otherwise, no matter how carefully they attempt to avoid the subject of price and to obtain strictly independent

28

nominations for future lifting. Certainly the concerted action toward which oligopolists tend to move becomes easier.

In the Middle East the ownership of concessions interlocks at many points. The precise pattern can be seen in Table I on page 11. With minor holdings and ownership percentages excluded, the following presents the basic pattern:

Operating companies	Parent companies
Iraq Petroleum Company (IPC)	British Petroleum Royal Dutch–Shell Compagnie Française Jersey Standard Socony Mobil
Arabian American Oil Company (Aramco)	Standard of California Texaco Jersey Standard Socony Mobil
Kuwait Oil Company (KOC)	British Petroleum Gulf Oil
Iranian Oil Exploration and Producing Company and Iranian Oil Refining Company	The Consortium British Petroleum Royal Dutch–Shell Jersey Standard Socony Mobil Standard of California Texaco Gulf Oil Compagnie Française

The greater possibility of concerting action tacitly or explicitly, as a consequence of these meshed arrangements, can be seen in the multiple directorships held by particular representatives of the parent companies. In 1957, for example, P.

29

J. Anderson of Jersey was on the boards of the Consortium and IPC, and Brandon Grove of Socony was on the same two boards. The Hon. Maurice R. Bridgeman, C.B.E., was on the following boards: British Petroleum (the parent company), BP (Kuwait) Ltd., the Consortium, IPC, and KOC.[14] One is led to believe that the pattern of interlocking ownerships, along with membership of parent-company representatives on the boards of directors of two or three concession companies, checks at least somewhat the tendency of the owners to compete in oil lifted from separate joint enterprises.

4. Joint Marketing and Joint Refining

The oil of the Middle East is marketed jointly with less frequency than it is produced jointly, but a number of joint ventures in marketing do exist. By decreasing the number of independent sellers, these joint-marketing enterprises tend to reduce competition in particular markets or regions.

We have already mentioned the joint marketing of Royal Dutch–Shell and British Petroleum. These two companies market jointly in the United Kingdom, Republic of Ireland, Cyprus, Syria, Lebanon, Jordan, Egypt, Sudan, Ethiopia, Somalia, Aden, East and Southeast Africa, the Union of South Africa and British-administered Territories, Madagascar, and Ceylon. Standard of California and Texaco, through the California-Texas oil companies ("Caltex"), market jointly in seventy countries in the Eastern Hemisphere, covering Europe and lands East of Suez. Under the Gulf-Shell contract, already discussed on pages 26–27, Gulf and Shell are associated in a profit-sharing agreement for the production and marketing of a large quantity of Kuwait oil. Until 1960 Jersey Standard and Socony Mobil, through an affiliated firm, Standard-Vacuum ("Stanvac"), marketed jointly in South Africa, East Africa, the Indian Ocean, India, Australasia, and the Far East. Then Stanvac split up, with

[14] Iranian Oil Participants, Registration Statement, on file at Company Search Office, Bush House, London.

30

Jersey and Socony apparently planning to compete with one another in these markets. (Jersey agreed to the division of Stanvac as part of a consent decree in the Cartel Case, discussed in Chapter VI; Socony, although a defendant in this case, is not a party to the consent decree.)

The companies described earlier as being engaged in joint production (IPC, Aramco, and the others) are engaged also in some joint refining. Likewise, joint-marketing firms such as Caltex refine jointly. But the basic character of these enterprises, their impact on the competitive situation, is little altered by the additional activity of refining. In a few markets, however, ventures in joint refining unite firms into new combinations and quite possibly reduce competition in such areas, perhaps through conservative partners who slow down the rate at which new capacity is developed, perhaps through common costs of refining which furnish a basis for tacit or explicit concerted action on prices. In Turkey a refinery owned jointly by Socony, British Petroleum, and Royal Dutch–Shell is expected to go on stream late in 1961. In the Republic of Ireland, Jersey Standard, Caltex, and "Shell Mex and BP" (an affiliate of Royal Dutch–Shell and British Petroleum) refine jointly. In Ceylon a joint refinery has been proposed by Shell-BP, Stanvac, and Caltex. And Stanvac, Caltex, Shell, and Burmah Oil plus local capital have proposed a refinery for Pakistan.

It is true that one or two refineries of optimum scale may be enough to supply an entire market when the market is small; whenever refining is a natural monopoly, joint refining is entirely rational. Since joint refining, however, may check competition, governments should probably act to protect consumers against monopoly prices.

5. Jointly Used Pipelines and Terminals

In the Middle East there are two large jointly owned pipeline systems, and in a number of small markets, particularly in Africa, terminals are used jointly in various combinations by major companies. Do these joint facilities strengthen the market control held by sellers of Middle East oil?

The pipelines of the Iraq Petroleum Company run from Kirkuk in northern Iraq to the eastern Mediterranean at Banias and Tripoli. The pipeline of the Trans-Arabian Pipeline Company ("Tapline"), with the same ownership as that of Aramco, runs from Dhahran, on the Persian Gulf in Saudi Arabia, to Sidon on the eastern Mediterranean. Terminals are used jointly in several small West African markets,[15] for example, in the Republic of the Congo and the countries formerly comprising French Equatorial Africa.

It is generally because of the economies of large-scale operation that pipelines and terminals are used jointly. In pipelines these economies are strikingly great; transport costs per barrel per thousand miles decline all the way up to a throughput of 400,000 barrels per day, though the curve tends to flatten out at 150,000 or 200,000 and the decline after 300,000 is quite small. Pipeline costs decline because "there is less friction incurred per barrel of oil carried in a large-diameter pipe than in a small-diameter pipe." [16] In the Middle East, pipelines tend to be large: in March, 1960, the capacity of the 30–31-inch Tapline was 463,900 barrels per day; in January, 1960, the three IPC pipelines (12 inches, 16 inches, and 30–32 inches) had a capacity of 583,000 barrels daily and it was announced that their capacity "shortly" would be raised to 730,000 barrels a day.[17] By way of comparison it may be noted that the average production of

[15] The joint producing companies in the Middle East have jointly used terminals of course, but we will not deal with them specifically since joint ownership of such facilities does not alter the basic character of the operations in joint production which we have already discussed.

[16] Leslie Cookenboo, *Crude Oil Pipelines and Competition in the Oil Industry* (Cambridge: Harvard University Press, 1955), pp. 20, 26. See also John G. McLean and Robert W. Haigh, *The Growth of Integrated Oil Companies* (Boston: Graduate School of Business Administration, Harvard University, 1954), p. 185.

[17] *Petroleum Press Service*, September, 1958, p. 343; January, 1960, p. 7.

crude oil in Saudi Arabia during 1959 was 1,095,399 barrels per day, in Iraq 837,000 barrels daily and in the entire Middle East 4,587,108 barrels daily.[18] In the case of terminals the economies of scale are not so great. Apparently it is economical for each of a number of sellers in a large market to possess a separate terminal. In a small market, however, one or two terminals of optimum scale are sufficient, and the most economical delivery can be obtained by the several sellers only through joint owner-ship or use of these facilities.

Another reason for joint use of pipelines and terminals is the limited number of suitable routes or sites, though such con-siderations may be of little importance for pipelines in much of the Middle East with its wide, nearly empty deserts.

In attempting to decide whether or not market control by the major companies is augmented by joint use of pipelines and terminals, we should ask two questions: (1) Is it likely that such joint use will check competition among the large companies? (2) Does it put smaller, independent, nonaffiliated sellers at a competitive disadvantage?

It appears that jointly controlled pipelines and terminals in-crease the possibility of concerted action, tacit or explicit, among the majors. A greater part of costs are common to the several firms, providing an enlarged basis for concerted action on price, and representatives of the participating firms meet more often to discuss matters of common interest. Further, at least some of the owners may feel that facilities should be developed slowly. One of the less dynamic owners, one preferring a slower, less vigorous, potentially less competitive development, may find it easier to veto heavy investment expenditures for looping,[19] new pumping stations, enlarged docks, than to veto the relatively small costs of developing an oil field already discovered.

But perhaps a more substantial increment of market power by

[18] *World Oil*, February 15, 1960, p. 95.
[19] An increase in capacity achieved by laying a second line next to the first along some sections of the pipeline.

the majors as a result of their joint use of pipelines and terminals arises from the competitive disadvantage of nonaffiliated, independent firms. The latter may not be large enough to build their own large-volume, low-cost pipelines or terminals. If such independents are kept outside the joint arrangements, they will find themselves at a disadvantage. And they may be kept out because no government is able or willing to declare the facilities common carriers, because rates or the minimum tenders acceptable for delivery through a pipeline are maintained prohibitively high, or because they would be subjected to discriminatory exclusion when the line or terminal is at capacity and therefore would be unable to depend on the facilities at all times. Particularly if the outsider discovers oil far from tidewater will he be in no position to cut price in order to win a larger share of the market, for truck transport, rail transport, or transport through small-diameter pipelines is very costly. Even if independents find oil near the coast of the Persian Gulf, the most likely place, they will not, as long as they are outsiders, have the advantages of cross-desert transport at low cost through a 1,068-mile, large-diameter pipeline but probably will have to send their oil by tanker 3,221 miles around the Arabian peninsula (actually a 6,442-mile round trip for a tanker). The chances of their engaging in serious competition clearly will be smaller than if they had access to low-cost transportation. Similarly a nonaffiliated firm which has to build and operate its own small terminal and compete with the majors which are using a large terminal jointly is at a disadvantage, though probably less so than it would be if it had transportation difficulties, since terminal costs usually amount to a much smaller part of total delivered costs than do transportation costs, perhaps in some cases one twenty-fifth of the total as compared with one-quarter or one-third.

Of course independents may be taken into the ownership of joint pipelines or terminals. When the economies of scale are great, there is a strong motive for bringing in everyone as a means of building volume and attaining lower costs—though there might be a stronger inclination to exclude the nonaffiliated firm if it was thought that it would cut prices and disorganize markets. Even independents permitted to join the majors in a joint venture may not be in a position to compete: the large companies may be slow to agree to an expansion of capacity, not permitting an aggressive independent to increase its throughput; or high rates charged on small volumes may leave the independent, nonaffiliated firm too small a margin for it to reduce prices substantially.

Several oil companies—Socony Mobil, Shell, Texaco, Petrofina, British Petroleum, and perhaps one or two others—have developed a program for supplying a number of West African countries with petroleum products, the "West African Replenishment Plan." This program, which grew out of arrangements for supplying West African terminals during the Second World War, is basically a project for joint deliveries to a series of terminals. In some ports each of the participating firms possesses its own separate terminal; in others a terminal is used jointly. It would be uneconomical for each of the companies to send a tanker to supply its own relatively small wants in these ports when one tanker could be sent to take care of all their requirements. So the Plan calls for the co-operating firms to take turns in providing a ship, loading it with products, and making the deliveries. Each company nominates its requirements for each port and obtains delivery accordingly, and an individual company is entitled over a period of time to supply ships and products for the whole operation in proportion to its own particular requirements. The loading and delivering company sells the products to the others at a delivered price which is calculated in accordance with an agreed formula, the "low of Platt's" at the U.S. Gulf Coast plus a freight rate awarded by a London brokerage firm.[20]

[20] "West African Replenishment Plan," *Emergency Oil Lift Program and Related Oil Problems* (Washington, D.C., February, 1957), Part 3, pp. 1782–1799, Joint Hearings before Subcommittees of the Committee

The West African Replenishment Plan, argue its supporters, does not contribute in any way to market control. It is, they say, purely a matter of logistics. Each firm can obtain through the Plan all of its product requirements, and a dynamic, competitive firm can request and receive larger and larger deliveries. A dynamic firm can nominate larger amounts as time passes and supply a correspondingly greater part of the transport needed for the operation. In effect the expanding firm increases its investment (in ships) with its nominations and cannot be charged with making a profit on another firm's investment. (Where terminals are used jointly, terminal fees, which in any case represent a small part of total delivered costs, are negotiated outside the Plan.)

In this program of joint supply the companies participating do not have common costs. Over the long run each firm puts into the program, in petroleum products and transportation, as much as it takes out. Hence its costs over a period of time are the costs of its own oil and its own ships. The Plan is an exchange program; in fact the companies considered setting it up purely as a barter of physical quantities (barrels of oil and ton-miles of transportation) but decided against this because of the heavy paper work involved. (There are, to be sure, net cash balances in the program, because of price and rate changes between the times a participant supplies oil and transportation and the times it receives oil delivered in the ships of other participants, but these balances are small.) Members of the Plan, then, engaged in an exchange of oil and transportation, do not have common costs as a basis for concerted action on prices. One company,

on the Judiciary and Committee on Interior and Insular Affairs, United States Senate, 85th Congress; hereafter these hearings will be cited as *Emergency Oil Lift Program*. Platt's is a price-reporting service, and "low of Platt's" is the lowest sale price reported on a given day. There is reason to believe that most recently the freight rate used is the AFRA rate, the Average Freight Rate Assessment, calculated by a panel of London brokers.

36

Socony Mobil, states explicitly that the prices it charges its affiliates in West Africa are not the same as the prices at which exchange quantities are invoiced among members of the Plan. (Presumably, Socony charges its affiliates prices which reflect its own costs of product and transport.) And apparently other participants bill their affiliates at prices which differ from settlement prices in the Plan.

Nevertheless, the West African Replenishment Plan could serve in some degree to moderate competition. Though the costs of all its members differ, the low-cost firms may not seek to improve their positions. Instead all of the participants might use, tacitly or explicitly, the intercompany settlement prices as the basis for concerted action on sale prices. The mutual consultation necessary to the operation of the program would make such behavior easier. Finally, it is possible that outsiders would have difficulty in entering the Plan, and if they were forced to make their own small deliveries, they would remain at a disadvantage. These reservations may not, however, be very significant. Firms which want to concert their price behavior do not need a joint-supply program to derive a uniform delivered price but can rely on published data of product prices and tanker rates; such firms could, for example, without the program we are examining, all use the "low of Platt's" at the U.S. Gulf plus the AFRA tanker rate. Hence the West African Replenishment Plan does little to increase the possibilities of concerted action on price. In the absence of knowledge that outsiders have been kept out of the program, one is inclined to give the West African Replenishment Plan a clean bill of health and to suggest that probably it has not served to moderate competition in a significant degree.

Common costs in jointly operated pipelines and terminals, consultation among the participants, and control by the laggards of investment in these facilities may together check competition among firms participating in such joint ventures. And it may be that independents, disadvantageously kept on the outside or controlled when permitted to enter, will not be in a position to challenge the majors.

6. Role of the Independents in Middle East Oil

In the preceding section we touched on only one aspect of the situation of the independent, nonaffiliated firms. What is their situation generally? What is their present place and what their likely future in Middle East oil?

At the outset we should observe that an independent is not to be thought of as the repository of all virtue in international oil. Indeed some students of petroleum economics doubt that the word "independent," with its favorable connotations, should be used in a scientific work; they suggest that companies which are not integrated, vertically or horizontally, should be designated by the more neutral terms "nonaffiliated" or "nonintegrated." Though in sympathy with those who want a neutral terminology, the writer is inclined to feel that the word "independent" is of value in a study of the oil industry. Nonintegrated firms do have greater independence of action than the majors; with less to lose, they are freer to cut prices, freer to act in ways which undermine price stability. But while using the word "independent," we do not want to forget that these firms are often irresponsible, uninformed about their own costs, addicted to short-run gains, and not very concerned to take care of their customers' interests during a shortage of oil.

In the discussion to follow it should be realized that some of the firms we will refer to as independents are nonintegrated only outside the United States; in the U.S. they are partially or fully integrated and are thought of as majors.

At present there are only two independents with any substantial degree of production in the Middle East—American Independent Oil Company ("Aminoil") and Getty Oil Company, both in the Neutral Zone between Kuwait and Saudi Arabia. Together they averaged 113,819 barrels a day in 1959 out of a total Middle East production of 4,587,108 barrels daily, or 2.5 percent of the total.[21] Neutral Zone costs of production are probably a good deal higher than the average in the Middle East, output per well is relatively low, and much of the oil is of poor quality, requiring special treatment. Moreover, Neutral Zone oil is lifted by tanker and does not have the advantages of low-cost cross-desert transport. Given its magnitude and costs, it is doubtful that production from Aminoil and Getty has influenced very substantially the price of Middle East oil. To be sure it has been reported that Jersey Standard and Socony Mobil cut their prices for Safaniya, low-gravity, Saudi Arabian crude by 15 cents a barrel to meet the low prices posted by Getty for heavy crudes from the Neutral Zone.[22] But generally Neutral Zone competition has probably not been serious.

In the later fifties some new entries into the Middle East occurred, and people began to think that the situation might change. The Italian state-owned Ente Nazionale Idrocarburi ("ENI") headed by Enrico Mattei obtained exploration rights in Iran, as did Standard Oil Company (Indiana), a major in the United States but without foreign markets. A Japanese firm, the Arabian Oil Company, acquired a concession in the offshore area of the Neutral Zone and in January, 1960, discovered oil. Moreover, the world price of oil, and hence the price in the Middle East, may be influenced by a host of new independent entrants into Venezuela, many of which have made very handsome discoveries. Old patterns are breaking up and new ones emerging.

One view of the future is that for a time at least world markets may be rather badly disorganized and that over the long run they will be a great deal more competitive. The independents have paid large sums for their concessions, perhaps overpaid for them; if they discover oil, they are going to want to develop them rapidly and they may be pushing large quantities of oil

[21] *World Oil*, February 15, 1960, p. 95.
[22] *Petroleum Press Service*, October, 1958, p. 397.

into the markets of the world. Some who had hoped to sell their oil in the United States have found it shut out by import controls. There is no doubt that the marketing problems of an independent producer are serious. Only a few independent refineries exist outside the United States; they are in Italy, Switzerland, Sweden, and Japan. The independent producer usually cannot sell crude oil to the independent refinery and then take the products back, as can the major producer, because he lacks marketing outlets for products. Often the independent must give its crude to a broker who gets what he can for it. "We are naked," said one independent producer to the writer. An independent finds it difficult to get out of its exposed position by building a marketing network. A substantial volume is necessary for this to be economical, and a high investment is required. One estimate is that to refine and market only 10,000 barrels per day of crude oil requires an investment of $33.6 million.[23] Moreover, an independent trying to build markets for petroleum products will run into the problem of "specifications." The international majors, according to Dr. G. Tugendhat, managing director of the Manchester Oil Refinery, a nonintegrated firm in England, have special relationships with the defense services and government departments of European countries because of certain standard product specifications. It would be difficult for a newcomer to push his way in. "Only in low-grade industrial fuels would it be possible to gain entry," in the view of Dr. Tugendhat.[24]

But independent oil may not disorganize world markets as much as the foregoing would appear to indicate. Governments in the consuming countries may give preference to independent oil produced abroad by their nationals. Oil which has been discovered in the Persian Gulf by the Arabian Oil Company, a Japanese firm, can expect preferential treatment in the Japanese

[23] *Economist*, December 7, 1957, p. 886.
[24] *Petroleum Times*, quoted in the *Observer*, September 28, 1958, p. 2.

market.[25] Of course this will shut out some major-company oil, but the majors have a large stake in price stability and they may not try to push displaced oil into other markets. The majors might even voluntarily step aside to make room for new oil in countries where it enjoys no preference, checking their rates of growth in order to avoid price competition. If a competitor who commands but 5 percent of what a major is selling can upset the latter's markets, then common sense will tell the major to make considerable sacrifices in order to prevent this from happening.[26] In addition to, or alternatively to, making way for the independents, the majors might buy some of their oil. It would not be the first time majors have purchased "distress" oil which threatened to spoil the market. Laurent Wolters, managing director of Petrofina, a dynamic Belgian "minor major" rising into prominence on the world scene, has suggested that the majors buy the independents' oil but at the same time require them to cut back production.[27] In the autumn of 1957 there was talk in London that the majors would buy or had bought independent oil at a discount of 20 percent off posted price. But an independent interviewed by the writer in New York in the spring of 1958 ruefully reported that the international majors had not purchased any of *his* oil.

Much depends on the magnitudes involved. The majors can step aside and make room for some independent oil, and they can buy some distress oil. But governments in the producing countries will not agree to large cutbacks of major production nor even accept substantial failures on the part of the majors to grow with demand. Moreover, no one major can afford to buy large quantities of distress oil for the benefit of the others, and a co-operative group program "in restraint of trade" certainly would attract the unfavorable attention of the U.S. De-

---

[25] *Petroleum Week*, February 5, 1960, p. 11; February 19, 1960, p. 84.
[26] P. H. Frankel, *Essentials of Petroleum: A Key to Oil Economics* (London: Chapman & Hall, 1946), p. 86.
[27] Burck, "World Oil: The Game Gets Rough," p. 128.

partment of Justice. And then the majors may decline to buy independent oil simply in order to demonstrate to the governments of producing countries that the independents cannot find markets.

There is the possibility that the majors will not buy independent oil but will purchase the independents themselves, at knockdown prices. Independent producers struggling to find markets may in time become happy to sell out to the large companies, as the saying most appropriately goes, "lock, stock, and barrel." Producing-country governments, on the other hand, will oppose such sales if they are seeking independent avenues to market for their oil in order to escape major-company control.

Some short-run disorganization of world markets may well occur. The independents have paid large amounts for their concessions, they are going to be eager for a return on their investments, and they may try to push large quantities of oil into the market—quantities so large that the majors can neither stand aside for them nor purchase them. As time passes, however, disorganization probably will disappear. More independent refineries and marketers may come into existence as independent crude becomes more readily available in world markets, and such refineries will absorb some crude oil that would otherwise cause trouble. Some independent producers may integrate vertically themselves. Aminoil has signed a fifteen-year agreement to supply Persian Gulf crude to a new refinery in Germany, the refinery to be financed by Aminoil, Gottlieb Duttweiler, an independent Swiss marketer, and others. Getty Oil Company recently acquired a 51 percent interest in an Italian refinery. Indiana Standard and a newly formed Swedish Petroleum Company will build a refinery with a capacity of 36,000 barrels a day in Sweden.[28] The largest independents will develop an interest in stability if they see their activities tending to undermine the existing price structure. Badly placed independent operators may be purchased

[28] *Petroleum Week*, July 7, 1957, p. 51; October 11, 1957, p. 83; October 3, 1958, p. 72; October 24, 1958, p. 6.

by the majors, perhaps with the approval of the producing-country governments, who have learned to dislike markets which are disorganized.

But more interesting than the problem of short-run disorganization is the question of whether or not the market, over the long run, will become more competitive than it was before the independents entered production. Will these firms provide "the ventilation which prevents the powerful firms from making it 'too hot' for the public at large"? [29] One is very much inclined to doubt it. In the first place the majors still control a large part of the most promising acreage, though the Arabs are insisting more and more that they relinquish some of their holdings. Then it remains to be seen whether or not the new entrants will find low-cost oil on the concessions they have acquired, oil which in the long run will be competitive, and whether or not these companies can obtain, where necessary, low-cost cross-desert transportation. Wolters states that Petrofina has not entered the Middle East because oil found under the new concession terms will not be "cheap oil," with large bonuses and payments to governments of more than half of the profits. He even suggests that it may turn out to be more costly than Venezuelan oil.[30] Even if the newcomers do find low-cost oil, it seems doubtful that they will remain small and independent indefinitely, for an oil company's interest in security and stability is very great. When a large investment is at risk in production, the desire for secure markets is exceedingly strong. Similarly the owners of refineries and marketing facilities are very much interested in secure sources of supply. Vertical integration becomes almost inevitable. At times a major company will eliminate an unstable situation by purchasing an awkward independent. At other times an independent may integrate vertically on its own or combine with other independents. Absorption of the independents, then, by the international majors or their combination into new, rela-

---

[29] Frankel, *Essentials of Petroleum*, p. 85.
[30] *Petroleum Week*, November 14, 1958, p. 104.

tively large units would seem to be the most likely long-run developments in the institutions of world oil. Later in this chapter (see Section 10) it is suggested that Middle East oil is a "natural oligopoly."

Even if a number of low-cost independent producers remain in existence, it is doubtful that governments in the producing countries will allow them to act as serious competitors. It seems probable that, following the precedent of Texas, Oklahoma, and Louisiana, these governments will control independent output with the expectation of sharing in the profits of oligopoly.[31] Quite possibly the pattern of the future will be world-wide "pro-rationing," that is, a world-wide balanced control of output, jointly administered, though probably not explicitly concerted, by the international majors and the governments of the main producing areas. Perhaps action concerted by governments should not be ruled out. "The producer countries might one day call for an international order for oil as a means of securing for them-selves an 'equitable' share in the markets."[32]

7. Competition with Oil from Other Regions

Middle East oil competes with oil from the other major pro-ducing regions, but, as we shall see, mostly on the periphery of its marketing area. Oil from minor producing areas—in France, West Germany, Italy, Turkey, and other countries—is not seri-ously competitive. Small in magnitude, high in cost, it tends to shelter under an umbrella of world oil prices established in the Middle East, the Caribbean, and the Gulf of Mexico, as well as to seek the protection of tariffs, import quotas, and exchange controls.

Indonesian oil is of substantial magnitude, an average of 365,658 barrels per day in 1959 compared with 4,587,108 barrels

[31] Early in 1960 the Venezuelan government halted discount sales by Superior Oil Company, Signal Oil and Gas Company, and San Jacinto Petroleum Corporation, new independents in Venezuela (*Petroleum Press Service*, April, 1960, p. 142).

[32] P. H. Frankel, "A Turning Point," *International Oilman*, 1957, A.P.I. issue.

daily in the Middle East during the same period.[33] Yet one doubts that this oil exerts a significant influence on Middle East oil prices. One doubts that Indonesian oil is required to struggle for a position in Far Eastern markets inasmuch as it is under the control of several of the international majors—Royal Dutch–Shell, Stanvac (Jersey Standard and Socony), and Caltex (Standard of California and Texaco). These companies probably are inclined to make room for it rather than have it fight their oil from the Middle East.

North African oil must be taken more seriously. Some of it is likely to provide substantial competition for Middle East oil.

The French expect production in Algeria (they prefer to call it the "French Sahara") to increase rapidly; by 1963 Algerian production is expected to supply the entire French market and by 1965 to produce a large exportable surplus. The French, however, may be unduly optimistic. The variable (and in some places low) permeability of the biggest field (Hassi Messaoud) leaves uncertain the magnitude of recovery from the formation, and the 460-mile pipeline from this field to the coast runs through the Atlas Mountains, in which the Algerian rebels are strong; hence it may be blown up periodically. Should Algerian production grow as rapidly as the French expect, it will compete with Middle East oil. Already the French government has announced that in the early sixties refiners in France will be required to take 80 percent of the Algerian output. The international majors with refineries in France may not refine the light Algerian crudes there (where they are not very suitable), but they will have to dispose of them somewhere; hence this production may displace Middle East oil or slow up its rate of growth. A more serious problem is that the French are now trying to get special preference for Algerian oil in the European Economic Community.[34] Should they succeed—and they are very determined—Middle East oil might find itself, about 1965, at least

[33] World Oil, February 15, 1960, p. 95.
[34] Petroleum Week, December 18, 1959, pp. 20–21; Economist, December 26, 1959, p. 1256.

partially shut out from the countries in the Common Market. Oil from the Middle East displaced by Algerian oil might be pushed into other markets and might put pressure on prices in these markets. Even if Algerian oil did not displace Middle East oil but only threatened to check its rate of growth, Algerian oil might exert pressure on prices. The Middle East might insist on maintaining its share of world markets, and the ensuing struggle might lead to price reductions. On the other hand, the international majors and the Middle Eastern governments, with their strong interest in stability, might defend world oil prices by holding back output in the Middle East in order to make a place for Algerian crude. Much depends on the magnitudes involved.

When the oil of Libya is added to that of Algeria, the volume of North African oil almost certainly will be great enough to have a substantial impact on the market for Middle East oil. Libyan discoveries are more recent and less immediately a threat to the world price structure, but they are nearer the coast (about 100 miles inland), in a politically stable area, and very low in cost. Jersey Standard has already ordered the pipe for a 30-inch Libyan pipeline with an initial capacity of 200,000 barrels per day and an eventual capacity of 500,000 barrels daily. Two other pipelines for Libya are being planned by other companies.[35] It is significant that at least two independents have found oil in Libya—Conorada (Continental Oil, Ohio Oil, and Amerada) and Libyan American (Texas Gulf Producing and W. R. Grace).

It seems fairly certain that by 1963 or 1964 Middle East oil will find a higher degree of competition West of Suez as it encounters oil from North Africa. It is less likely that North African oil will have an impact on markets east of the Suez Canal. Of course if oil which could be sold only at less attractive prices in the West (less attractive because of competition from North Africa) were pushed into eastern markets, these might become more competitive, but the international majors will be slow to undermine price stability east of the Canal by such

[35] *Petroleum Week*, December 11, 1959, p. 52; January 15, 1960, p. 32.

actions, and Middle Eastern governments probably will support them in their caution.

Russian oil has recently begun to appear in substantial quantities in Eastern Hemisphere and Latin-American markets, and the Russians are talking about large increases in production in years to come. Soviet bloc exports to the non-Communist world averaged about 340,000 barrels per day in 1959.[36] "The Russian sales policy is one that cannot be met by private companies," says Laurent Wolters. "Not only do the Russians sell oil at low prices, but they offer to buy—at world prices—the excess production of whatever other commodities . . . [an oil-purchasing] country cannot sell." [37] Soviet sales at low prices may well occur even though Soviet oil is not particularly low in cost. Cost accounting is less developed in the Soviet Union and less systematically applied; one state enterprise or one industry may subsidize another. And a state trading enterprise which can arrange barter transactions readily has a competitive advantage in soft-currency areas.

Probably it is too early to forecast the Soviet impact on the market for Middle East oil. Before too much is expected from the Russians in the way of short-run disorganization or long-run competition, it should be recalled that they do have an interest in getting the best prices they can for their exports, though of course political objectives may at times override this interest. It is worth noting that, while disorganizing some markets in the thirties, the Russians did come to terms, during the same period, with the "as is" group of companies (the cartel) in a number of other markets.[38] And in January, 1960, Soviet Russia agreed to sell all of its western exports of diamonds to the Diamond Corporation of South Africa, which will in turn market them through the Central Selling Organization of the de Beers group of com-

[36] *Petroleum Press Service*, April, 1960, p. 123.
[37] Quoted in *Petroleum Week*, November 14, 1958, p. 104.
[38] FTC Report, pp. 236, 239–240, 278. See Chapter VI for a discussion of the cartel question.

47

panies. The de Beers group supplies 90 percent of the world's diamonds.[39]

Middle East oil competes mostly with oil from the other *major* producing areas, and this competition is largely on the periphery of its marketing area. No doubt competition with Venezuelan oil is moderated by the fact that the largest part of Venezuelan production is controlled by international majors who are also active in the Middle East, though independents in Venezuela probably will become increasingly important. Jersey Standard, Royal Dutch–Shell, and Gulf, the big three in Venezuela, plus Socony Mobil and Texaco, were together responsible for 90 percent of 1958 Venezuelan crude production.[40] U.S. Gulf Coast oil is a limited competitor of Middle East oil because of its high cost.

Still there is a certain amount of competition between the major producing regions in peripheral markets. In Europe, oil from the Middle East meets Caribbean fuel oil; in South America, Middle East oil meets Caribbean crude and products; on the East Coast of the United States, though competition is checked by import quotas, Middle East oil encounters Caribbean oil and oil from the U.S. Gulf; and on the West Coast of North America, oil from the Middle East confronts oil from California and Canada. Now that import quotas have checked the free entry of oil into the United States, it is probably the competition of Middle East oil with Caribbean oil in South America that provides the most important interregional competition, and Middle East prices are probably in some measure influenced by this encounter. But in an oligopolistic market the impact of peripheral competition will be felt only slowly in the interior of a price "basin." Though prices on the periphery tend to decline and realizations on border sales to fall, oligopolists, inclined to protect prices in their interior markets, are slow to withdraw supplies from distant markets and

[39] *Observer*, January 24, 1960, p. 3; *Economist*, January 23, 1960, pp. 332–333.
[40] *World Oil*, August 15, 1959, p. 142.

48

ship them into those nearby (where they may depress prices). In the ECA Case, discussed in Chapter V, the U.S. government alleged that competition in peripheral markets was not reflected in lower prices to purchasers nearer the Middle East.

8. The Competition of Substitutes

Besides experiencing the rivalry of companies with petroleum for sale, an oil producer or marketer may find himself in competition with sellers of coal, natural gas, water power, or nuclear energy, and perhaps one day in competition with oil produced from shale or tar sands.

Coal has been the most serious competitor in recent years, though its long-run future is not so promising. In the later fifties the demand for energy and heat increased more slowly than hitherto, as first the United States and then Europe experienced economic declines. At the same time coal output in Europe, especially of inferior (small) coals, continued to rise, stocks accumulated, and low ocean freight rates made prices of American coal delivered in Europe very attractive. Increased installations of dual-firing equipment made competition between fuel oil and coal more acute. The consequences of all these circumstances varied from one locality to another in Europe, but in many places fuel oil has been selling at lower prices because of the competition of imported or indigenous coal (or in some cases because of the competition of local lignite).[41]

Coal is less likely to be seriously competitive with oil over the long run; at least European coal is not a likely competitor. With governmental policies of very full employment plus rigid wage structures, Europe has had great difficulty in getting workers into the mines. This problem and increasingly unfavorable geological conditions of exploitation have made it very hard for Europeans to obtain an increase in coal output. One forecast is for "an average rate of increased output of 1 percent per annum until 1965 and the maintenance of the output in that year until

[41] *Petroleum Press Service*, June, 1958, pp. 203–206.

1975." [42] When world economic advance is resumed, then, the postwar shortage of coal in Europe is apt to be renewed. Moreover, fuel oil has many advantages over coal, in efficiency, flexibility in meeting changes in heat requirements, ease of handling, cleanliness, etc.—advantages which vary, of course, with use and equipment. An original assessment of these advantages was made by Dr. Regal, deputy director of the Economics Division of the High Authority of the European Coal and Steel Community. He found that if it were assumed that the consumer paid the same price for fuel oil and coal of the same calorific content (the same price for one ton of fuel oil and 1.4 tons of coal), the economies obtained by using oil would represent an over-all cost saving of between 20 and 50 percent. And he found that in many of the consuming centers of the Community the price of fuel oil in terms of effective calories is below the price of coal, following a continued decline in the ratio of fuel oil to coal prices over some years. In addition, in some expanding sectors of consumption, such as automatic central heating, coal today does not rank at all as an alternative to oil.[43]

Coal is not entirely out of the running, however. While the total output of coal increases very slowly, the output of the inferior grades, small in size, with a high ash, water, and, usually, sulphur content, will probably rise more rapidly. A larger quantity of inferior coals will be mined because exhaustion of the best seams always leads to deterioration; coal-mining machinery, increasingly in use, tends to break the coal and raise the proportion of dirt; and more water is being used in modern mining operations.[44] Two power stations under construction in England were recently switched from fuel oil to coal because of the increased availability of small coal in that country. Should the authorities

[42] Organization for European Economic Co-operation, *Europe's Growing Needs of Energy: How Can They Be Met?* (Paris, 1956), p. 23.
[43] *Petroleum Press Service*, February, 1958, pp. 67–68.
[44] G. H. Daniel, of the Ministry of Power in England, in a paper cited by *Petroleum Press Service*, January, 1958, p. 27.

in various European countries decide to reduce prices of the inferior coals, which they hesitate to do, perhaps in some cases because they have docile, monopolistic state enterprises as large buyers, these coals might provide fuel oil with considerable competition, though the general difficulty of increasing coal output probably will act at least as a partial check on this development once world economic growth is resumed. Coal from America may remain a serious competitor with fuel oil in Europe.

Very great progress in mechanization has been made in recent years and output per man-shift underground in U.S. bituminous coal mines has nearly doubled since the war to reach nearly 11 tons, compared with about 1.6 tons in the U.K. and in the Ruhr. Operating under far better geological conditions, American mines are producing more cheaply and are more easily adaptable to sudden changes in demand than those in Western Europe. There is in the U.S.A. a large production potential for high-grade coals, including coking coal, of which there are local shortages in Europe, and the loading capacity provided in U.S. ports is now far in excess of the highest demand hitherto experienced.[45]

Despite the costs of transport (50 percent or more of the delivered costs) and the fact that payment for U.S. coal must be made in dollars, European imports from the United States have become substantial and, unless Europe becomes very protectionist, are likely to continue to be a significant factor in the market for fuel.

At the very least, indigenous and imported coal will put a ceiling on the price of fuel oil in Europe. What is more, it may provide a measure of serious competition, though the distance of American coal, protectionist sentiments in Europe, the general difficulties of expanding European coal production, and the economies of fuel oil consumption will limit the importance of coal in the fuel oil market. And of course coal is no substitute at all

[45] *Petroleum Press Service*, June, 1958, pp. 204–205. Quoted by permission.

51

for gasoline; the motorist gains no protection from the competition of coal with oil, though he might at some future date through the production of liquid fuels from coal.

Natural gas is a competitor of oil. The consumption of natural gas in western Europe increased eightfold from 1950 to 1957, much of this increase being in Italy. Future large increases are expected in France, and probably increases will occur in West Germany, Austria, and the Netherlands.[46] Natural gas competes effectively with fuel and heating oils for several reasons: the calorific content of natural gas is high—twice that of manufactured gas—gas-burning equipment is often more efficient than equipment using other fuels, and gas is clean and easy to handle. Hence at point of delivery natural gas can often command a premium over oil (and coal) per b.t.u. However, its cost of transportation in pipelines per b.t.u. is high, higher than that of oil, which restricts the area in which it can effectively compete. Natural gas consequently is and will be an important competitor with fuel oil and heating oil in some areas, such as northern Italy and southwestern France, but it probably will not be in others. If experiments in the sea transport of natural gas prove successful, however, natural gas delivered from North Africa, Venezuela, or the Middle East in ships may enter a number of regions at present without supplies of natural gas. In any case natural gas does not compete with gasoline; hence its sale gives the motorist no protection against the prices of oligopoly.

Water power is a competitor of fuel oil in some areas and its future is not without promise. It has been estimated that in Europe (in the countries which are members of the Organization for European Economic Co-operation) only 27 percent of the "economically workable" hydro power actually has been harnessed. Moreover it is believed that the production of hydroelectric power in Europe will increase at a rate of 4.2 percent per annum until 1975, compared with an estimated rate of growth in oil imports of 5.1 percent per annum. By 1975 Europe

[46] *Ibid.*, September, 1958, pp. 336–340.

will be getting about 11 percent of its energy from water power.[47] Hydroelectric power again is of no help to the motorist.

Nuclear energy obtained from nuclear fission has entered the picture and will grow in importance as a competitor of fuel oil in the years to come. Its greatest impact will be on the generation of electricity. The British estimate that possibly by 1965 they will be able to build nuclear plants capable of generating electricity that will cost no more than electricity produced in the best conventional power stations. But they realize that they may not succeed in doing this by 1970.[48] Britain is well ahead of the rest of the world, but a number of other countries are pressing forward in this area, especially France, Germany, Italy, the Benelux countries, and Japan.

The economies of scale in the production of nuclear power are presently very great. Capital costs are high; the most economical nuclear plants are very large and must be run at a high load factor, i.e., as near to twenty-four hours a day as possible. For this reason, progress in nuclear energy in the advanced industrial countries after the next decade is problematical. Once nuclear power is producing the entire base load, the entire quantity of electricity demanded on a twenty-four-hour basis, additional capacity installed will not be used around the clock, capital costs will be spread over fewer and fewer working hours a year, and costs per kilowatt of electricity produced will be higher. That is, costs of nonbase load capacity will be higher until smaller plants can be designed and the enriched fuels they require made cheaper. Hence it is possible that in the advanced industrial countries it will remain more economical to produce electricity in excess of the base load with coal or oil. What of the less-developed nations? A few years ago it was thought that nuclear energy would be a particular boon to regions dependent on

[47] OEEC, *Europe's Growing Needs of Energy*, pp. 22–23, 73, 105.
[48] "Can Nuclear Power Compete?" *Economist*, May 9, 1959, p. 543; "Euratom's Diminishing Target," *ibid.*, November 14, 1959, p. 646; "Nuclear Power in the Sixties," *ibid.*, February 13, 1960, p. 639.

imported coal or oil, because the costs of transporting uranium are extremely low. More recently difficulties have been recognized. In most underdeveloped countries electricity is produced in small, widely dispersed stations with very low load factors. Fifty percent or less of capacity in these countries, frequently less than 30 percent, is used twenty-four hours a day. Until small, economic nuclear power stations are designed and cheaper enriched fuel is developed, electricity produced from nuclear energy will be of interest to few underdeveloped regions.

As progress is made in designing small reactors, nuclear power will become of greater importance in transportation. Nuclear-powered merchant ships, surface and submarine, are being studied, and in some cases being built, and the U.S. Air Force is attempting to construct a bomber driven by nuclear power. But it is doubtful that atomic energy will be used in automobiles, where the weight of the necessary lead shielding will be prohibitive. In the foreseeable future, energy for small mobile units, apart from the costly energy stored in batteries, will be supplied entirely by petroleum, unless an economical liquid fuel from coal should be developed.

There remain two potential competitors of Middle East oil which should be mentioned—oil extracted from shale and oil from tar sands. The largest deposits of oil shale and tar sands are not very advantageously located, in the western United States and western Canada respectively, and extraction of the oil is still in the stage of experiment, but it is conceivable that in the future shale oil or oil from tar sands might put a ceiling on Middle East oil delivered into some markets.

At the least coal, natural gas, water power, and nuclear energy will put an upper limit on the prices of fuel oil in various markets. Better, one or another of these sources of energy and heat, or all of them, may provide serious competition for fuel oil, though perhaps only in some markets and at some times. But none of them can compete for the custom of the motorist; none of them are likely to supply energy for small mobile units.

9. Nonprice Competition

Economists, it is often said, put too much emphasis on price competition. Rivalry to improve quality and service, say businessmen, and expenditures on advertising benefit consumers, and these should not be neglected in analysis of a market. It is certainly true that consumers may benefit from nonprice competition—but, as we shall see, they may also lose by it.

There is no doubt that the oil industry is a dynamic one. Product quality and service are improving constantly. It is difficult to build a refinery that is not obsolete in some respects before it is completed, and in scarcely more than a generation we have seen the "filling" station develop into the "service" station.

Almost certainly the oil companies of the Middle East, like all oligopolists, prefer nonprice competition. Such competition does not cut so deeply and is "less likely to degenerate into unbridled warfare." While advertising or variations in product or service will be matched by changes in the behavior of rivals, these responses occur "less easily, less quickly, and less certainly," thus giving the aggressive firm a better chance of gaining an edge.[49]

Nonprice competition may not be an unalloyed benefit, however. The costs of such competition, the costs of product variation, additional services, and advertising, may be greater than the value of the benefits to the consumer. The buyer might prefer a simpler, cheaper product with less service, but not be given an opportunity to make this choice. In petroleum nonprice competition may have resulted in an undesirably high octane level for gasolines and additives which ordinary automobiles have not been able to utilize effectively. Dr. P. H. Frankel speaks of the octane inflation in Europe which gave the motorists a quality of fuel far above the capacity of their cars to benefit therefrom; and on the lunatic fringe of the competitive field we saw a craze

[49] Joe S. Bain, *Pricing, Distribution, and Employment* (New York: Henry Holt, 1948), p. 201.

for additives designed to improve motor fuels which, however sound their conception might have been on the testbed, fell inside the margin of error of the average car, that most patient but therefore not very discriminating contraption.[50]

Nonprice competition may also have led to an uneconomic multiplication of small service stations. Unwilling to seek volume by price cutting, the majors tend to try to enlarge their volume by establishing additional outlets. In Britain, for example, though the total number of stations has fallen in recent years as small curb sites have given way to new multipump stations, the average throughput of each station is below that achieved in several other countries, and the average throughput per pump "is still only about 40,000 gallons a year, a poor showing by international standards." [51] And the majors intend to build new company-owned stations on "virgin sites." Less nonprice competition and more price competition might check station-building programs, eliminate the least profitable dealers, increase the average station output, and lower costs.

Nonprice competition may result in undue expenditures on advertising. Of course defenders of sales promotion call attention to its educative function, suggest that it enables firms to obtain large volumes and low costs, and point out that it supports television entertainment and the publication of journals and periodicals. But much advertising simply offsets other advertising; if one firm advertises to maintain its position against another firm which advertises, neither gains at the expense of the other, neither obtains a larger volume and lower costs; indeed, total costs, and prices, may be higher. When advertising does enable a firm to obtain the economies of scale through large volume, the volume might have been obtained without advertising or with less advertising, perhaps by cutting prices. And of course the quality of entertainment and periodical literature supported by advertising, aimed at a mass audience, leaves much to be desired.

[50] "A Turning Point."
[51] "Competition at the Pump," *Economist*, December 7, 1957, p. 886.

It seems quite certain that the "gross" rate of product development in oil is more rapid and the number of service stations larger *because* price competition is moderated. But it is not certain that the improvements in quality and the gains in service and convenience are worth the additional costs. Perhaps the consumer would have preferred an opportunity to choose lower quality, less service, less convenience in location, less advertising—and lower prices. The writer, like many if not most economists, remains skeptical of nonprice competition as a substitute for rivalry in price.

10. Is Middle East Oil a Natural Oligopoly?

We have characterized the market for Middle East oil as oligopoly, a market of sellers so few in number that any one of them can detect an influence on price of a change in its output. Is this market, we may ask, inevitably oligopolistic? Is it a "natural" oligopoly? A natural oligopoly occurs when the economies of large-scale production are very great, so great that a small number of firms of optimum scale can supply the entire market. The market for Middle East oil would be naturally oligopolistic if the economies of scale in finding, producing, refining, and distributing this oil were so large that a few firms of optimum scale could supply all the quantity demanded. We must ask ourselves, then, what the optimum-sized unit for exploration and production in the Middle East is, and say a word about the size of the optimum transportation, refining, and marketing operation.

Little has been written about the economies and diseconomies of oil exploration and production. The most appropriate scale of operation varies a great deal with the location and the character of the terrain being explored or the oil fields being developed. Certainly an exploration and production firm in the Middle East of optimum scale is larger than one elsewhere in the world. Exploration in the desert requires the difficult provision of fresh water, in many cases the provision of air-conditioned,

57

mobile dwelling units, the provision of special vehicles, aircraft, and so forth. A large firm can keep this expensive equipment more fully occupied than can a small one. Of course a smaller firm can have geological work, geophysical work, and drilling done on a contract basis by specialized companies, but it must pay large sums to get these people to bring their equipment into a remote area, and the job will cost them more than it would a bigger firm which can assure a contractor a greater volume of business. On the other hand, as more independent firms enter the Middle East, they will be able, collectively, to keep specialized geological, geophysical, and drilling companies busier and they will obtain, as a consequence, better terms from them. But for some time to come it appears that the majors will have a cost advantage over the independents in Middle East exploration, though probably not a strikingly large one.

As for producing Middle East oil once it is found, the economies of scale here are substantial. Oil fields in the Middle East tend to be large, and some of them are very large; the Ghawar field in Saudi Arabia is at least 140 miles long and the Kirkuk field in Iraq is about 60 miles long. For a most economical operation an oil field should be produced as a unit; large fields are best handled by large producing companies. When a number of firms lift oil independently from the same field, either there is wasteful competitive lifting, which reduces the total oil extracted from the field, or the government must regulate production and prorate it among the several parties, which is cumbersome. And since in the latter case the lifting firms do not compete with one another in the oil of the field (they produce to quota and could not get additional oil from the field if they enlarged their sales), a critic who wanted to see a higher degree of competition in Middle East oil would not advocate that a single field be produced by a number of firms. The economy of unit operation and the fact that the degree of competition cannot be increased by putting several firms in a given field—these point to a pattern of large companies for the large fields of the Middle East.

58

Moreover, the economies of scale in production equipment give advantages to big firms. Gas-oil separation plants (degassing plants) and crude oil stabilization units are the most important items. Arabian American Oil Company has standardized on gas-oil separation plants with a capacity of 100,000 barrels per day. There are economies of design and engineering in such standard units, they can be added one at a time as more capacity is desired, and they are suitable for thin, dispersed fields where larger units cannot be employed. Economies can be obtained by grouping these plants, which means that a degassing operation of 300,000 or 400,000 barrels a day would have lower costs than one of 100,000 barrels daily—but probably not a great deal lower. Aramco has some crude stabilization plants of 150,000 barrels per day capacity and some of 220,000 barrels per day, but it also operates at least one stabilization plant of 60,000 barrels daily. Apparently stabilization units are rather like refineries in that the curve of declining costs tends to flatten out as volume exceeds 60,000 barrels per day. The economies of scale in secondary recovery techniques, water and gas injection, are very substantial; one oil man in a major company suggested that the smaller independents are not likely to engage in secondary recovery unless forced to do so by governments. Economies of scale in the production of electricity and in water distillation plants are considerable, but the costs of electricity and water are not a significant part of total costs.[52]

Large firms in the Middle East can obtain real economies in transportation, especially in transportation over land. In pipelines, costs per barrel per thousand miles decline all the way up to a throughput of 400,000 barrels per day, though the curve tends to flatten out at 150,000 or 200,000 barrels a day, and the decline after 300,000 is quite small. (See Section 5 of this chapter.) Because of its great volume a large firm can afford to build a long pier far out into the shallow waters of the Persian Gulf, a

[52] The information in the foregoing paragraph was obtained in private interviews with oil men.

pier capable of loading at one time several of the economical, giant supertankers. Or it may build an artificial island terminal out in the Gulf.

Finally, there may be economies of scale in research, finance, and legal work, and discounts may be obtained on the purchase of materials in quantity.

On the other hand, oil companies may experience diseconomies in large-scale organization; management tends to become un-wieldy and inflexible as administration grows. Still, in an industry as highly automatic as the oil industry, equipment increases more rapidly than personnel, and top management can administer a large operation with a relatively small body of executives. Bu-reaucracy is slower to proliferate.

Along with economies of scale in exploration, production, and transportation, resulting in a few large companies, an oligopoly, we observe lesser economies of scale in refining and marketing and the possibility of a greater number of firms in these later stages. The curve of declining costs in refining flattens out, and "the most substantial economies of scale are realized by the time ca-pacities in the range of 60,000 to 100,000 bbl/day are reached." [53] Moreover, it seems quite certain that marketing can be carried on economically in rather small units. With the economies of scale in refining and marketing less than in exploration, produc-tion, and transportation in the Middle East, several firms can join together in production (and in exploration and transport) but refine and market separately in smaller units. Joint produc-tion and separate marketing provide a higher degree of com-petition in Middle East oil than would joint production and joint marketing with the marketing carried on at the same scale and with the same number of firms as production, and they make the market less of an oligopoly. The student cannot, however, measure the degree of competition by looking at the size and number of marketing companies alone, for as we have seen (in

[53] Daniel C. Hamilton, *Competition in Oil* (Cambridge: Harvard University Press, 1958), p. 45.

60

Section 3 of this chapter), joint production tends to moderate the competition of the separate marketing firms.

The market for Middle East oil, it appears, is naturally oligopolistic—but may not always be so. The large fields of the Middle East and the economies of scale in exploration, in gas-oil separation plants, in crude oil stabilization units, in secondary recovery techniques, and in transportation—all give the big company of, say, 500,000 barrels per day substantially lower costs, and these factors no doubt explain in part the large size and small number of firms in Middle East exploration, production, and transportation. But the cost advantages which the large companies have over smaller ones are not strikingly great. Should a small, well-managed independent find a good field on or near tidewater, one which produced 100,000 barrels daily and did not require secondary recovery activities, it might be quite profitable; he might give even the majors a run for their money. A number of such independents could transform the market for Middle East oil. Although this market is a natural oligopoly, new discoveries could change its character.

The writer has characterized as oligopoly the market for Middle East oil—but in using the term he has frequently been misunderstood by oil men who are not familiar with the literature of formal economic analysis. Perhaps it would be useful to say what the word oligopoly does *not* mean. In the first place oligopoly is not simply a term of abuse; rather it is a precisely defined concept which characterizes a particular kind of market structure. (Section 1 of this chapter gives an exact description and an analysis of oligopoly.) Moreover, oligopoly is not a synonym for monopoly. No doubt Wanda Jablonski does not expect to be taken seriously when she refers to oligopoly as a "monopoly with a college education"; and she should not be, for the two are different. While oligopolists tend to restrict output and maintain high and rigid prices, the degree of output restriction and price maintenance is less, often much less, than in the case of monopoly. Actually, the concept of oligopoly covers a wide range of market situations, from near-monopoly to "workable competition," with the exact classification dependent upon the number of small firms on the sidelines in the industry, the extent to which outsiders threaten entry, the closeness of substitutes, and other factors. The writer would place the market for Middle East oil somewhere in the middle of the range, perhaps a little closer to workable competition than to an oligopoly which is nearly a monopoly. But oligopoly it is, and scientific analysis requires that it be so labeled.

Repetition of the term (which is necessary in a work of this sort), far from being evidence of prejudice against the oil industry (oil men have cited it as evidence of such), indicates a desire on the part of the writer to ground his statements in analysis, a desire to substitute thought for fancy.

Having examined the structure of the market and concluded that it is oligopoly, that it is orderly but less competitive than might be desired, we will find it of value to study available data on costs, prices, and profits in Middle East oil in order to determine whether or not these reflect the character of the market as we have seen it.

III

Costs and Profits in Middle East Oil

THE generally prevailing impression is that costs in Middle East oil are remarkably low and that profits are remarkably high. What is known of the production pattern in the oil fields of the Middle East tends to support this view: daily output per well in the United States in 1958 amounted to 12 barrels and in Venezuela to 250 barrels, but in the Middle East it was 3,860 barrels.[1] Middle East oil is, however, situated at a great distance from its principal markets, and it usually sells at a price about one dollar per barrel below Caribbean oil. Moreover, it is produced in the desert under circumstances of great difficulty. The oil companies usually have to build their own roads, erect schools, hospitals, theaters, and churches, and they bear the risks of adverse governmental policies, one of these risks being the possibility of nationalization. It will be worth our while to study carefully the subject of costs and profits in Middle East oil.

1. Profits per Barrel in Production

A considerable amount of data is available which can be used to calculate the margin of profit in crude oil. One method of

[1] Calculated from data in *World Oil*, August 15, 1959, p. 102.

63

estimating profit margins in Middle East crude relies on what is known of royalties and taxes paid to host-country governments. Since these payments, made under concession agreements, amount to approximately 50 percent of net profits, it can be assumed that, oil company profits after taxes equal the sums paid to the governments. By dividing net profits calculated in this manner by annual production of crude oil, one can obtain an estimate of profits per barrel.[2] The method is imperfect: refinery profits, though usually small, are often mixed in; annual payments to a government do not always reflect current production; and annual payments, since they are based on posted prices rather than actual sale prices, give the governments more (and the oil companies less) than half of the profits when sales are made at a discount. With these reservations in mind, the reader can usefully look at Table III, which presents profit margins calculated in the manner described. The profit margins as calculated are seen to range from 75 to 90 cents per barrel, the average being 82 cents.

In three cases it is possible to obtain independent figures representing profit margins, and these figures tend to support the validity of calculations based on oil company payments to host-country governments. In information submitted by Aramco to a Congressional committee, it is stated that profits per barrel in Aramco were 77 cents during 1955.[3] In the oil agreement signed in 1952 by Iraq and the Iraq Petroleum Company, Article 9 (b) (v) states, with some qualifications, that the actual costs of oil produced after 1952 shall be taken to be 13 shillings per long ton (approximately 24 cents a barrel).[4] Let us assume that the agreement accurately forecasts cost in southern Iraq through

[2] The secretariat of the Economic Commission for Europe calculated Aramco profits in this manner in its study, *The Price of Oil in Western Europe* (Geneva: United Nations, 1955), pp. 14–15, though it erroneously overstated these profits by including in them the sums which were being paid to the Saudi government. This study will be cited as the ECE Report.

[3] *Emergency Oil Lift Program*, p. 1442. The year to which data supplied on page 1442 is applicable can be ascertained by reference to page 1240.

[4] *Iraq Government Gazette*, No. 3,063, February 18, 1952.

1959. If to the 24 cents we add half of the difference between 24 cents (lifting costs) and the posted price (since half of the profits must be paid to the Iraqi government), if then we subtract this total from the posted price in the Persian Gulf, the remainder

TABLE III

PROFITS PER BARREL IN THE MAJOR CONCESSIONS
OF THE MIDDLE EAST

Concession	Year	Payments to government (millions)	Crude production (millions of barrels)	Profit margin per barrel	Sources of data Pay-ments	Sources of data Pro-duc-tion
Saudi	1958	$310.7	367.9	$.85	g	g
Arabia	1957	296.9	353.0	.84	g	g
	1956	280.0	360.0	.78	b	e
	1955	280.0	352.1	.80	a	e
Kuwait	1958	415.0	511.7	.81	g	g
	1957	365.0	418.2	.87	g	g
	1956	306.0	401.4	.76	g	g
	1955	305.0	398.8	.76	g	e
Iraq	1958	235.0	261.3	.90	g	g
	1957	136.2	159.2	.86	c	c
	1956	193.0	231.0	.84	a	a
	1955	206.4	252.1	.82	f	e
Iran	1958	246.0	277.4	.89	g	g
	1957	216.7	261.0	.83	d	d
	1956	146.0	195.5	.75	a	e
	1955	90.0	119.7	.75	a	e
Average				$.82		

a. Petroleum Information Bureau, London.
b. *Petroleum Press Service*, April, 1957, p. 154.
c. *Petroleum Press Service*, February, 1958, p. 75.
d. *Petroleum Week*, February 14, 1958, p. 58.
e. Aramco, *Middle East Petroleum Data*, p. 5.
f. Iraq Petroleum Company.
g. William S. Evans, *Petroleum in the Eastern Hemisphere* (New York, 1959), p. 21.

represents oil company profits per barrel of production in southern Iraq. For the years 1959 and 1958 respectively, profits so calculated are 80 and 87 cents per barrel. It is widely believed in the industry that the lifting costs of Kuwait oil are about 10 cents per barrel, and in fact this figure is cited by *Fortune*, though the source is not given.[5] If to the 10 cents we add half of the difference between 10 cents (lifting costs) and the posted price (since half of the profits are paid to the Kuwait government), then subtract the resulting total from the posted price, the remainder represents oil company profits per barrel. For the years 1959 and 1958 we get, with such calculations, 80 and 88 cents. (The foregoing calculations of profits in Iraq and Kuwait do not take into account the fact that some oil is sold at a discount off posted price; actual profits per barrel may have been somewhat lower than here represented.)

It seems reasonable to conclude that at the end of the fifties the profits of the major concessions in the Middle East averaged something less than 82 cents a barrel. Such profits, oil men have argued, are not unduly high. When Arabian American Oil Company margins were called into question by the secretariat of the Economic Commission for Europe, Jersey Standard asserted that

cost-price relations for Middle East oil do not differ substantially from those existing elsewhere. . . . Figures taken from the annual reports of the six largest oil companies in the U.S. which confine their activities to crude production (and whose operations are therefore comparable to those of Aramco) show that net profits per barrel of oil in 1952 ranged from 56 cents to $1.43.[6]

Data from more recent years tend to support the view that profit margins in the Middle East do not differ a great deal from

[5] Burck, "World Oil: The Game Gets Rough," p. 128. The same figure is cited (without a source) on page 20 of a memorandum, *Middle East Field Report* (August 16, 1957), prepared by the Research Department of Laurence M. Marks & Co., a brokerage firm of New York City.

[6] Mimeographed press release, Standard Oil Company (New Jersey), March 17, 1955.

margins in the United States. In fact they seem to be lower: they average 82 cents (or less), while the average for six large producing companies in the United States, shown in Table IV, is 87 cents.

But a comparison of profit margins in the two areas is not

TABLE IV

PROFITS PER BARREL OF SIX LARGE PRODUCING COMPANIES
IN THE UNITED STATES

Company	Year	Net income (millions)	Crude production (millions of barrels)	Profit margin per barrel
Amerada	1958	$22.5	29.2	$ .77
Petrol. Corp.	1957	29.9	32.1	.93
	1956	26.5	32.9	.81
	1955	25.4	31.2	.81
Honolulu	1958	11.8	11.7	1.01
Oil Corp.	1957	14.5	13.2	1.10
	1956	13.8	13.4	1.05
	1955	13.7	11.6	1.18
Seaboard Oil Co.	1957	11.2	14.7	.76
	1956	9.4	14.7	.64
	1955	7.5	13.2	.57
Superior Oil Co.	1958	16.6	27.5	.60
	1957	18.9	26.4	.72
	1956	5.0	25.1	.20
	1955	3.4	22.4	.15
Texas Gulf	1958	4.0	4.5	.89
Prod. Co.	1957	6.8	5.1	1.34
	1956	5.7	4.9	1.14
	1955	6.7	4.8	1.40
Texas Pacific	1958	6.2	6.8	.91
Coal & Oil Co.	1957	7.2	7.4	.98
	1956	7.2	7.6	.95
	1955	7.9	7.5	1.05
Average				$ .87

Source: *Moody's Industrial Manual*, 1956, 1958, 1959.

very meaningful. Volume per well in the Middle East is far greater than it is in the United States, and returns on capital invested may be, as a consequence, a great deal higher. A larger measure of competition in the Middle East might (and perhaps should) have reduced returns on invested capital and driven profits per barrel down to a point at which they would have become substantially lower than those in the United States. There is no reason to believe that profit margins in the Middle East should be equal to margins in the United States. We will find it more meaningful to look at the rate of return on the capital which the oil companies have invested. Unfortunately, data for such an investigation is difficult to obtain, though some is available. A substantial amount of information has been published on the Arabian American Oil Company for the years 1955 and 1956.

2. Profits on Capital Invested in Aramco

Profits in Aramco reflect net investment in Aramco itself as well as the net investment of Trans-Arabian Pipeline Company (owner of "Tapline"), since Trans-Arabian Pipeline is operated as a nonprofit service company which charges fees to Aramco just high enough to cover costs. In Table V an attempt has been made to calculate the combined net worth of Aramco and Tapline and then to estimate return on investment. Part of the cross-desert pipeline is owned by Aramco and is included in the net worth of Aramco (line 1). The remainder, 70 percent of the mileage (as measured on a map), is owned by Trans-Arabian Pipeline Company; hence we have allocated 70 percent of the gross investment in the pipeline to Trans-Arabian (line 3). (Investment in terminal facilities and pumping stations may not in fact be so proportioned.) After depreciating this investment at the rate which is permitted under the agreement with the Saudi government (line 4), the writer has added it to the net worth of Aramco to get the net worth of the combined operation (line 5).

Net income in an oil company often is a misleading figure: it may vary a great deal from year to year as programs of explora-

TABLE V

PROFITS ON INVESTED CAPITAL IN ARAMCO

(millions of dollars)

	1956	1955	Sources
1. Net worth of Aramco	$471.4	$491.5	a, b
2. Gross value of Tapline investment	230.0	230.0	c
3. Gross value of Tapline owned by Trans-Arabian Pipeline Co. and not included in Aramco assets (70% of line 2)	161.0	161.0	d
4. Depreciated value of Tapline owned by Trans-Arabian Pipeline Co. (at 6.67% per year beginning with 1951)	96.5	107.2	e
5. Net worth of Aramco and Tapline (line 1 plus line 4)	567.9	598.7	
6. Net income of Aramco	280.8	272.3	a
7. Exploration and development expenses	14.8	14.1	a
8. Depreciation	47.0	44.5	a
9. Losses on materials and supplies	5.0	6.7	a
10. "Net cash income" or "cash flow" (sum of lines 6, 7, 8, and 9)	347.6	337.6	
11. Net income as percentage of net worth	49	45	
12. "Net cash income" as percentage of net worth	61	56	

a. *Emergency Oil Lift Program*, p. 2839.

b. *Ibid.*, p. 1237.

c. U.S. vs. California Standard and Texas Co., Stenographers' Minutes, April 15, 1957, p. 28.

d. Tapline owns the section from Quaisumah to Sidon, 744 miles, as measured on the map, or 70% of the published total mileage of 1,068 miles (Aramco, *Middle East Oil Development*, 4th ed. [n.p., 1956], p. 23; *World Oil's 1958 Middle East Oil Map*, published as a supplement to *World Oil*, August 15, 1958).

e. Permitted rate of depreciation given in Royal Decree 4,589, Saudi Arabia, ratifying the Tapline Convention, signed in Jiddah, October 24, 1949.

tion and development are accelerated or decelerated, the reason for the variation being that the costs of dry holes as well as intangible development costs (such as costs of labor, fuel, repairs, roadmaking, surveying, and geological work) are charged against income as expenses of the year during which they are incurred. Moreover, there is a considerable variation in the rates at which companies depreciate and deplete their properties. Security analysts have developed, consequently, a concept of "net cash income" or "cash flow," which they believe provides a better indication of oil company earnings and provides figures which are more comparable over the years and from one firm to another. To net income are added the figures for depreciation and depletion, dry hole costs, intangible development expenses, and charges against income for lease abandonments. The writer has attempted, still on Table V, to calculate net cash income for Aramco in the manner indicated (lines 6–10), and then has computed net income as a percentage of net worth (line 11) as well as net cash income as a percentage of net worth (line 12). Net income was 45 and 49 percent of net worth in 1955 and 1956 respectively, and net cash income was 56 and 61 percent of net worth in the two years. This seems to be high income, higher than producing companies earn elsewhere in the world, but these figures may overstate the actual return obtained on Saudi Arabian oil.

3. Profits in Transportation, Refining, and Marketing

In the spring of 1959 it became clear that during the second half of the fifties the international majors were realizing little or no profit on the transportation, refining, and marketing of Middle East oil. Virtually the entire profit on the operation of producing and distributing this oil was in production. Under these circumstances, "production" profits have been earned by the majors on capital invested in the later stages as well as on capital invested in production itself, and such profits overstate the profitability of Middle East oil when taken as a percentage of capital invested in production alone.

Let us look at the evidence on the lack of profitability in transportation, refining, and marketing. For 1956 the seven international majors (Jersey Standard, Socony, Standard of California, Texaco, Gulf Oil, Royal Dutch–Shell, and British Petroleum) reported total net profits of $2,562 million on their world-wide operations in production, transportation, refining, and marketing, while their combined crude production was 8.42 million barrels a day. Their net earnings, therefore, on all their operations averaged only 83.4 cents per barrel of crude produced. Net earnings for 1957, similarly calculated, came to 83.0 cents a barrel.[7] Profits on crude production alone average about 82 cents a barrel. (See Section 1 of this chapter.) When company profits on the several phases of activity in petroleum are compared with profits on production alone, it becomes clear that the international majors have been earning little if any profits on refining, transportation, and marketing. But here we have been talking about profits world-wide. William S. Evans of the First National City Bank of New York has made a study of oil profits in the Eastern Hemisphere.[8]

For the years 1953 to 1958 he has compared total net income from the Eastern Hemisphere operations of the seven international majors with payments to governments in Eastern Hemisphere producing countries. Under the assumption that profits in crude production are shared equally by the companies and governments, the payment figure provides an indication of company profits on production. Table VI is a reproduction of one of Evans' tables with some modification of the headings to make them more descriptive. The table demonstrates that the international majors have been making most of their profits in the Eastern Hemisphere on production and that they have been earning very small profits or experiencing losses in transportation, refining, and marketing.

In considering the profitability of Middle East oil, British

[7] Wanda M. Jablonski, "When the Pinch Leads to Blisters," *Petroleum Week*, March 20, 1959, p. 24.

[8] First National City Bank of New York, *Petroleum in the Eastern Hemisphere*, published by the bank, apparently in the spring of 1959.

Petroleum Company, Ltd., is of particular interest because it gets a very high proportion of its oil from the Middle East—in a fairly normal year such as 1958 about 97 percent.[9] For the years 1958 and 1959 it paid to producing-country governments in the Middle East under the fifty-fifty profit-sharing principle

TABLE VI

A COMPARISON OF NET INCOME ON ALL EASTERN HEMISPHERE
OPERATIONS WITH PAYMENTS TO PRODUCING-COUNTRY
GOVERNMENTS
(millions of dollars)

	1953	1954	1955	1956	1957	1958
Total net income *	$766.9	$862.0	$948.2	$1024.3	$1075.1	$ 976.9
Adjusted government payments †	602.1	697.1	898.1	958.8	1047.4	1237.0
Indicated nonproducing income	$164.8	$164.9	$ 50.1	$ 65.5	$ 27.7	$–260.1

Source: Slightly modified from a table in William S. Evans, *Petroleum in the Eastern Hemisphere* (New York, 1959), p. 12.
* From all Eastern Hemisphere operations of the seven international majors.
† Payments to governments in the Middle East and to the governments of Borneo, Indonesia, and other countries.

£119 and £115 million sterling respectively while its own reported income for each of these years was £63 million.[10] Taken at face value, these figures indicate that British Petroleum made money on production but lost a great deal on transportation, refining, and marketing. One has some reservations about the very low reported company income of £63 million; a large

[9] *Economist*, April 18, 1959, p. 253.
[10] Statements by Sir Neville Gass, chairman, British Petroleum Company, Ltd., *Annual Report and Accounts*, 1958, pp. 13, 18; *ibid.*, 1959, pp. 14, 27.

72

allowance for depletion or large outlays on exploration (treated as expenses) could lower income a great deal. But even if the item "Depreciation and Amounts Written Off" (£49 million in 1958 and £47 million in 1959), which includes depletion and expenditure on exploration, is added back in, the resulting BP "net cash income" is only £112 million in 1958 and £110 million in 1959, still less than its payments to producing-country governments (still less, that is, than its approximate net income on production).

It seems quite certain, then, that the international majors, in the second half of the fifties, have been making very small profits on the refining, transportation, and marketing of Middle East oil, even at times losing money on these operations. One can point to a number of factors all or part of which may explain this rather strange situation: (1) With fewer sellers in crude oil than in products, there is less competition in crude and crude prices are more rigid. (2) Before U.S. import quotas were made compulsory in the spring of 1959, the American majors may have been concerned to protect the U.S. price level by maintaining high prices on Middle East crude. They may have been seeking to defend the value of their investments in the United States or trying to prevent the introduction of compulsory quotas. (3) All of the oil companies may have kept crude oil prices high because of the general European hostility to profits; oil men may have felt that should crude prices be lowered governments would use price controls to eliminate any profits that opened up in refining and marketing. (4) The governments of Britain and France, holding shares in Middle East production (through stock ownership in British Petroleum and Compagnie Française des Pétroles), have received profits arising out of high crude prices and consequently may not have minded the lost tax revenues associated with low income in refining and marketing. (5) The governments of other consuming countries may not have reacted to high prices for crude oil (and lost tax revenues) because their countries are at a distance and benefit from freight absorption (that is, purchasers may not actually have been paying high posted prices for crude), because they do not understand that they lose tax money when crude prices are high and profits in refining and marketing low, or because they have not wanted to engage in state trading or threaten to restrict imports in order to get better prices for crude oil. (6) Finally, crude prices may have been kept high to satisfy the demands of the Arabs and Iranians who share in the profits of production.

Whatever the cause of high crude prices and low profits in transportation, refining, and marketing, it seems clear that "production" profits actually have been earned by the majors on capital invested in all the stages of production itself. These profits could not have been earned without both the profitable investment in production and the very nearly non-self-supporting investment in refining, transportation, and marketing. Under the circumstances, it appears that Aramco net income of 45 and 49 percent on net worth in 1955 and 1956 and Aramco net cash income of 56 and 61 percent of net worth in the two years (net worth, in both cases, not including tankers, refineries, and marketing facilities) overstate the profitability of Saudi Arabian oil, but it is difficult to say by how much.

4. Profits in Kuwait Oil

We have a different sort of knowledge concerning another concession, the concession in Kuwait. We do not have direct information of the profits which are earned on capital invested in production there, but we do know something of over-all profits on production, transportation, refining, and marketing.

The oil industry generally believes that profits in Kuwait production are much greater than Aramco profits in Saudi Arabia, a belief which gains substance from the undisputed facility with which the oil in Kuwait is extracted and brought to tidewater. Kuwait oil-producing sands are more than 1,000 feet thick, and their porosity and permeability are the highest in the Middle East; there is a natural water drive of great efficacy serving to

74

lift the oil to the surface; the oil, taken from wells only a few miles from the harbor, is pumped up to the Ahmadi Ridge, 390 feet in elevation, from which it flows by gravity into tankers at the terminal. By contrast, Saudi Arabian oil sands are mostly less than 200 feet thick, gas provides the principal drive, though a rather ineffective water drive exists (costly projects for gas and water injection are under way at the present time), and the oil fields are much farther from the coast.[11]

Although profits in Kuwait production are known to be exceptionally high and some data on net profits have become available through publication, figures on net investment in oil production in Kuwait have not been published. Hence an estimate of the rate of return on investment in production alone is impossible. An indication, however, of the over-all rate of return on investment in Kuwait oil—the rate of return on investment in production, transportation, refining, and marketing—can be obtained by examining the Eastern Hemisphere operations of Gulf Oil Corporation, which owns 50 percent of the Kuwait Oil Company. Gulf's activities in Kuwait oil are the largest part of its operations in the Eastern Hemisphere: in 1959 the Kuwait production of Gulf represented 90 percent of its Eastern Hemisphere production and Gulf's refining in Kuwait amounted to 70 percent of its Eastern Hemisphere processing.[12] Other operations of Gulf in the Eastern Hemisphere comprise production in Sicily, France, and Iran, refining in France and Iran, and marketing in Europe and the Far East. Almost certainly, however, Gulf's Kuwait investment is more profitable than its Eastern Hemisphere investments outside Kuwait. In all likelihood, therefore, its rate of return in Kuwait is higher than its over-all Eastern Hemisphere profits on net capital which averaged 67 percent over the years 1956 through 1959. (See Table VII.) Perhaps knowledge of exploration expenses deducted from Eastern Hemisphere receipts or knowledge of the

[11] Laurence M. Marks & Co., *Middle East Field Report*, pp. 15–16, 20.
[12] Gulf Oil Corporation, *Annual Report*, 1959, p. 26.

depletion allowance deducted would demonstrate that the return on Kuwait oil is very substantially higher than these figures indicate.

TABLE VII

PROFITS ON INVESTED CAPITAL IN THE EASTERN HEMISPHERE
OPERATIONS OF GULF OIL CORPORATION
(millions of dollars)

	1959	1958	1957	1956	Four-year average
Net income (consolidated)	$106.0	$202.0	$137.0	$109.6	
Net assets (consolidated)	269.0	262.0	174.0	149.0	
Net income as a per-centage of net assets	39	77	79	74	67

Source: Gulf Oil Corporation, Annual Report, 1959, p. 12; ibid., 1958, p. 12; ibid., 1957, p. 12; ibid., 1956, p. 16.

5. The Level of Necessary Profits

In attempting to appraise the magnitude of profits in Middle East oil, one looks in vain for a competitive market which might be used as a rough norm. Quite apart from the fact that profits in U.S. crude do not reflect political risks or the risks of trading across international boundaries comparable to the risks borne by oil companies in the Middle East, these profits reflect the powers of the state conservation commissions (principally in Texas, Louisiana, and Oklahoma) to control production and to maintain prices and profits in U.S. crude oil. Hence the greater part of the market in U.S. crude is not competitive. And we have already pointed out that Venezuelan oil has been under the control of a small number of firms which undoubtedly have behaved as oligopolists. Still, it will be of some value to see how profits in the Middle East compare with those in the other major producing areas. Production profits on invested capital in the United States

are shown in Table VIII, and profits on invested capital outside
the United States in the Western Hemisphere are shown in Table

TABLE VIII

PROFITS ON INVESTED CAPITAL OF SIX LARGE PRODUCING COMPANIES
IN THE UNITED STATES

Company	Year	Net income (millions)	"Net cash income" (millions)	Net worth (millions)	Net income as percentage of net worth	"Net cash income" as percentage of net worth
Amerada	1958	$22.5	$58.7	$156.5	14%	37%
Petrol.	1957	29.9	69.5	146.6	20	47
Corp.	1956	26.5	66.1	129.0	21	51
	1955	25.4	64.0	115.1	22	56
Honolulu	1958	11.8	22.3	86.6	14	26
Oil Corp.	1957	14.5	25.5	82.3	18	31
	1956	13.8	24.8	75.2	18	33
	1955	13.7	21.7	67.8	20	32
Seaboard	1957	11.2	30.6	79.3	14	39
Oil Co.	1956	9.4	27.4	72.5	13	38
	1955	7.5	24.3	52.6	14	46
Superior	1958	16.6	63.4	145.9	11	43
Oil Co.	1957	18.9	64.0	129.3	15	49
	1956	5.0	51.6	110.4	5	47
	1955	3.4	43.9	105.4	3	42
Texas Gulf	1958	4.0	11.6	41.4	10	28
Prod. Co.	1957	6.8	13.6	39.9	17	34
	1956	5.7	11.5	35.3	16	33
	1955	6.7	11.6	29.4	23	40
Texas Pa-	1958	6.2	14.4	73.0	9	20
cific Coal	1957	7.2	15.0	60.9	12	25
& Oil Co.	1956	7.2	14.4	57.2	13	25
	1955	7.9	14.6	53.4	15	27
Average					15%	37%

Source: *Moody's Industrial Manual*, 1956, 1958, 1959. "Net cash income" is equal to net income plus, as reported, depreciation, depletion,
intangible development costs, costs of dry holes, exploration expenses,
and lease relinquishments.

IX. Where possible, the writer has calculated "net cash income" or "cash flow" as a percentage of net worth in order to reduce the distortions arising from variations in rates of depreciation and

TABLE IX

OIL COMPANY PROFITS ON INVESTED CAPITAL OUTSIDE THE UNITED
STATES BUT WITHIN THE WESTERN HEMISPHERE

Region or Company	Year	Net income (millions)	"Net cash income" * (millions)	Net worth (millions)	Net income as percentage of net worth	"Net cash income" as percentage of net worth
Venezuela: all companies [a]	1957	2,765 bolivares		8,507 bolivares	33%	
	1956	2,115 "		7,213 "	29	
	1943–55				19	
Creole Petroleum (Venezuelan affiliate of Jersey Standard) [b]	1958	$235.7	$339.0	$846.2	28	40%
	1957	396.9	481.3	889.9	45	54
	1956	336.4	405.5	802.0	42	51
	1955	292.9	363.8	756.6	39	48
Sinclair Venezuelan Oil Co. [c]	1958	$ 16.5	$ 25.7	$ 84.9	19	30
	1957	10.1	17.5	74.4	14	24
	1956	9.2	17.2	64.3	14	27
	1955	5.0	13.2	55.2	9	24
Gulf Oil (Western Hemisphere outside U.S.) [d]	1959	$ 32.0		$367.0	9	
	1958	50.0		333.0	15	
	1957	81.0		269.0	30	
	1956	59.3		254.0	23	

Sources: (a) Ministry of Mines and Hydrocarbons, Venezuela. Reported in *Petroleum Week*, June 27, 1958, p. 52; June 13, 1958, p. 68. (b) Creole Petroleum Corporation, *Annual Report*, 1958, pp. 30–31; *ibid.*, 1957, pp. 30–31; *ibid.*, 1956, pp. 34–35. (c) *Moody's Industrial Manual*, 1958, 1959. (d) Gulf Oil Corporation, *Annual Report*, 1959, p. 12; *ibid.*, 1958, p. 12; *ibid.*, 1957, p. 12; *ibid.*, 1956, p. 16.

* "Net cash income" is equal to net income plus depreciation, depletion, cost of dry holes, etc. The Western Hemisphere operations of Gulf Oil outside the United States are mostly in Venezuela and Canada.

depletion as well as those caused by the expensing of intangible development costs and the costs of dry holes.

Net income as a percentage of net worth seems high in the Middle East in relation to this percentage in the Western Hemisphere—something less, possibly a good deal less, than 45 to 49 percent in Aramco and more than 67 percent in Kuwait, as compared with an average of 15 percent for six large producing companies in the United States and an average of about 30 percent for all companies in Venezuela. "Net cash income" as a percentage of net worth is high in the Middle East, but it is not so high relative to similar figures in the Western Hemisphere as is net income. It is 56 to 60 percent or less in Aramco as compared to an average of 37 percent for the six American firms, 40 or 50 percent for Creole, and 25 to 30 percent for Sinclair Venezuelan. Actually it is doubtful that these figures prove very much about profits in Middle East oil. We do not know by how much to reduce Aramco profits on capital invested as a consequence of our knowledge of the low or nonexistent profits in refining, transportation, and marketing. Although, no doubt, the extraordinarily high returns the companies earn on Kuwait oil are mostly oligopoly profits, they are, in all probability, partly economic rents; they represent in part returns attributable to the especially prolific fields of Kuwait, which the Kuwait government, the "landlord," has not yet succeeded in capturing. (Economic rents in Middle East oil will be discussed later in the book.) Perhaps the most one can say is that study of the limited data available leaves one with the *impression* of unusually high profits in Middle East oil. It is, moreover, an impression which, in the writer's experience, is borne out by conversations with oil men who are familiar with the facts. The writer is inclined to believe that his earlier analysis of the structure of the market in Middle East oil, an analysis which led him to conclude that the market could best be described as an oligopoly, gains support from the data on profits which have been reviewed. He is inclined to believe that the profits observed in Middle East oil represent in part oligopoly profits, particularly when he recalls that the lower Western Hemisphere profits with which he compared these returns have themselves been earned in controlled markets—controlled in the United States by the state conservation agencies and in Venezuela, in all likelihood, by the few majors.

Many will contend that high profits in the Middle East are necessary if firms are to carry the risks of investing in a politically unstable area and of trading across international boundaries. And there is no doubt that the profits of innovation must be high, whether the innovation involves the development of new products, the introduction of new equipment, or entry into new regions. Schumpeter presents a strong case for the proposition that short-run monopoly profits are necessary if innovation is to take place. (See p. 7.) As time passes, however, it is desirable that imitators and followers enter, thereby eliminating the gains of temporary monopoly. Admittedly, risks are considerable in Middle East oil in view of the ever-present possibility that trade barriers will be erected against the oil, that currency difficulties will interfere with its sale, or that an oil firm may find itself the object of a drive for nationalization. But it may be true that profits in Middle East oil are too high even while allowing for these risks; perhaps the extraordinary profits of innovation have endured too long. With pre-emption of the most promising acreage by the major companies, with control of markets by these companies, with Middle East oil a natural oligopoly, it seems likely that entry has not been sufficiently free to eliminate the earlier gains of innovation. Unusually high profits probably have been earned in the Middle East for some years now; the major concessions attained a production of 500,000 barrels per day in the following years: Iran, 1948; Saudi Arabia, 1950; Kuwait, 1951; Iraq, 1953.[13]

[13] *World Oil*, August 15, 1958, p. 130. During the Mossadegh regime Iran virtually shut down, of course, and was below 500,000 barrels a day from 1951 through 1955.

The idea that profits in Middle East oil have declined too slowly and that they are higher than necessary gains support from recent developments in Venezuela. Net profits on invested capital were about 30 percent there in 1956 and 1957 and averaged 19 percent from 1943 to 1955. Venezuelans are intensely nationalistic, and in its political affairs the country has been only precariously stable. Nevertheless, when new areas recently were opened up by the government for exploration, numerous "independent" firms from the United States paid large sums in bonuses for concessions, a total of $392 million in 1956 and $420 million in 1957.[14] It appears that the level of profits necessary to attract capital to the Middle East is lower than the profits we have discovered in Saudi Arabia and Kuwait.

The oil companies do point out that their profits world-wide are not unusually high. Over the years 1956, 1957, and 1958 the average return on capital invested (net income as a percentage of net worth) for the five American international oil companies plus the Royal Dutch–Shell group was 13.2 percent; this figure compares with an average return for a group of leading U.S. manufacturing corporations, for the same three years, of 12.2 percent.[15] The companies go on to argue that high Middle East profits are necessary to offset the lower profits, or the losses, which are experienced in other geographical areas. Now there is no denying that early, high profits associated with entry into a new region may simply offset losses endured in other parts of the world or that in many cases they represent no more than the proper reward for bearing the risks of innovation. But one is inclined to doubt that high profits, oligopoly profits, can be defended indefinitely on these grounds. Over a period of time less venturesome firms should enter and eliminate the gains

[14] *Petroleum Press Service*, July, 1958, p. 248.

[15] Return of oil companies calculated from data in *Moody's Industrial Manual*, 1959; return of manufacturing corporations from *Monthly Letter* of the First National City Bank, New York, April, 1958, p. 46; April, 1959, p. 40.

of innovation. That is, over the long run, profits in any one sector of the economy should be just high enough to cover the usual risks of doing business in that sector. Nor can the international majors defend enduringly high, oligopoly, returns in the Middle East on grounds that funds are earned thereby for investment all over the world. The consumers of Middle East oil should not be expected indefinitely to finance (to subsidize) investment for the benefit of consumers supplied from other regions, nor should the governments or peoples of the Middle East. If oil is scarce in other parts of the world, if the amount supplied is less than the amount demanded, prices in these regions will rise until it is profitable to explore for and develop oil there, or until it is profitable to ship in oil from the Middle East.

To be sure, the companies might argue that they are seeking to redress the inequities arising from the uneven distribution of natural resources in the world, that they are seeking to give to distant, poorly endowed peoples some of the advantages which accrue to those fortunately situated in the vicinity of rich oil reserves. And oil men might observe that in the absence of a world government to redistribute income from the natural wealth of the earth, the international oil companies can perform a most useful function in this respect. But it is doubtful that the international majors possess the moral authority to fill such a role; staffed in their upper echelons mostly by westerners, it is unlikely that they can command the respect of all the parties whose conflicting interests they might try to reconcile. A defense of high profits in Middle East oil, then, which suggests that funds are earned in this way for investment all over the world must be viewed with some skepticism.

The limited data available suggests, in the writer's opinion, that the profits of oligopoly are being earned in the Middle East. But a warning is in order at this point. Much remains to be said in later chapters concerning factors which influence the price of Middle East oil, and much must still be presented with respect to changes which have been proposed for improving the situation.

The reader would do well not to jump to conclusions. The market for Middle East oil is complex, the interests engaged are numerous and frequently conflicting, and the difficulties associated with alternative patterns are large, often far larger than they appear at first glance to be.

IV

The Price of Middle East Oil in
the Pattern of World Oil Prices

UP to this point we have not sought to discover how the price of Middle East oil varies as it moves from one point to another on the surface of the earth, and we have considered only briefly the consequences to its price of encounters with oil flowing from rival producing areas. Now, to repair these omissions, we turn to the subject of geographical differences in the price of Middle East oil.

1. The Theory of Geographical Price Differences

We have recognized that short-run imperfections in competition may be desirable in the interest of both innovation and stability. Hence we will confine ourselves here to asking how prices of a commodity vary through space in the long run at equilibrium under conditions of competition. We will assume a uniform blanket of buyers (with similar tastes) on the earth's surface, and we will assume a number of discrete centers of production. Supplies in the various producing regions reach out into surrounding areas for customers. From prices at points of origin, f.o.b. prices, there will be an increase of prices with distance, these delivered prices, or c.i.f. prices,[1] rising from each producing region to the points at which supplies from the different regions meet. The lines formed by these points of contact constitute "watersheds" of maximum delivered prices and boundaries between the various marketing regions. (See Figure 1.)

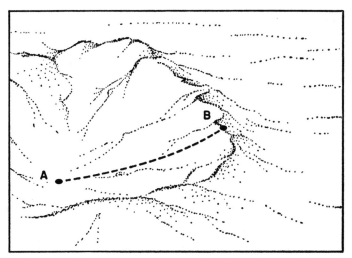

Figure 1. Customer on watershed of maximum delivered prices. *A,* factory, mine, or oilfield. *B,* customer.

With numerous centers of production one can imagine a number of natural marketing areas, the prices in each forming a sort of price crater or price basin: factories or mines with f.o.b. prices at low points in the interiors, customers on the surrounding hills ("price hills," not real hills) paying higher and higher delivered prices as they are farther away from a center of production until those on the peaks, or watersheds, look down into more than one basin and have a choice of regional centers from which they

[1] When f.o.b. prices are quoted, the buyer takes delivery at the factory or mine and the seller's responsibility ends when the goods are placed "free on board" the proper conveyance or ship. With c.i.f. prices the goods are shipped some distance to the seller and the price includes "costs of insurance and freight."

may buy. August Lösch has suggested that a uniform distribution of customers and plants would lead to a series of basins or craters which would be hexagonal in shape, since a pattern of hexagons would minimize total transportation costs.[2] In practice the price basins would be of different sizes, for a low-cost center of production would be capable of dominating a large area (though of course the costs of freight would check the reach of any center).

One other point about this long-run competitive equilibrium: Under it there would be no geographical price discrimination. Sellers would realize the same amount on all sales, distant or nearby; that is to say, their "netbacks" (prices of sale minus freight costs) in all cases would be the same. All f.o.b. sales would be at the same price no matter what the destination of the merchandise, and delivered prices for all destinations minus actual freight costs would yield the same amounts. In sum, the price of any good would vary in space only by the costs of transportation.

This situation can be understood best by contrasting it with the state of affairs in a market very imperfectly competitive. With a strongly entrenched oligopoly, sellers are likely over a long period of time to top the crest of the watershed and drop down on the other side, cutting prices to take business away from more advantageously situated suppliers. Of course they realize less on such distant sales than on those to nearby customers; they have not charged for the extra freight costs incurred and this "freight absorption" results in lower netbacks. Geographical price discrimination of this sort (the sellers are discriminating against nearby customers) makes sense to them because, if their realizations on additional sales cover the marginal costs involved, with a little extra which can be devoted to fixed costs, total profits are enlarged. And oligopolistic sellers do not choose to push the additional output into nearby markets in which netbacks are higher because they want to protect the price structure in these markets. They know that price cuts would be matched by their

[2] Stefan Valavanis, "Lösch on Location," *American Economic Review*, September, 1955, pp. 637–638.

few rivals and that they would end up here selling the same volume at a lower price.

But the picture is quite different in a market exceedingly competitive, the number of sellers being so large that no one of them can detect any influence on price of changes in his output. Here suppliers enter nearby markets if netbacks are high and withdraw from markets in which netbacks are low, until prices in all markets differ by no more than the costs of transportation, and realizations on all sales are equalized.

Suppose now in a competitive market change occurs; costs and prices at one center of production decrease. A shift in the watershed will take place, though the movement may not be rapid and indeed may be accompanied by difficult and rather painful adjustments in price and output. Suppliers in a production center with lower costs will tend to increase output and to cut prices, cutting prices beyond the watershed as well as inside it. As a consequence they will tend to win new territory, and the watershed of maximum delivered prices will tend to shift. (See Figure 2.) These lower-cost sellers may win a very large increment in their market territory almost immediately, or they may make

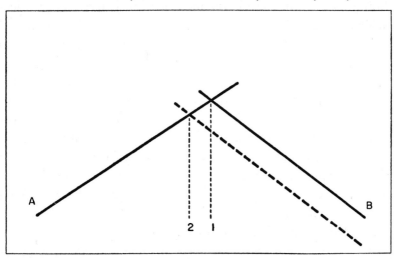

Figure 2. Shift of the watershed. The sloping lines represent delivered prices rising from production centers *A* and *B*. Reduced costs at *B* lead, sooner or later, to a shift of the watershed from *1* to *2*.

small gains at first followed by more substantial gains as time passes, depending upon the elasticity of demand for their product and the size of the territories (or "price basins") invaded. Let us consider the possibilities. Sellers in an adjacent center of production which has been encroached upon will tend to withdraw from the periphery of their territory, where new competition has been encountered and prices are lower, and to move their products into nearby markets. This of course tends to transfer the price declines from the edge of their territories to the center. If demand is elastic and the territory invaded large, goods withdrawn from the edge of the area will be readily absorbed in the remainder, price declines will be small, established sellers in the disputed border area will give way readily, and a movement in the watershed will be immediate and substantial. If, however, demand is inelastic or the territory invaded small, goods withdrawn from the periphery and sold nearer the center will cause large declines in price. With reduced prices in their hinterland sellers will be less inclined to withdraw in the face of new competition on the border, and the watershed will be slower to move. In the short run these sellers will of course be prepared to sell both on the border and in the interior of their territory at prices which cover only variable costs. As time passes, however, and existing facilities depreciate, sellers in the invaded territory who have been marketing at prices below their long-run average costs, will not replace productive capacity; then supplies in the market will decline, prices in the part of the territory not entered by the lower-cost producers will tend to return to their old level (or even to go higher if costs in a region with reduced volume are now greater), and suppliers in the territory invaded will retreat from peripheral markets to markets with more attractive netbacks. A reduction in costs, then, in any one production center sooner or later under competition will lead to a shift in the watershed of maximum delivered prices.

One other point should be noted. If demand is inelastic or the territory invaded small so that substantial price changes occur during the course of the adjustment, these price changes may spread to regions which do not even border on the center of reduced costs. Suppliers in production center A with reduced costs start selling across the watershed into the territory of production center B; reduced prices on its now-contested border will spread across its market area to other borders and lead to price declines in the region of production center C. Of course in time all the price changes outside the initially disputed border area will be reversed as depreciated productive capacity is not replaced by suppliers who have been selling at prices below long-run average costs.

Since no theory is a complete explanation of reality, the foregoing analysis takes us only a little way toward understanding the multifarious facts of the workaday world. Yet we will find it of some value as a sort of base camp in our further explorations.

2. International Oil Prices before the Second World War

Though there were a number of centers of oil production before the war, world prices for both crude and products were set, in the main, as though there were only one, the coast of the United States on the Gulf of Mexico. The formula for this system was "U.S. Gulf plus." Apart from the relatively few exceptions to be discussed shortly, a buyer anywhere in the world paid the U.S. Gulf price plus freight from the Gulf even though the oil actually was delivered to him from a nearer field. From the U.S. Gulf Coast the price rose with distance over the entire international market; it was almost as if the whole world were a single price crater or price basin with the U.S. Gulf at the center (though the geometry becomes awkward when a depression in a sphere is said to envelop the sphere).

There were, of course, innumerable day-to-day minor exceptions from the general pattern, and there were a few rather considerable variations. The most notable variation was in the vicinity of Rumania. For a time Constanta in that country became an export base and relatively independent prices were

89

quoted f.o.b. Constanta.[3] Rumania thus was in the center of a small price crater distinct from the very large one centered on the U.S. Gulf Coast. No doubt there were, at least part of the time, additional distinct regions. Dr. P. H. Frankel mentions Galicia and Russia,[4] and one suspects that some existed in the interior of the United States, though these last would not have involved trade across national boundaries. But most if not all of the separate market territories were but minor blemishes or pockmarks on a smooth face of world prices delineated by "U.S. Gulf plus."

What can be said for or against such a price system? It has been pointed out that before the Second World War a large part of world demand was met by exports from the Gulf Coast of the United States, which was the main source of supply for independent importers in consuming countries.[5] But neither of these observations is a defense of the predominance of U.S. Gulf prices. The question we must ask is why certain other areas— the Middle East or Venezuela—did not carve out their own separate market areas and form their own distinct price craters? In 1938 the Middle East was producing close to 120 million barrels of oil a year out of a world production of 1,988 million barrels, or about 6 percent of the total,[6] and Europe was getting almost a quarter of its imports from this source.[7] In the same year Venezuela produced 188 million barrels and Rumania produced 48 million barrels.[8]

There are two ways of explaining why the international majors did not struggle for distinct marketing territories in the Middle East and Venezuela: (1) the U.S. companies may have been

[3] Walter J. Levy, "The Past, Present and Likely Future Price Structure for the International Oil Trade," *Proceedings Third World Petroleum Congress*, Sec. X, Preprint 16 (Leiden, 1951), p. 5.

[4] "The State of the American Oil Industry," reprint of a series of articles published in *Petroleum Times*, May–August, 1946, p. 13.

[5] P. H. Frankel, *Essentials of Petroleum*, p. 115; Levy, *op. cit.*, p. 4.

[6] *World Oil*, August 15, 1958, pp. 129, 130.

[7] Levy, *op. cit.*, p. 16.

[8] *World Oil*, August 15, 1958, pp. 129, 131.

interested in protecting their investments in U.S. production, and
(2) all the majors may simply have been acting as true oligopolists. Serious price cutting by the companies producing in the
Middle East and Venezuela might have pushed the United States
out of world export markets and even captured some U.S. markets from domestic producers. This would have reduced the
value of some of the U.S. holdings of American companies. But
for the present we will set this suggestion aside; in Chapter VIII,
Section 1, we consider very carefully the question of whether or
not Middle East development has been held up to protect investments elsewhere. It is quite possible that the price of "U.S. Gulf
plus" was accepted so widely simply because the major companies were acting as oligopolists. In Rumania, which did carve
out a separate territory and establish a distinct price structure,
there were many independent suppliers, probably about thirty,[9]
and it was difficult to control their sales, though attempts were
made to do so. In the Middle East and Venezuela the few producers were aware that price cuts would be matched by their
rivals; rather than cut price to nearby buyers and develop separate market areas, they seem to have chosen to live and let live
under an umbrella of U.S. Gulf Coast prices.

Of course a policy of this sort might be defended by reference
to the intellectual atmosphere of the twenties and thirties which
tended to approve "orderly" markets, but it should be clearly
recognized that "U.S. Gulf plus" almost certainly provided quite
a different pattern of world oil prices than would have existed
had the industry been more competitive.

3. Oil Prices during the War: The End of "U.S. Gulf Plus" in the Middle East

A marked change in the pricing of world oil occurred during
the Second World War. The formula "U.S. Gulf plus" for Middle East crude and products was abandoned. The Auditor General of the British government objected to purchasing bunker

[9] Letter to the writer (dated March 11, 1959) from an oil executive
formerly associated with the Rumanian oil industry.

oils in Middle Eastern and Indian Ocean ports at a price equal to the U.S. price plus freight from the United States, and after discussions with the oil companies he "accepted f.o.b. prices for Persian Gulf centres approximating the f.o.b. prices in the Gulf of Mexico." [10] In 1945 the U.S. Navy, which was buying crude oil for France under the Lend-Lease Act, obtained a Persian Gulf crude price of $1.05 per barrel, which was equal to the price at the U.S. Gulf, and shortly after this it agreed to buy Persian Gulf products at prices equal to those on the U.S. Gulf Coast. The Navy purchases have since been criticized in Congress, where it was suggested that the price paid did not reflect the lower costs of Middle East oil, and the authors of the FTC Report have noted that earlier, from 1942 to 1945, Caltex supplied the Navy with products in the Middle East at a special contract price somewhat *below* U.S. Gulf quotations.[11]

Although the oligopolistic character of the market for Middle East oil may have kept its price from declining as rapidly as it would have under competition, nevertheless the changes made during the war were very great and it is quite inaccurate to call them "minor modifications," as the FTC Report does.[12] The Persian Gulf actually became a new basing point, and this production center then began to develop its own distinct marketing area and price structure. (See Figure 3.) In effect Persian Gulf f.o.b. prices were lowered by an amount equal to the costs of transportation from the U.S. Gulf Coast to the Persian Gulf; the f.o.b. crude oil price, for example, was lowered from something like $2.95 per barrel to $1.05.[13] Such a change can scarcely be called minor.

[10] Report of the Auditor General, quoted in FTC Report, p. 356.
[11] FTC Report, p. 359.
[12] *Ibid.*, p. 355.
[13] To get the figure $2.95 the writer calculated what the price would have been at the Persian Gulf had the "U.S. Gulf plus" formula remained in use, adding to the U.S. f.o.b. price of $1.05 the USMC freight rate from Ras Tanura to the U.S. Gulf Coast. (The USMC freight rate is the rate set by the U.S. Maritime Commission during the war.)

The Second World War ended with the Persian Gulf established as a distinct marketing territory with its own price structure. Postwar discussions of world oil prices and the many disputes that occurred mostly were concerned, as we shall see, with

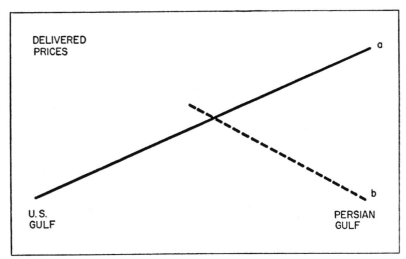

Figure 3. New basing point in the Persian Gulf. Prewar "U.S. Gulf plus" is represented by the solid line. Wartime establishment of Persian Gulf as a basing point is represented by the broken line. The Persian Gulf f.o.b. price was consequently lowered from *a* to *b*.

the size of this new territory and the rate at which it should expand. After the war the prices of crude oil and products in the Middle East began to diverge, and we will find it useful to treat crude prices and product prices separately.

4. Postwar Developments in Crude Oil Prices

Though "Persian Gulf plus" had now replaced "U.S. Gulf plus" in the pricing of Middle East oil, there was still a direct tie between the two markets as long as prices in the Persian Gulf were equal to prices at the U.S. Gulf Coast. But this tie was soon to be broken. When in 1946 price controls were removed in the United States, crude oil prices at the U.S. Gulf started on a series of increases until in December, 1947, they had reached a level

93

$1.46 per barrel above the wartime price. Middle East crude prices followed, but not all the way: they reached a peak in March, 1948, only $1.17 above the wartime price. (See Figure 4.) Middle East prices, it appeared, had acquired a degree of

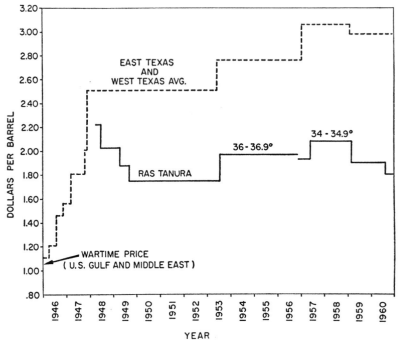

Figure 4. Crude oil prices at the U.S. Gulf Coast and in the Middle East. An average of East Texas and West Texas (sour) crude oil prices is generally thought to be representative of prices at the U.S. Gulf Coast, and these crudes are considered to be comparable to Middle East crudes. The price at Ras Tanura is representative of Persian Gulf prices in general. The increases which occurred in the price of Middle East oil from the wartime price of $1.05 to the 1948 price at Ras Tanura of $2.22 were not published.

Sources: Platt's Oil Price Handbook, annual editions; *Petroleum Week,* various dates; W. J. Levy, "Middle East Crude Prices," *Oil Forum,* November, 1953, p. 399.

independence from U.S. prices. Then while U.S. prices remained constant, Middle East prices began to decline in May, 1948, in part perhaps under the pressure of the Economic Co-operation Administration (this point will be considered in the next chapter), but in any case by July, 1949, they had fallen 47 cents a barrel and were 76 cents below prices at the U.S. Gulf Coast. The direct link between Persian Gulf prices and U.S. Gulf prices clearly was broken. When U.S. Gulf Coast prices increased in 1953 and 1957, Middle East prices followed by smaller amounts, and when U.S. prices declined in 1959, Middle East prices fell by larger magnitudes. In 1960 prices in the Middle East dropped while prices at the U.S. Gulf remained unchanged. At the beginning of 1961, then, Middle East crude oil prices were $1.18 per barrel below U.S. Gulf Coast prices.

To say that the direct tie between Middle East and U.S. crude prices was severed is not to say that it was severed as soon as it should have been or that the rate of decline of Middle East prices relative to those in the United States has been as rapid as would have been desirable. We are dealing with a market of oligopoly, and in such a market prices tend to be rigid or "sticky." But the direct link has been broken, Middle East oil has attained a degree of independence, and contrary to often-expressed views the post-war world price structure of crude oil is quite different from that of the wartime or prewar period.[14]

[14] See the FTC Report, pp. 362–363, for one of the contrary views. The authors of the report suggest that the decline of Persian Gulf prices relative to prices at the U.S. Gulf Coast was of little significance; they observe that it "did not actually result in a price reduction . . . because its effect was more than offset by the rising level of United States Gulf prices, to which the Persian Gulf price was linked." This statement, of course, confuses the general upward movement of world oil prices in the postwar period, attributable no doubt to inflationary forces, with the relative movements of prices in different oil centers. Persian Gulf prices did decline relative to U.S. prices, and this was a new competitive factor in numerous markets. To put it another way, as prices at the U.S. Gulf increased, Persian Gulf prices increased less than they would have if they had not broken their direct tie to the U.S. Gulf. Moreover, the authors of the FTC Report fail to recognize that the nature of the link between the two markets had changed. Instead of the wartime direct link, Persian Gulf prices equal to U.S. Gulf prices, prices in the two regions now were related only indirectly, linked, in fact, only through

PRICE OF MIDDLE EAST OIL

There is one possibility that could throw doubt on the degree of independence gained by Middle East prices in the postwar period. Perhaps they declined relative to prices in the United States simply because freight rates had increased. With higher freight rates, the more distant Middle East oil may have been at a greater disadvantage. Far from representing a new, meaningful, and at least moderately competitive development, Middle East price changes may simply have represented an attempt to hold existing markets when costs of transportation had increased and a locational handicap become more serious. There are two reasons for rejecting this interpretation of postwar price changes in the Middle East: (1) the trend of tanker rates since the war has if anything been downward, and (2) in the postwar period Middle East crude oil has steadily enlarged its marketing territory while the watershed between Middle East and Caribbean oil has constantly moved west through Europe and toward the United States.

Tanker rates in the postwar period have been plotted in Figure 5. The tendency, revealed to some extent in the figure, is for rates to decline as a consequence of the new, larger, and more economical tankers that are now being built. It seems clear, therefore, that the price of Middle East oil has not fallen relative to U.S. Gulf Coast prices because of a postwar increase in freight rates.

But the best evidence for the view that the decline of Middle East crude prices relative to those in the United States represents a new accession of independence, an essentially competitive development, lies in the postwar enlargement of the marketing area for Middle East crude oil and the movement of the watershed between Middle East and Caribbean oil west through Europe and toward the United States. (Cf. Figure 2, p. 87.) As the output of Middle East oil grew rapidly, from 700,000 barrels per day in 1946 to 1,400,000 barrels daily in 1949,[15] the watershed

---

a struggle for customers in the vicinity of the watershed. (The precise nature of this new bond will be discussed later.)

[15] *World Oil*, August 15, 1958, p. 130.

of maximum delivered prices swept dramatically westward until it reached the Atlantic and then, perhaps, crossed the ocean. (One says "perhaps" because this point has been much disputed and indeed, as we shall see later, makes up much of the controversy in the ECA Case.) With Western Hemisphere crude oil, except for specialty oils, by 1949 very largely displaced from

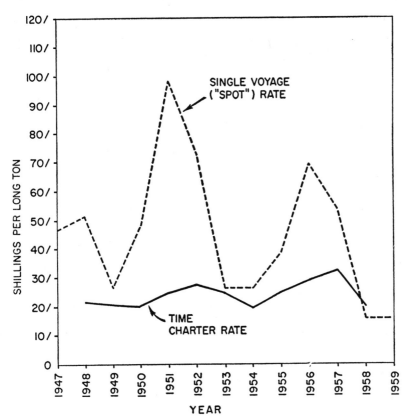

Figure 5. Postwar tanker rates (yearly averages). Single voyage rate: yearly mean; dirty; shillings per long ton per voyage, Curaçao to London to Curaçao. Time charter rate: yearly mean; shillings per dead weight ton per month; dirty, 16–20,000 d.w., delivery 24–36 months after fixing, charter period 5–7 years. No tonnage was fixed in the time charter market during 1959.

Source: Harley, Mullion & Co., Ltd., *Tanker Freight Statistics* (London, March, 1960), pp. 1, 23.

Europe by crude oil from the Middle East, it seems certain that in the postwar period the price of Middle East crude oil had declined substantially relative to the price on the U.S. Gulf Coast and that Middle East crude prices had attained a considerable degree of independence.

It is important to realize that as crude oil prices in the Persian Gulf declined and the market territory of Middle East oil expanded, the watershed of maximum delivered prices East of Suez moved eastward at the same time that the watershed West of Suez moved west. While the latter swept through Europe toward the East Coast of the United States, the former crossed the Pacific from Japan toward California, though Middle East crude oil did not, East of Suez, meet Caribbean crude in quantity. The wide Pacific plus oil production in Indonesia and California have separated on the far side of the globe the two major producing areas of the world.

Of course Middle East oil did meet Caribbean oil West of Suez, and, as we have observed, the watershed of maximum delivered prices in the postwar period moved constantly westward, driving oil from the Caribbean before it. When the watershed reached the Atlantic Ocean, a new situation arose and a new and interesting theory was developed to explain it.

5. Watershed at the Atlantic: The Theory of Walter Levy

In our earlier theory of geographical price differences we assumed a uniform blanket of buyers on the surface of the earth, supplied from a number of discrete centers of production. But when through price declines the market for Middle East crude oil had expanded through all Europe and arrived at the Atlantic, it had come to a break or gap in the blanket of customers. What would happen to the price of Middle East oil now that this wide expanse devoid of potential buyers had been attained? Sometime after the Atlantic had been reached and crossed, substantial deliveries of crude having been made on the East Coast of the

United States, Walter Levy, the noted student of world oil prices, suggested that the price of Persian Gulf crude had established itself with a range, the upper limit of which

would permit Caribbean crude oil to compete with Middle East crude oil in Western Europe, while its lower limit would permit Middle East crude oil to compete with U.S. crude oil at the U.S. East Coast. Actual prices within this range depend on both the competition between Middle East and Caribbean oil as reflected in the supply pattern and that between the various suppliers in the Middle East.[16]

Levy's theory has on occasion been called the "high and low of the range" theory. In effect he was suggesting that when the watershed of maximum delivered prices was still on the western coast of Europe, the price of Persian Gulf crude would be at its upper limit and that when the watershed had crossed the Atlantic to the eastern coast of the United States, the price of this crude would have dropped to its lower limit. (See Figure 6.) Persian Gulf crude prices, then, would fluctuate within limits set by the delivered prices of Western Hemisphere crude, delivered prices

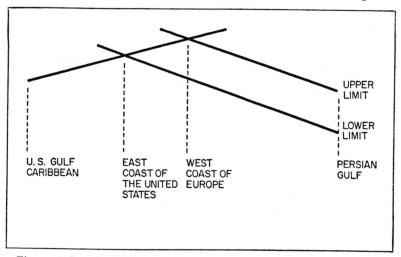

Figure 6. Levy's "high and low of the range" theory. Sloping lines represent delivered prices.

[16] Levy, op. cit., p. 1.

on the western coast of Europe or delivered prices on the eastern coast of the United States. Levy did not attempt to forecast where the watershed actually would be, and indeed he left open the possibility that it would jump back and forth across the Atlantic. Output in the Middle East at one time might have been great enough to supply all Europe and some of the needs of the U.S. East Coast. Then at a later date it might have lagged behind European demand so that prices in the Eastern Hemisphere would have risen to attract supplies from the U.S. Gulf Coast and the Caribbean Sea. As it turned out, the watershed has tended to stay on the East Coast of the United States and the crude oil price at the Persian Gulf has tended to settle at its lower limit.

Levy's "high and low of the range" theory is an elegant statement of the impact of the Atlantic Ocean on the structure of world crude oil prices. Although there is no basis for substantial criticism of the theory, two omissions should be noted.

First, Levy's theory is limited because he assumes a competitive market. In the article which we have just cited, a standard work on the price structure of world oil, he studies long-run trends of world prices in a market assumed to be competitive. Though he emphasizes that "it will require time before the price structure responds to changes in supply and demand,"[17] he apparently is speaking only of the normal time of long-run competitive adjustment, for he starts his article with the assertion that "the structure of world oil prices is *intimately* related to the pattern of competitive world oil supplies and demand"[18] and frequently thereafter refers to competitive factors in the market. In line with his assumption of competition, Levy apparently expects long-run competitive forces to eliminate geographical price discrimination, in crude oil at least, in all but "far distant and marginal markets."[19] Levy's failure to treat imperfections in competition does not make his theory incorrect but it does mean that the theory

[17] *Ibid.*, p. 2.
[18] *Ibid.*, p. 1, my italics.
[19] *Ibid.*, p. 11.

must be supplemented by additional analysis. A pattern of world oil prices such as he envisages probably emerges in time, but socially undesirable delays and dubious geographical price discrimination which may occur in the interim are phenomena not covered by his theory.

In addition to omitting a treatment of market imperfections, Levy fails to bring out the interaction between Middle East crude prices and prices in the Western Hemisphere. Though he recognizes that these prices interact, his extensive discussion of the fluctuations of Middle East prices within limits set by the delivered prices of Western Hemisphere oil leaves the impression that the latter are relatively fixed and beyond the influence of the former. Now Levy no doubt feels that he has given adequate reason for omitting a discussion of the interaction between prices in the two hemispheres when he asserts that his study "does not go into the dynamic inter-relationship between the price levels" in the major centers of supply "but refers only to the static relationship between the f.o.b. prices in the major exporting centers of the world." [20] But in fact he does deal with the dynamic inter-relationship of world prices when he depicts a Middle East crude price which fluctuates within limits and changes its relationship to prices in the Western Hemisphere. He fails, however, to make clear that the Middle East price may influence the Western Hemisphere price as well as respond to its influence. At the same time as the price of Middle East crude oil is fluctuating between two limits, it may itself change the limits. Suppose the watershed between the two regions were in Europe, and Middle East prices were tending to decline and to drive Western Hemisphere crude oil off the continent. If the people controlling production in the Western Hemisphere insisted on maintaining existing volume or insisted on continuing a predetermined rate of increase, then competition between the regions could lead to a fall in Western Hemisphere prices and a decline in the upper limit on Middle East prices. Or suppose that the watershed were on the East

[20] *Ibid.*, p. 4.

Coast of the United States with Middle East prices tending to decline and Middle East oil tending to take a larger share of the U.S. market. If those controlling production in the United States sought to maintain output and defend these East Coast markets, then U.S. prices might fall and the lower limit on Middle East crude oil prices decline.

Although Middle East prices are almost certain to have some influence on U.S. prices, Levy's failure to make this observation is not very serious. For in the period following the appearance of his article in 1951, the likelihood was that Middle East crude prices would decline and Western Hemisphere prices remain relatively fixed. Tremendous quantities of low-cost oil had been found in the Middle East, and as this oil-producing region sought its place in the sun, its low costs were almost certain to lead to price reductions. Western Hemisphere oil, particularly U.S. oil, on the other hand, represented relatively high-cost production; its price was apt to be defended by withdrawal from exposed markets, such as those in Europe, by control of output, and through protection where this was obtainable, as in the United States. Developments in the last few years have been along these lines and the general emphasis of Levy's analysis has been shown to have been correct: prices in the Western Hemisphere do not appear to have been influenced very much by Middle East crude prices.

Apart, then, from two relatively unimportant omissions—consideration of imperfectly competitive factors in the market and discussion of the interaction of Western Hemisphere with Middle East prices—Levy's "high and low of the range" theory is very fine. It is a clear statement of the consequences to price of a gap in the blanket of customers such as occurs over the breadth of the Atlantic Ocean. And, though he does not develop the point, the theory indicates the circumstances under which prices of a commodity in two regions would be completely independent of one another: Middle East prices move in complete independence of prices in the Western Hemisphere when they are within the range set by Levy's upper and lower limits, and they are within this range when Middle East oil has pushed Western Hemisphere oil out of Europe but has not begun to penetrate the United States. Middle East prices, then, are fully independent of U.S. Gulf Coast prices when each producing region has its own distinct and separate market area (divided by the Atlantic Ocean on the one side and the Pacific Ocean and the U.S. West Coast area on the other). We can generalize from Levy's theory and suggest that the prices of a commodity produced in two regions will be entirely independent of one another only when supplies from the two areas at no point meet in volume and compete for peripheral customers.

6. Postwar Developments in Product Prices

As we observed earlier, during the Second World War Persian Gulf product prices (along with crude prices) declined from "U.S. Gulf plus" to an equality with U.S. Gulf Coast prices. No longer were the costs of freight from the Gulf of Mexico added to the price at the Gulf to get the price f.o.b. Persian Gulf (or to get the delivered prices of Persian Gulf oil). After the Second World War, though crude prices in the Middle East continued to fall relative to Western Hemisphere prices and ended up about one dollar per barrel below these prices, product prices in the Persian Gulf remained equal to prices at the U.S. Gulf Coast until 1957, when a slight tendency to break away became evident. By January, 1960, many products which sold for nine or ten cents a gallon were a quarter- or a half-cent per gallon cheaper in the Persian Gulf than they were on the U.S. Gulf Coast; others were a little higher in the Middle East than on the Gulf of Mexico. (One-half cent a gallon would be 21 cents on a barrel of 42 gallons.)

Why have product prices in the Middle East not been more independent of product prices in the Western Hemisphere?

Levy writing in 1951 thought that they would become independent,[21] and there is, indeed, no obvious rationale for an equality of Persian Gulf and U.S. Gulf product prices.

It appears that quite fortuitously Persian Gulf product prices equal to U.S. Gulf Coast prices may have been "about right" for the period following the Second World War. Although crude prices in the Middle East were lower, the pattern of refinery output was different, less high-value gasoline being turned out than in the Western Hemisphere and more low-value fuel oil, so that Middle Eastern refinery profits may not have been out of line with refinery profits elsewhere. E. A. Higgins of the Shell Petroleum Company has suggested that "the gross margins earned on refining to the pattern of demand in the Indian Ocean area are much the same as those applicable to refining to the pattern of demand ruling on the East Coast of the United States." [22] Estimates of refinery margins for the years 1948 to 1954 made by the secretariat, Economic Commission for Europe, show that margins in the Middle East are about equal to those obtained on the U.S. Gulf Coast.[23] Of course refineries in the Persian Gulf tend to be larger than in the United States, and similar gross margins on a larger volume may be translated into higher profits on capital invested. Still it is possible that Persian Gulf product prices close to prices at the U.S. Gulf are not unreasonable even though crude prices in the two areas are quite different. Without further information, however, one hesitates, for two reasons, to affirm that product prices in the Middle East are satisfactory. One, the structure of the market is oligopolistic and an economist expects

[21] Op. cit., p. 12.

[22] Petroleum Press Service, January, 1958, p. 9.

[23] ECE Report, Annex, p. 8. The authors of the study explain on page 50 that the refinery margins for the Middle East shown on their Table 18, Annex, p. 8, are overestimated. When one averages the Middle Eastern margins (for the years 1948 to 1954) presented on this table and corrects the average by the estimates of error provided on page 50, one obtains a figure remarkably close to an average of the U.S. Gulf Coast margins which are set forth on the same table.

to find rigid or sticky prices under such circumstances. Two, refining is a complex affair, the economics of which apparently are not widely known. Perhaps exaggerating, an astute student of oil prices in a major company said to the writer that petroleum economists do not understand refineries while refinery engineers do not understand economics. It does seem that less thought has been given to product prices than to the price of crude oil. The officers of one international major had not even been able to affirm positively that product prices in the Persian Gulf were about right until challenged by the Australian government to prove that they were so; these officers had simply had a feeling that they were satisfactory. In a sector in which knowledge is lacking, it would not be surprising to discover that the *status quo* had become particularly attractive and that a superficially plausible price, the price at the U.S. Gulf Coast, should acquire a spurious authority.

Whether Persian Gulf product prices about equal to prices at the U.S. Gulf are fortuitously correct or dubiously adherent, it seems probable that in time they will diverge markedly from U.S. prices. What pattern might then emerge?

In 1951 Levy believed it unlikely that future product prices f.o.b. Persian Gulf would be determined on a netback basis, "by equating the delivered price for such products to that of products from the United States or the Caribbean in their marginal market West of Suez, or to that of products from California or the Dutch East Indies in the East of Suez area." He observed that "in the future only a small stream of refined products will move from the Persian Gulf area to West of Suez countries, which would not appear to offer a proper basis for the establishment of a price structure." And he suggested that Middle East product prices would not be determined on the basis of East of Suez netbacks because "the quantities of refined products available in the Persian Gulf are so large that the Persian Gulf will easily constitute the major source of supply for East of Suez markets, while the Dutch East Indies and California would contribute only limited quantities." [24]

If Levy is right about future world movements of oil products, his observation that netbacks in peripheral markets, East or West of Suez, would not be used in establishing prices is certainly correct. In effect he is saying that Middle East products are not likely to meet products from other regions in quantities large enough to be significant. European and Western Hemisphere refineries will process most of the oil consumed West of Suez, and East of Suez the Pacific Ocean will separate products from the Eastern and Western Hemispheres (while products refined in Indonesia remain relatively small in volume). Because of the separation in product-marketing areas, product prices in the Middle East will be completely independent of U.S. product prices, just as because of the occasional Atlantic separation of crude markets (backed up by a Pacific Ocean and U.S. West Coast separation on the other side of the world) there is a range of complete independence in Middle East crude prices. In products, however, Levy does not speak of a range only, within which prices would move independently, probably because he sees no likely price which would allow products from the Middle East to reach out across the Pacific in quantity to meet products from California or to move West of Suez in volume, and no price which would allow Western Hemisphere shipments in volume west across the Pacific. Hence he does not see upper and lower limits, only within which would product prices fluctuate independently. (But it is interesting to speculate on the possibility of a lower limit for Middle East product prices which would permit products from the Middle East to move in significant volumes into the U.S. East Coast.)

At all events, if, contrary to Levy's 1951 expectations, Middle East products at some time do meet Western Hemisphere products in quantity, East or West of Suez, then netbacks from the watersheds between marketing areas should be an important fac-

[24] Levy, *op. cit.*, p. 13.

tor in price determination. In addition to costs and profit margins, oil companies would want to consider netbacks earned on large sales to distant and stable markets. Of course the watershed from which netbacks were calculated would vary from one product to another; for example, the price basin for Middle East gasoline might be larger than the basin for fuel oil.

In all cases it should be recognized that enduring variable netbacks are indefensible. Under competition, discrimination between geographical regions would be eliminated as sellers so numerous that they had no visible influence on price withdrew from low netback markets and entered those with high realizations. But in practice there appears to be a great deal of geographical price discrimination in products from the Middle East, evidently more than in crude oil. Levy tells of this discrimination, administered through freight allowances,[25] and the FTC Report discusses an interesting postwar case of geographical price discrimination. While Persian Gulf product prices, along with crude prices, were dropped during the Second World War from "U.S. Gulf plus" to approximately the U.S. Gulf Coast prices, the exact Middle East f.o.b. product price varied with destination until 1948. The "high of Platt's" at the U.S. Gulf was used on Persian Gulf shipments to China, the "mean of Platt's" on shipments to all other markets East of Suez, and the "low of Platt's" on shipments West of Suez.[26] This system apparently was abandoned in 1948, but it appears that much discrimination in products remains. One wonders whether the oligopolistic structure of the markets has not led to an unduly slow elimination of geographical price discrimination, the oil companies adjusting prices on nearby sales too slowly as the Middle East market basin enlarges and too slowly pulling out of distant, marginal markets where low netbacks are likely to endure indefinitely. The entire subject of geographical price discrimination will be explored more fully in the next chapter.

[25] *Ibid.*, p. 7.
[26] FTC Report, p. 371. "Platt's Oilgram" is a price-reporting service.

Though product prices in the Persian Gulf have shown only a slight tendency to break away from an equality with U.S. Gulf Coast prices, it is possible that fortuitously this structure has been about right for the postwar period. Crude prices at the Persian Gulf are approximately a dollar per barrel below crude prices at the U.S. Gulf. The product demand pattern in the Middle East calls for a smaller output of valuable gasoline and a larger volume of fuel oil so that gross refinery margins are apparently about the same as elsewhere in the world and net profits on capital invested may not be too high. It is possible, however, that, given the oligopolistic structure of the market and a lack of knowledge of refinery economics (with the conservatism that follows from limited understanding), oil men may be attached too firmly to an outdated product-pricing formula and too ready to accept geographical price discrimination in products. In the future as product prices in the Middle East diverge more from prices at the U.S. Gulf, they are likely, in accordance with Levy's 1951 observations, to become quite independent of prices in the United States, with netbacks on small deliveries into peripheral markets of the Western Hemisphere of little importance in price determination. Relatively small quantities of Middle East products will be shipped West of Suez, while the breadth of the Pacific Ocean will separate Eastern and Western Hemisphere markets east of the Canal. If at any time Middle East products should begin to meet Western Hemisphere products in quantity, however, then along with costs and profit margins oil men, in establishing prices, would want to consider netbacks on sales to watershed markets.

7. Oil Prices at the Eastern Mediterranean

Oil men, government people, and others have debated at length the relationship in the Middle East between oil prices in the Persian Gulf and oil prices at the eastern Mediterranean. Logically eastern Mediterranean prices should exceed Persian Gulf prices by the costs of transportation; one would find such a spread in a perfectly competitive market. But there are two modes of transportation here—the cross-desert pipelines and tanker transport around the Arabian peninsula and through the Suez Canal—and their costs have differed. Which should prevail? Which costs should be used to determine the difference between prices in the Persian Gulf and at the eastern Mediterranean?

Apparently when the 1,068-mile Trans-Arabian Pipeline began operations late in 1950, some officials of the Mutual Security Agency (successor to the Economic Co-operation Administration) estimated that costs of transportation through the pipeline were 26 cents per barrel.[27] At the same time the 6,442-mile tanker journey around the peninsula to the eastern Mediterranean and return cost about 70 cents a barrel (the USMC rate). It is not clear that the pipeline costs of 26 cents included necessary profits on capital invested. Moreover, the cost differential between the two routes may have narrowed since 1950 and may narrow more in the future: the supertanker is tending to reduce the costs of sea transport, while the Arabs are insisting on (and the companies in principle have conceded to them) half of the pipeline profits.

For the purposes of this discussion we shall assume that differential transportation costs remain in existence. Certainly there is reason to believe that various modes of transportation will be used in carrying oil to the West. Because capacity operation is so important in obtaining low-cost pipeline transport, it is doubtful that large-diameter pipelines will ever be installed to carry all of the oil moving to markets west of the Suez Canal; lesser quantities probably always will be transported in smaller pipelines or in tankers. Indeed 5 or 10 percent of the Middle East oil which reaches the Mediterranean may be invariably carried by tanker, simply because such transport is more suitable for the irregular shipment of marginal supplies.

With different modes of transportation likely to remain in use, differential transport costs are a continued possibility. Such differences in costs create pricing problems. In the Middle East

[27] Read in a private but nongovernmental memorandum of the period.

prices at the eastern Mediterranean have tended to reflect the costs of tanker transport around the Arabian peninsula rather than the apparently lower costs of pipeline transportation across the desert. Under these circumstances, large-diameter pipelines earn a surplus, a gain of natural monopoly. It is a return which resembles the rent earned by a well-located or particularly fertile piece of land. Practical procedures for the elimination of this surplus are difficult to devise. No feasible price changes which the oil companies might make will remedy the situation. Suppose we consider the possibilities.

Eastern Mediterranean prices based on the lower costs of land transport would have one of two effects. The oil companies would have to discriminate between customers, giving some the advantages of eastern Mediterranean prices which reflect low-cost pipeline transport while forcing others to pay for higher-cost tanker transport (to their competitive disadvantage). Alternatively the companies would have to lower their prices on oil shipped by tanker to the West and in effect absorb freight on these shipments. For example, suppose pipeline costs (including necessary profits) are 30 cents per barrel, tanker costs around the peninsula are 40 cents, the f.o.b. price in the Persian Gulf is $2.00 a barrel, and the price at the eastern Mediterranean is $2.30. Western European customers who buy at the Persian Gulf and pay the higher tanker transportation costs find themselves at a competitive disadvantage; by the time their oil reaches the eastern Mediterranean it has cost them $2.40. If the oil companies lower to $1.90 the Persian Gulf price on tanker shipments to the West, they are absorbing freight on those shipments; they net less than on oil shipped through the pipeline. And they are now discriminating against their other Persian Gulf customers, buyers lifting oil for nonwestern destinations, who are still paying $2.00 per barrel.

Perhaps it will be suggested that the companies reduce prices on all tanker shipments, that they set prices at the eastern Mediterranean and on the Persian Gulf which are the same for all purchases at a given point and which yield an adequate return on total capital invested in production, pipeline transport, and tanker transport. For example, if as before pipeline costs are 30 cents a barrel (including necessary profits) and tanker costs 40 cents, an f.o.b. price of $1.95 in the Persian Gulf (to all buyers there) and a price of $2.35 at the eastern Mediterranean might provide a satisfactory return on total invested capital. To be sure, the companies would net $2.05 on their pipeline deliveries and $1.95 on their tanker sales; but prices would have been selected which provide an average netback just high enough to yield an adequate return on capital invested in production, and no purchaser would have been given an advantage by the differential netback. Nevertheless, this pricing system is unsatisfactory. The fact that in order to maintain a proper average netback prices would have to be changed periodically as the proportions of oil carried by pipeline and tanker varied is perhaps not serious. Nor would advocates of this system have to take seriously a contention that customers who receive oil through pipelines were being discriminated against because company netbacks were higher on these shipments; all purchasers at a given point would be paying the same price for oil and none would be at a competitive disadvantage. The really serious criticism is that in effect the oil companies still would be absorbing freight on tanker deliveries, and that it would be the high netbacks on pipeline shipments which made possible the low f.o.b. prices on deliveries to tankers. As a consequence of this freight absorption the smaller producing companies in the Middle East without access to cross-desert pipelines would be at a real disadvantage in trying to match f.o.b. prices which were in reality subsidized by netbacks received on pipeline shipments. In the preceding example a Persian Gulf price f.o.b. of $1.95 would be one thing to a company netting $2.05 on part of its shipments and quite another thing to a firm which received only this price on its sales.

It seems very doubtful that there is a scheme of pricing open to the oil companies in the Middle East which will solve the problems created by the existence of differential costs of transportation to the West. Prices at the eastern Mediterranean will have to reflect the higher costs of marginal transport through smaller pipelines or around the peninsula in tankers, and f.o.b. prices in the Persian Gulf, rather than being lowered to absorb freight, will have to reflect actual costs of production (including of course necessary profits). Eastern Mediterranean and Persian Gulf prices so established will yield a surplus, a gain of natural monopoly, to the owners of large-diameter pipelines (as long as they are a lower-cost mode of transport).

Perhaps an ideal, but impractical, solution would be for a supranational authority to identify and to tax away the surplus, and then to pay the proceeds of the tax to all purchasers of oil West of Suez in proportion to purchases. This solution, likely to be approved by the ghost of Henry George, would give the benefits of low-cost desert transportation to all buyers west of the Canal. One can even conceive farsighted and detached oil companies recognizing a surplus and allaying criticism by paying it out to buyers West of Suez as a kind of "patronage dividend."

But the problem of dealing with surpluses earned by large pipelines merges into the problem of treating surpluses in Middle East oil generally. Whether they are excess pipeline profits or oligopoly profits in production, numerous problems present themselves, not the least of which is the fact that in all likelihood the Arabs and Iranians will be disinclined to forgo a share in these gains. We will consider carefully in later chapters the extremely difficult problems of change and reform in Middle East oil.

8. Are Middle East Prices Tied to the U.S. Gulf Coast?

Critics of the international oil companies often state that Middle East oil prices are tied, or too closely tied, to prices at the U.S. Gulf.[28] We have already touched upon this subject many times, but now it will be advantageous to draw together the various strands of our analysis.

[28] FTC Report, pp. 360, 377–378; ECE Report, pp. 4–5, 21–23.

Neither Middle East crude nor products are linked by the old prewar formula of "U.S. Gulf plus," under which Middle East prices changed their relationship to U.S. prices only when freight costs changed. The direct tie of Middle East prices equal to U.S. Gulf Coast prices has held product prices in the Middle East longer than it held crude oil prices: only since 1957 has there been a tendency, and then a relatively slight one, for product prices to break away. But crude prices broke the tie in the early postwar period, and by January, 1961, Persian Gulf prices were $1.18 per barrel below U.S. Gulf prices. (See Figure 4, p. 94.) Nevertheless, although Middle East crude oil prices now clearly have a degree of independence from Caribbean crude prices, they are not, except in the range between Levy's upper and lower limits, completely independent. Crude oil prices in the Middle East tend to be indirectly linked to U.S. Gulf prices as a consequence of the encounter between Middle East crude and Caribbean crude in watershed markets on the U.S. East Coast or in South America. Since oil from the two regions competes in these border areas, an increase in U.S. Gulf Coast prices tends to increase Middle East prices, and a reduction in U.S. prices tends to reduce them. As U.S. prices rise, peripheral buyers are inclined to shift to Middle East suppliers, putting a certain amount of upward pressure on Middle East prices unless Middle East supply is very elastic. When U.S. Gulf prices drop, peripheral buyers are inclined to shift away from Middle East oil, and in the absence of an elastic Middle East supply the price of Middle East oil tends to decline. Of course if the long-run tendency is for Persian Gulf prices to fall relative to U.S. prices, as has been the case in crude oil since the Second World War, Persian Gulf prices will be slow to rise with Western Hemisphere prices (they probably will not rise the full amount of any Western Hemisphere increase) and quick to decline with any Western Hemisphere reduction (probably declining more than in the Western Hemisphere). But as long as oil from the two regions meets in substantial quantities in some markets, Middle East prices in the short run will tend to move with prices at the U.S. Gulf Coast. Perhaps, however, this is a tendency which ought not to exist. It might be argued that, given the low costs of Middle East oil, its price should not rise with U.S. Gulf prices. Rather than follow U.S. prices up, sellers in the Middle East might supply at existing prices customers who want to shift to them from Western Hemisphere sources. They might thus move the watershed more quickly west and enlarge more rapidly the Middle East market basin. This is of course a variation on the theme that Middle East prices have not declined relative to Western Hemisphere prices as much or as rapidly as they should have. But there may be no objection to short-run, parallel movements in prices in the two hemispheres even though over the long run it is desirable for them to diverge. At times the short-run supply in the Middle East may be inelastic and there may be little or no excess capacity with which to take care of the wants of customers seeking an escape from higher U.S. Gulf prices. These higher U.S. prices and the consequent shift toward Middle East suppliers, at least temporarily, may be followed by higher prices in the Middle East. Certainly we can say that short-run movements of Middle East prices with prices in the Western Hemisphere are not in themselves evidence of imperfect competition, for, given areas in which supplies from the two producing regions meet, such movements probably would occur in perfectly competitive markets.[29]

A complete independence of prices between two producing areas, an absence of all ties whatever, can occur only if the markets of the two regions are completely separate and distinct. In crude oil this happens, for a range of Middle East prices, when Middle Eastern and Caribbean market basins are separated by the Atlantic Ocean on the one side and by the Pacific Ocean and the U.S. West Coast area on the other. In products, price independence will develop when Middle Eastern and Caribbean market

[29] See Section 1 of this chapter for a detailed discussion of price movements from one market basin to another under competition.

basins are separated by European and Western Hemisphere refineries West of Suez and by the Pacific Ocean and the U.S. West
Coast area east of the Canal.

Nothing we have said in this section concerning links, or the
absence of links, between Persian Gulf and U.S. Gulf Coast
prices rules out the possibility that in recent decades the former
have declined too slowly and too little relative to the latter—rules
out the possibility, that is, that the international majors, as oligopolists or as oil men interested in protecting Western Hemisphere holdings, have maintained Middle East prices higher than
low costs in the area warranted. But we have, it is hoped, made
it clear that Middle East prices are much less closely tied to Western Hemisphere prices than they have been in the past, that short-
run links may be justified by conditions of inelastic supply and
might in any case exist under competition, and that all assertions
alleging a tie between regional prices must be carefully stated
and cautiously interpreted.

V

The ECA and the Oil Companies: A Study in Geographical Price Discrimination

A LARGE part of the aid given under the European Recovery Program, the "Marshall Plan," was devoted to the purchase of crude oil and petroleum products. The Economic Co-operation Administration (ECA) and its successor, the Mutual Security Agency (MSA), were very much concerned to see that these funds were well spent, that prices paid for oil were appropriate and reasonable. From its beginning in 1948 ECA or MSA[1] was constantly probing oil prices. It corresponded with the oil companies, called them in for consultation, studied documents, and appointed a panel of five consultants as advisers to the agency. On some occasions following the attentions of ECA, the companies reduced their prices, apparently in part at least as a consequence of ECA pressure; at other times they resisted efforts of ECA to get price reductions. Eventually ECA asked several oil firms for refunds on a large number of transactions, and upon refusal of the firms to pay it turned its claims over to the De-

[1] Henceforth referred to simply as "ECA."

partment of Justice for possible litigation. When the Justice Department sued for recovery of over $50 million, it created the ECA Case, which involved a number of subtle legal questions and some very interesting economic theory.[2]

We will concern ourselves only with the economics of the dispute, but at the same time we shall go beyond the ECA Case proper, since some parts of the controversy which were not brought to trial are of considerable interest to the economist.

The comparatively unimportant statutory provisions concerning price in the various acts which established the European Recovery Program are not relevant to our study. The pertinent law is to be found in regulations promulgated by the ECA administrator. These stated that ECA would finance only purchases which were made at "lowest competitive market prices" and at prices no higher than those charged on comparable sales to other buyers.[3] As can easily be imagined, much of the controversy between ECA and the oil companies hinged on what prices were in fact competitive.

There were actually two disputes, one over the price of crude oil and another over the price of refined products. Only the first reached the courts.

1. The Price of Crude Oil

During the period of Marshall Plan aid the watershed of maximum delivered prices between crude oil from the Middle East and crude from the Gulf of Mexico was about to change from one side of the Atlantic Ocean to the other, or did change, depending on one's point of view. Indeed much of the controversy

[2] U.S. vs. Standard Oil Company of California, the Texas Company, and several ("Caltex") affiliates, 155 F.Supp. 121, henceforth cited as "U.S. vs. Standard of California and the Texas Company." Only the case against Caltex was tried; the government lost in a U.S. District Court and lost in the U.S. Court of Appeals. Then similar cases against Jersey Standard and Socony Mobil were dropped (*Petroleum Week*, August 28, 1959, p. 15; January 8, 1960, p. 16).

[3] *Federal Register*, 14 F.R. 2166.

was over precisely this question. The government held that the watershed, or boundary between the marketing areas, had moved to the East Coast of the United States when the companies contended that it was still in western Europe. In any case it is clear that Levy's "high and low of the range" theory provides the best analytical background for understanding many of the points at issue. Levy, it will be recalled, suggested that the price of Persian Gulf crude had established itself within a range, the upper limits of which "would permit Caribbean crude oil to compete with Middle East crude oil in Europe, while its lower limit would permit Middle East crude oil to compete with U.S. crude oil at the U.S. East Coast." [4] He was suggesting that when the watershed of maximum delivered prices was still on the western coast of Europe, the price of Persian Gulf crude would be at its upper limit, and that when the boundary between the two marketing areas had crossed the Atlantic to the East Coast of the United States, the price of this crude would have dropped to its lower limit. (See Figure 6, p. 99.) In view of the fact that crude oil from the Middle East was flowing to the eastern coast of the United States, ECA contended, with some qualifications to be discussed later, that the lower limit of Levy's range was the appropriate one. The oil companies, however, argued that crude deliveries from the Middle East to the United States were transitory, that the watershed really was still in western Europe, and that ECA should finance shipments priced at the upper limit of the range. A brief review of the sequence of events will clarify the dispute.

When ECA began operations in the spring of 1948, the f.o.b. price of crude oil in the Persian Gulf was $2.22 per barrel. By September, 1949, at least partly as a result of the prodding of ECA, the price had dropped to $1.75, and when the panel of consultants appointed by ECA met for the second time, it approved this price. It reported:

[4] Levy, *op. cit.*, p. 1.

Your committee notes with approval that, since its last meeting, the price of crude oil f.o.b. Persian Gulf ports has declined by 28¢ a barrel. [It had just previously been $2.03.] The present figure appears to be close to the delivered price at American East Coast ports less tariff and competitively determined transport costs from the Persian Gulf.[5]

In this statement one detects an emerging East Coast watershed, since it suggests that the price had been calculated on the basis of an East Coast boundary between Middle East oil and oil from the U.S. Gulf Coast. (If the price had been so calculated it was at the lower limit in Levy's not yet published theory.) But the panel quite explicitly stated that it "expresses no opinion on the prospective world flows of crude petroleum," thereby abstaining from a suggestion that the watershed had been firmly established on the U.S. East Coast. The panel did, however, recognize a possibility that the watershed had been established there when it recommended

that any substantial rise of crude oil prices above U.S. East Coast prices, less tariff and competitively determined transport cost from Persian Gulf ports, should call for renewed examination by ECA of the price at which it finances shipments of crude oil from Persian Gulf ports.[6]

ECA accepted the $1.75 f.o.b. price of crude for some months, until the tanker rate for single voyage charters began to rise in the latter half of 1950. Then, since it had come to believe that the watershed was in fact solidly established on the U.S. East Coast, it challenged this price, arguing that with higher freight costs the oil companies were realizing less than $1.75 a barrel on their sales to the United States and that they should lower correspondingly their Persian Gulf f.o.b. prices,

[5] U.S. vs. Standard of California and the Texas Company, 155 F.Supp. 139.
[6] *Ibid.*

the prices charged on sales to Europe. Failure to lower these prices, ECA held, would constitute geographical price discrimination (discrimination against Europe) and would mean that the companies were absorbing freight on shipments to the United States. When the oil companies refused to reduce prices further, ECA continued to finance shipments at the $1.75 figure for many months but eventually, as we have observed, turned refund claims over to the Justice Department for collection and in time ceased altogether to finance shipments of crude from the Middle East.

2. The Netback Formula

The government made its case by calculating company realizations on sales to the U.S. East Coast. It used a relatively simple netback formula, deriving the realizations from Venezuelan f.o.b. prices and from certain c.i.f. prices. To the Venezuelan f.o.b. price of $2.65 per barrel the government added freight to New York of 38 cents; the sum of $3.03 presumably gave the delivered price of crude oil on the East Coast of the United States. From it the government subtracted freight costs of $1.70, the costs of shipping crude oil from the Persian Gulf to New York; the resulting figure of $1.33 a barrel, it alleged, was the actual amount the oil companies realized on New York shipments. This was of course much lower than the $1.75 Persian Gulf f.o.b. price charged to Europeans. The freight rate used was the single voyage charter rate, the "spot rate." [7] In view of the fact that the oil companies concerned were buying the oil from their affiliate, Aramco, at a price of $1.43, the government inserted a

[7] U.S. vs. Standard of California and the Texas Company, U.S. District Court, Southern District of New York, Civ. 78-152, Stenographers' Minutes, April 15, 1957, pp. 22-23. The government also obtained netbacks of around $1.33 when it calculated them by subtracting freight costs from the c.i.f. prices mentioned in several specific contracts for the delivery of Middle East oil to the Western Hemisphere. In its appeal it put more emphasis on these calculations than on its derivations from the Venezuelan f.o.b. price.

"floor" into its formula. Since the companies could not be expected to sell oil at a loss, it suggested that the price properly
chargeable to European buyers was not the netback of $1.33 but
a floor price of $1.43.

The government's netback formula was equivalent to the
"Atlantic Coast minus" formula of Dr. P. H. Frankel, who had
suggested that the f.o.b. price of Persian Gulf crude oil be set
at a figure equal to the delivered price of crude on the East
Coast of the United States minus the cost of freight from the
Persian Gulf to the East Coast.[8] Of course Dr. Frankel's formula
placed the watershed on the East Coast of the United States
and, when used, eliminated geographical price discrimination
against Europe.

Many, happily not all, industry people responded to the government's formula with a severely practical approach. We are
oil men, they said, and do not know anything about this "new
fangled netback theory" (the quoted words were used by one
witness). In any case we do not sell our oil on that basis; we
just price it to meet competition. Not a soul in Europe (with
one exception which can be explained) has been able to buy oil
at prices lower than ours. But having indulged in these antitheoretical sentiments, of which, it must be said, America has
more than it can afford, and having put forth a series of irrelevant
arguments,[9] they generally settled down to the more valid approach of criticizing the formula and its application. They argued
that the flow of oil to the U.S. East Coast was temporary and
marginal and that the government's use of the single voyage spot
rate was indefensible. They contended that the necessity of
attaching an arbitrary floor to the formula to deal with negative
netbacks and netbacks below cost invalidated the theory or
proved that the wrong marine rate was being used. And they

[8] "American Oil in a Changing World," *Oil Forum*, November, 1950,
p. 449. Without using the exact words "Atlantic Coast minus," Dr.
Frankel had suggested as early as 1948 that this might in time become
the appropriate formula.

[9] This charge of irrelevance will be substantiated shortly.

pointed to what I shall call the Stocking anomaly. Dr. George W. Stocking, one of the panel of consultants called in by ECA, had noted:

With fluctuating freight rates, the formula leads to highly anomalous results. The demand for ocean tankers is a derived demand reflecting changes in the demand for petroleum and its products. An increase in the demand for crude and its products would ordinarily bring an increased demand for ocean tankers and an increase in ocean tanker rates. Under the formula this leads to a lower not a higher f.o.b. price for Middle East crude. That is, as the demand for it increases Middle East crude sells for less. Conversely a decrease in the demand for petroleum and petroleum products leads to a decrease in the demand for tanker services, but under the formula it leads to a higher f.o.b. price for Middle East crude. That is, as the demand for it decreases, Middle East crude sells for more.[10]

Clearly the netback formula, or more particularly, as we shall see, its application, must be examined very carefully.

First of all let us dispose of what I have called the antitheoretical and irrelevant arguments of the defense. It simply will not do for oil men to talk about "theoretical netbacks" as though they were something discreditable, something in which only a hopelessly academic economist would be interested. For, as oil men well know, calculations of netbacks must be made, and are made, all the time by any company which wishes to sell merchandise over a wide area on a rational and sensible basis; such a company must compare realizations from sales in different markets. Businessmen may quite properly call attention to the difficulties of calculting netbacks and to the care with which they must be used when calculated, but they do not serve the goal of rationality in human affairs when they attack particular calculations or their applications as "theoretical."

It is irrelevant to meet a charge of geographical price discrimination by an allegation that "we price our oil to meet com-

[10] U.S. vs. Standard of California and the Texas Company, 155 F.Supp. 146.

petition." The charge is not that sellers have failed to match the prices of rivals but that they, being few in number, have chosen to push additional output into distant markets at reduced netbacks rather than undermine the price structure in nearby markets by seeking the larger realizations available there.

It is also irrelevant for the companies to suggest that "not a soul in Europe has been able to buy oil at prices lower than ours" when the charge is not that the oil companies were discriminating between European customers but that they were discriminating against all Europeans as compared with buyers in the Western Hemisphere.

We must, if we are to reach the heart of the matter, make a careful study of the netback formula. First of all, to what extent are f.o.b. and c.i.f. prices comparable?

3. The Comparability of F.o.b. and C.i.f. Prices

One expert witness for the defense, Willard L. Thorp, suggested that f.o.b. prices Ras Tanura (in the Persian Gulf) were not comparable to c.i.f. prices in the Western Hemisphere. "These are two different markets. The c.i.f. delivery involves the inclusion of more in the package which is being purchased by the buyer than a similar purchase in Ras Tanura, and these are not comparable markets." [11] This view, however, seems too extreme. The c.i.f. delivery does, of course, include more in the package, but often the additions are no more than the costs of transportation, or sometimes transport costs plus a tariff payment, and these can be measured, though frequently only with difficulty. By subtracting a careful estimate of freight costs from a c.i.f. price, one has a figure, a netback, which often can be compared with an f.o.b. price.

Often, but not always, other factors may make the two packages different. (1) The c.i.f. sale may be made for one currency

[11] U.S. vs. Standard of California and the Texas Company, Stenographers' Minutes, p. 1744. We defined the concepts of f.o.b. and c.i.f. prices in a footnote on page 85.

and the f.o.b. sale for another. These can be compared only if a foreign exchange rate, official or unofficial, can be found which reflects the true values of the two currencies. ECA, however, ran into no currency problems in comparing c.i.f. prices on sales to the United States with f.o.b. prices on sales to Europe, because oil company sales in the United States and European sales financed by ECA were both for dollars. (2) Realizations on distant sales would not be comparable to those obtained from nearby transactions if one or the other market was considered to be more secure. A businessman in a competitive situation might accept a lower netback from a distant market because he thought purchasers there were more likely to buy regularly or because he believed that trade policy in the area was more stable. There might be less likelihood that a tariff would be erected suddenly or import controls imposed in a certain distant market. In their dispute with ECA, however, the oil companies did not defend low realizations on U.S. sales by reference to the anticipated security of these earnings but instead emphasized the temporary nature of sales to the United States. (3) Netbacks on sales at a distance may not be comparable with those earned on nearby transactions if a firm is seeking geographical diversification in markets. A company in a competitive industry may not want to have all its eggs in one basket and may choose to enter and remain in a distant market in which it realizes less on sales simply because it does not wish to be entirely dependent on buyers who are closer.

There remains the question of whether or not one can compare f.o.b. prices with netbacks derived from c.i.f. prices when the netbacks are calculated from the data of an exchange or barter transaction. For example, in 1950 the Texas Company (now Texaco Inc.) agreed to deliver 6,000 barrels per day of Arabian crude to the Socony Mobil Oil Company at Naples, Italy, in return for which Socony would deliver 6,000 barrels a day of Guico crude to the Texas Company at Puerto La Cruz,

Venezuela. The Texas Company considered that the cost of transporting the Arabian oil to Naples was 96 cents a barrel, and on another contract it sold the Venezuelan crude which it received in exchange to McColl-Frontenac for $2.60 a barrel.[12] Can one compare its $1.64 realization on these transactions ($2.60 — $.96 = $1.64) with its f.o.b. price on European sales financed by ECA? The answer of course is that they may indeed be comparable, but that because of the greater complexity of exchange transactions such arrangements must be studied very carefully. Sometimes it may be very difficult to put a value on the oil received in exchange; in some cases book values placed on oil or on transportation may be doubtful; and it may be necessary to evaluate other consideration provided by one party or the other under the contract. In the example above the figure (96 cents) put on the books as the cost of carrying oil to Naples could be incorrect, and the $2.60 received for the Venezuelan crude may not have represented its real value since the Texas Company owns a majority of the stock of McColl-Frontenac and the transaction was not at arm's length.[13]

The general comparability of f.o.b. prices and c.i.f. prices can scarcely be denied. Businessmen seeking rationally and sensibly to market over a wide area compare them all the time. By subtracting freight costs, often, to be sure, estimated only with difficulty from delivered prices, they frequently obtain a figure which can be compared with f.o.b. prices. When the c.i.f delivery is made for a harder currency than is received in f.o.b. sales, when the c.i.f. delivery is made to a market considered to be more secure or one entered in the interest of geographical diversification, or when the c.i.f. price is obtained from the data of an exchange transaction, comparison of c.i.f. and f.o.b. prices becomes very difficult, and not seldom impossible. In the dis-

[12] *Ibid.*, pp. 1773–1774.
[13] U.S. vs. Standard of California and the Texas Company, 155 F.Supp. 158.

pute between the American oil companies and ECA, however, problems like these did not become serious, and valid comparisons between c.i.f. and f.o.b. prices could be made.

Having recognized the possibility of comparing c.i.f. and f.o.b. prices, we turn to applications of the netback formula by means of which they are actually compared. We want to consider how the formula is or can be used by competitive business, by businesses in oligopolistic markets, and by governments.

4. Application of the Formula

In a very competitive market, businessmen would use a net-back or realization formula (similar to that of the government in the ECA Case) in deciding where to ship their goods. A wheat farmer or dealer, for example, would subtract from anticipated prices in various markets the appropriate freight costs in order to decide in which one a sale would net the largest amount. In a competitive system, of course, a seller would not in any way use a netback formula to establish prices, for in such a system, with many buyers and sellers, dealers do not feel that they can influence price; they sell "at the market" and have no price policy.

In an oligopolistic market, a market of a few sellers, a business-man, like his counterpart in a competitive market, would use a netback formula in deciding where to ship his goods, though he would not, after subtracting freight costs from the delivered prices he would expect to get in different markets, necessarily ship into the market of highest realizations. He might choose to forgo high realizations in a nearby market in order to protect its price structure.

But unlike sellers in a market of perfect competition, the oligopolist may use a netback formula in setting prices. Recogniz-ing that output from a particular region is large enough and production costs are low enough for deliveries to reach into a certain distant market on a relatively permanent basis, an oligop-olist might decide that realizations on those distant (watershed) transactions should establish prices of sale for all regions. F.o.b. prices, as well as all c.i.f. prices less freight, then, would be equated to netbacks on border sales. An oligopolist might set prices in this manner for either or both of two reasons. He might be anticipating competitive developments, recognizing that high prices on nearby sales and wide profit margins are likely to attract rivals; that is, he might be seeking to prevent the entry of uneconomically numerous competitors. Or he might, while secure in his oligopoly position, feel that an intelligent imitation of the competitive pattern of prices would be the best way of serving the public interest and avoiding criticism. It seems to be fairly common for an oil company to select a distant market which it expects to supply regularly and permanently, calculate netbacks on shipments there, and establish prices on all other deliveries to realize the same amount. At least some of the oil companies used a netback formula in this way in establishing prices during the early days of ECA, choosing as the distant watershed market either western or northern Europe. On February 25, 1949, Jersey Standard or its affiliate Esso Export wrote to ECA as follows:

Before July 1, 1948, Esso Export's price for Arabian crude was solely on the basis of being competitive with Middle East crude from other sources, but on that date Esso Export went on the basis that the price of Arabian crude f.o.b. port of loading should be approximately equal to the Caribbean price for light Venezuelan crude of equivalent gravity plus freight at published USMC rates from the Caribbean to Western Europe less freight on the same basis from the Persian Gulf.[14]

We now come to the most interesting question of all: In what way can a netback formula validly be used by a government agency such as ECA? We shall see that it can often be used as

[14] *Emergency Oil Lift Program*, p. 1690. See page 1678 of these hearings for a statement dated March 23, 1949, in which Socony accepts this formula, and see U.S. vs. Standard of California and the Texas Company, 155 F.Supp. 135, for a similar calculation by Caltex dated March 22, 1949, using northern Europe as a watershed.

a test for competition, though it must always be used with care, but that it can never, by itself, be used as a device for determining competitive price. An agency of the government can use netback calculations as evidence in deciding whether or not a particular market is competitive, but if it decides that a situation is not competitive, it cannot, using these calculations alone, go on to conclude that netbacks obtained on distant sales, netbacks lower than those received in nearby transactions, represent the prices that generally would prevail under competitive conditions. The validity of the distinction we are making between different uses of the netback formula can be demonstrated by consideration of likely developments in a very competitive market.

There is no doubt that in a competitive market geographical price discrimination would, over a period of time, be eliminated. Under competition, realizations on sales to all destinations would end up the same; sellers would withdraw from markets yielding low returns and enter those promising a larger profit until delivered prices in all areas varied only by the costs of transportation.

However, competitive correction of a market situation with varying netbacks does not necessarily reduce prices paid by nearby buyers to the point at which realizations on these sales equal realizations formerly received on distant transactions. Supplies are withdrawn from distant markets and moved into nearby areas; prices afar tend to rise, prices nearby tend to decline, the magnitude of each movement depending upon the elasticities of demand in the various regions. Since price adjustments take place at a distance as well as nearby, one cannot assume that the entire adjustment will consist of a price decline on nearby sales, with realizations on these ending up equal to netbacks previously obtained on sales at a distance. Of course while competition is bringing a regional shift in supplies and a change in the relationships between the prices in the various regions, it may also be bringing an increase in output, perhaps the entry of new firms, and a decline in prices generally. Conceivably the new prices of sale to nearby buyers would net the seller an amount equal to his old realizations on distant sales. But a governmental agency could not take this for granted and assume that of necessity it would occur. Rather, having through use of a netback formula decided that a market was uncompetitive, it would then have to make a careful estimate of the prices which would be likely to result through an introduction of competition, taking into account a number of factors. It might study elasticities of demand in distant and nearby markets to see what would happen if supplies were shifted. Almost certainly it would consider the possibility of a different output under competitive conditions, which would lead it to an examination of the costs and profit margins of the sellers whose prices were being studied.

Recognition that a netback formula can be used as a test for competition but not as a device for determining competitive price enables us to clear up two difficulties that ECA ran into in seeking to decide upon a policy for financing oil purchases: (1) its awkward "formula floor" and (2) the anomaly pointed out by Dr. Stocking. Both of these difficulties arose out of attempts to use a netback formula in determining competitive price.

The government, it will be recalled, obtained a netback on Western Hemisphere crude oil shipments by adding to the Venezuelan f.o.b. price freight costs to New York and subtracting from this sum the costs of freight on the Persian Gulf–New York run. (See p. 120.) It used a spot freight rate and arrived at a netback of $1.33 per barrel, which compared with an f.o.b. price charged Europeans of $1.75 and a cost price paid by the companies of $1.43. At times during the period under consideration the spot rate went up, and went up so high that use of it in government calculations produced negative netbacks. To avoid netbacks below cost and negative netbacks, the government introduced a floor into its formula. Since the companies could not be expected to sell below cost, the floor price set, the price at which ECA was willing to finance shipments, was $1.43. However, the formula floor is necessary only because the formula is being misused; the government is attempting to calculate competitive price with it. But it is clear that in a competitive market when the freight rate increased, as it did in the second half of 1950, and netbacks on distant sales declined, suppliers would not have simply dropped prices to nearby customers correspondingly. Rather than reduce prices generally as a consequence of reduced netbacks on distant transactions, certainly rather than reduce prices to cost or to a figure equivalent to a negative netback (which would have amounted to paying buyers for carrying oil away), oil men would have begun to lose interest in distant transactions and begun to leave the Western Hemisphere in favor of Europe. Prices in New York would have tended to rise and netbacks on these sales to recover, while prices in Europe and the corresponding netbacks would have tended to decline. How much of the adjustment would have taken place in each hemisphere we cannot say without further study, but there is no reason for believing that the new competitive price in Europe would have been equal to cost, or the government's formula floor of $1.43.

By a similar analysis it is easy to show that the Stocking anomaly arises out of a misapplication of the netback formula, out of its use as a device for determining competitive price. Dr. Stocking had noted that under the formula an increase in the demand for crude and its products would bring an increased demand for tankers, increased tanker rates, and an, anomalous, decline in the f.o.b. price for Middle East crude, while a decrease in demand for petroleum, crude and products, would lead to a decreased demand for tankers, decreased tanker rates, and an, also anomalous, increase in Middle East crude prices. (See p. 122.) But properly applied, used only as a test for competition, the formula would not have these results. After the consequences of an increase or a decrease in demand had had time to work themselves out, an agency of the government might examine the resulting prices and realizations to see whether the realizations were the same for all markets. But if it understood what it was doing, it would not expect, in a competitive market, an actual decline in f.o.b. prices for Middle East crude to follow an increase in demand; it would not expect sellers to reduce prices at such a time just because tanker rates had gone up. Instead it would expect prices to rise and supplies to increase, *though it would expect prices to rise more in distant markets than in nearby ones* because higher tanker rates would make the far-away markets relatively less attractive and would lead to a slower increase in supplies there. (In a sense, therefore, f.o.b. prices would decline but only in the sense of declining relative to prices in distant markets.) Likewise a decrease in demand for petroleum and its products probably would lead to a decrease in all prices including tanker rates, with, however, prices at a distance declining more rapidly than nearby prices as supplies in these now relatively more attractive areas declined more slowly than in nearby regions. (F.o.b. prices would increase only in the sense of increasing relative to distant prices.) Hence properly understood and applied, a netback formula does not produce anomalous results. In due time after changes in demand had occurred, an agency would test prices with it to see whether or not netbacks were the same on sales to all regions. If tanker rates had changed, it would expect to find, in a competitive market, that regional prices had changed relative to one another, but it would not ordinarily expect to find price movements in a direction opposite to the movements in demand.

We might make one further observation concerning application of the netback formula. Once it is recognized that this formula cannot be used to calculate competitive price, it becomes clear that government computations of refunds due it in the ECA case are unsatisfactory. Even if the government had been sustained in its contention that oil was sold at noncompetitive prices, in determining the magnitude of the overcharge it should not have multiplied the volume of oil sold by the difference between the actual prices of sale and a "competitive price" computed by means of a netback formula. Instead, before making this computation it should have formulated a judgment as to competitive price by studying elasticities of demand in distant and nearby markets, the likely total output under competition, and perhaps costs as well as profit margins.

We have shown that a netback formula can be used as a test for competition, though not as a device for calculating competitive price, but that even in its relatively restricted sphere it must be used with great care. We turn now to consideration of a number of problems which arise in applying the netback formula.

5. Locating the Watershed

How is an agency of the government or a court to locate the proper boundary of a region's natural marketing area, its boundary of maximum delivered prices, the line within which all sales are to take place at prices which net suppliers equal amounts? Is a single sale in a peripheral area enough to draw it into the marketing basin, or are occasional sales, substantial and regular sales, or very large sales necessary?

In an extremely competitive market the watershed would be established in one place or moved to another by very small transactions. Suppliers would enter a distant market only if netbacks were as great as on nearby sales; hence even a small shipment would be evidence of a shift in the watershed. And sellers would pull out a supply which was very small if netbacks on distant sales declined. There would be no thought of freight absorption, no inclination to protect prices in nearby markets by sales in distant markets at low realizations. Under perfect competition the watershed would shift regularly as commodity prices and transportation costs fluctuated and suppliers from different producing regions moved into and out of peripheral areas. A free market in wheat might be a good example of this pattern.

Even if the numerous competing firms were vertically integrated and in possession of fixed assets in various marketing areas—terminals, warehouses, manufacturing or refining plant, marketing facilities—they would, where alternative supplies were available from more advantageously located producers, pull quickly out of low realization areas and move into markets where they realized more, protecting their investment in the low net-back areas as they did so by purchasing from the suppliers more advantageously situated. This can be seen most easily in the following table of deliveries of crude oil from the Middle East:

	To London	To New York
Sale price [15]	$2.50	$2.90
Transport costs	.50	1.00
Netback	2.00	1.90
Cost of production	1.00	1.00
Profit	1.00	.90

The firm here depicted would increase its crude profits per barrel by withdrawing supplies from New York and shipping them to London, at the same time protecting its investment in New York by becoming a crude purchaser in that area in the open market.

But of course the competitive model recognizes no value in stability. Economy, i.e., minimization of costs, is all. Businessmen, however, will seek stability, and society will tend to approve their efforts. A supplier will endeavor to obtain long-term con-tracts or the less formal "custom" of a buyer; when such ties have been established, he will be slower to pull out of a market when realizations from it decline. Prices and trade patterns will change more slowly and economic affairs become less hectic. The public probably will support some developments in this direction, though the exact balance between stability and change may be a matter of controversy.

In their dispute with ECA the oil companies argued that the watershed had not moved from Europe to the East Coast of the United States. They contended that shipments to the Western Hemisphere were marginal and temporary; the Korean War had broken out to upset regular supply patterns, and there were special shortages on the U.S. East Coast. The extent to which ECA and the courts accepted these arguments and the magnitudes

[15] Open market and intracompany transfer price.

of East Coast shipments which they considered to be significant probably reflected, as much as anything, the value which they attached to stability. At one time ECA said:

Movements . . . ranging from 1.9 percent . . . to 13.0 percent . . . and averaging 10.6 percent of total supplies . . . are not substantial and are properly characterized as marginal movements. A different case would be presented if such movements were of the order of one-third or more of total sales.[16]

Perhaps without being fully conscious of it, ECA is assigning a greater value to stability here than it did at another time when it sought price changes as a consequence of crude shipments to the Western Hemisphere amounting to only about 10 percent of Middle East production.

But in seeking to locate the watershed ECA had a further problem. In considering what scale of deliveries would be marginal and what scale large enough to require that an area be included in a particular market basin, ECA was faced with marked differences between total and net flows of crude oil as well as differences between the net flow of crude and the net flow of crude and products combined.

The total flow of crude oil to the Western Hemisphere during 1950–52 was at least 205,900,000 barrels, or 9.8% of Middle Eastern production and 2.3% of Western Hemisphere supply. The net flow of crude during the same period was at least 67,700,000 barrels, or 3.2% of Middle Eastern production and 0.7% of Western Hemisphere supply. . . . But the net flow of crude and products was toward Europe. During 1950–52 this net combined flow, after deducting all east-to-west shipments, totaled 362,300,000 barrels, or 4% of Western Hemisphere supply and 17% of Middle Eastern production.[17]

[16] Quoted in U.S. vs. Standard of California and the Texas Company, 155 F.Supp. 153–154. Probably the figures here cited are percentages of Middle East crude production.

[17] *Ibid.*, 143–144.

134

Which of these figures is significant in locating the watershed? How much importance should the authorities, who are trying to decide upon the natural market area for Middle East crude oil, attach to the reverse flow of crude or products from the Western Hemisphere?

We will consider first the reverse flow of crude oil. There are two possibilities. The crudes flowing from the Western Hemisphere may be of different or the same quality as Middle East crude. If they are of different quality, then probably the flow of crude to the Western Hemisphere is the significant magnitude, and the reverse flow of what is virtually another commodity is of little or no relevance. The fact that Europeans are purchasing some Western Hemisphere crude oil of a different quality would be of significance in deciding on the size of the natural marketing area for Middle East crude only if it could be shown that shortly Middle East oil would displace the Western Hemisphere oil because of new refining techniques being developed.

If the crudes flowing in opposite directions are of the same quality, we have what is called "crosshauling," which is a phenomenon of imperfectly competitive markets. Sellers have absorbed freight to cross over into other marketing areas and consequently have netted less on distant than on nearby sales; they have chosen to avoid the price competition that would result from firms in each region trying to win all of the nearby customers away from distant suppliers. Although the existence of crosshauling in this case might establish that the boundary of the natural marketing area for Middle East oil was still in Europe, if shipments each way across the Atlantic were about the same, it would raise additional questions as to the competitive character of Middle East prices. A critic would ask why the companies in the Middle East had not cut prices in Europe and pushed Western Hemisphere oil out of this area. Of course governmental agencies and courts might accept, along with temporary freight absorption, some concomitant, temporary, crosshauling, in the interest of stability. When freight rates rose, for example, a distant supplier might not immediately drop all buyers in a peripheral zone where it is now at a disadvantage but might, while declining to bid on new business, continue to serve its regular customers, and in doing so meet and pass, with the approval of the authorities, new supplies entering the zone. The amount of crosshauling likely to be acceptable to governmental agencies or the courts will depend upon the value which they place upon stability. However, even if the authorities are inclined to go along with a certain amount of crosshauling, one would think that companies trying to defend freight absorption into a distant, allegedly marginal market would be rather cautious in pointing to an uneconomic reverse flow of a similar crude.

The oil companies probably strengthened their case more when they spoke of a reverse flow of products. Such a flow might have been evidence of the temporary nature of crude deliveries to the Western Hemisphere. Upon completion of additional refinery capacity in Europe, the crude might have gone there directly for refining rather than go first to America and then back in the form of products. But a reverse flow of products is not necessarily temporary and may not be evidence that crude shipments to distant markets are transient. Particularly if only some products, say fuel oil, are going in the opposite direction may doubts be cast on the notion that they are temporary movements, for a flow of this sort may endure indefinitely when the pattern of demand in various markets differs from the optimum output pattern of local refineries.

In sum, it appears that when one is deciding upon the location of the watershed in the market for crude oil, the total flow of Middle East crude to the Western Hemisphere is likely to be the most important figure. A reverse flow of a crude of different quality or a flow of products from the Western Hemisphere would be significant only if such movements were temporary and soon to be stopped in favor of additional direct shipments of Middle East oil to Europe, made possible by refinery modifications or additions. Of course a reverse flow of crude of the same quality could establish that the watershed was still in Europe, but evidence of crosshauling of this sort would at the same time raise additional questions as to the competitive character of Middle East prices. And the amount of temporary crosshauling, like the magnitude of the "marginal," temporary shipments involving freight absorption, which the authorities accept when seeking to determine the proper location of the watershed, depends mostly on the values which they attach to change and to stability.

6. The Proper Tanker Rate

Another problem involved in application of the netback formula arises over choice of the appropriate tanker rate to be used in calculating Middle East netbacks. ECA selected the single voyage charter rate (the "spot" rate), but the oil companies challenged this selection and argued that a long-term charter rate or a weighted average of single voyage rates, long-term rates, and owned-ship costs should be used.

Selection of the spot rate can be defended on two grounds. First, in a highly competitive market, the single voyage rate almost certainly would be the most important of the marine rates in determining geographical price differences. With many buyers and sellers in all markets, each with adequate physical facilities for handling the commodity, oil prices would fluctuate a great deal, there would be a tendency to acquire transportation on a temporary rather than a long-term basis, and no seller could get a higher c.i.f. price (or no buyer pay a lower one) than the f.o.b. price plus the cost of carrying the oil on a single voyage charter. During his testimony in the ECA Case, Richard M. Bissell, economist for the government in ECA and earlier in the War Shipping Administration, suggested that in the world grain trade, a very competitive trade, the equivalent of spot rates were most important in establishing prices: "In the bulk grain trade, world wide, it is, I think, a spot charter market that will have the determining effect on prices, both at points of origin and points of destination." Though some grain is carried on liners, on vessels following regular schedules, "enough of the grain movement trans-Atlantic moves in tramps on single voyage charters so that a rise or fall of the tramp charter rate will promptly be reflected in Liverpool, Montreal, and Chicago prices." [18]

There is a second defense for the use of the spot rate in calculating netbacks. According to the opportunity cost theory, widely accepted by economists, the true cost of using any asset is the return it could get in its best forgone alternative opportunity. Even when an oil company owns a vessel or has chartered it for a period of years, it can, rather than carry its own oil, choose the alternative of "chartering out" the tanker for a single voyage. Hence, if the spot rate is high, the cost of transporting oil in owned ships or in ships on long-term charter is high, since the company is forgoing a high return. If the spot rate is low, the cost of transporting oil in owned ships or time-chartered vessels is low, even when the spot rate is below owned-ship costs or time-charter rates, because the latter higher historical costs or rates reflect mistakes of the past, overbuilding or unwise chartering, and are not relevant to decisions concerning future activities. Oil men, it is suggested, consider, or should consider, the alternative of chartering out a tanker in the spot market before they decide to use it in their own service; the true costs of using it, then, are the returns obtainable in this best forgone alternative.

The international majors, however, do not feel that the single voyage charter rate is the significant one in calculating netbacks and setting prices. Some oil men say: "We are not in the transportation business. We need our tankers to carry our own oil and putting them into the spot market is not a feasible alternative." This reply is, of course, very superficial. The international companies, along with producing, refining, and marketing oil, are

[18] U.S. vs. Standard of California and the Texas Company, Stenographers' Minutes, p. 581.

in the business of transporting it. Moreover, they do from time to time "charter out" surplus tankers into the spot market and no doubt generally keep this possibility in mind.

Closer to the real difficulty is the statement frequently heard that the oil industry could not function with prices tied to the fluctuating single voyage rate. Even this is an exaggeration. Many industries—copper, rubber, cocoa, and sugar are examples—live with fluctuating commodity prices all the time, or have done so in years past, and the oil industry, if it had to, could manage as well.

Perhaps the most effective defense of the oil company policy of using time charter rates or a weighted average of all rates in calculating netbacks and setting prices would concentrate on the values which inhere in stability. Single voyage charter rates fluctuate a great deal, and, though they might be most important in establishing prices in a highly competitive market and represent the true (opportunity) costs of carrying oil, their use would lead to very unstable prices and constantly shifting supply patterns. There is much to be said for watching trends in marine rates, as many companies do, setting up long-run supply programs, entering, or occasionally leaving, particular markets as emerging developments make this economical, and ignoring the day-to-day or week-to-week changes in the costs of moving oil.

Regulatory agencies and courts have to formulate a judgment and strike a balance; they have to choose between change and stability, between the disturbing oscillations of competition and the steady, perhaps lethargic, movement of oligopoly. If they accept time-charter rates in calculations of netbacks, they come down on the side of stability. Even if they insist on a weighted average of all rates—which in practice would weight owned-ship costs about 50, term-charter rates about 40, and single voyage rates about 10—they are to a degree simply accepting valuations which the international majors have put on stability, for they are approving a system for establishing prices which reflects the extent to which the companies have sought security through control of their marine transportation.

Industry interests in stability may produce prices which are higher than socially desirable—prices, for example, which decline more slowly than one who balances change against stability would approve. The authorities, without desiring to see prices tied to spot rates alone, might wish that the rate for single voyage charters were given greater weight than it is in usual industry practice. Of course they might feel that the current entry of non-affiliated independents into the Middle East would lead to greater price fluctuations, more single voyage tanker fixtures, and a greater influence of the spot rate on prices. Or, being less hopeful of these developments, the authorities might be inclined to turn to some sort of program of regulation or control, though the problems here, in a supranational industry, are most serious.

Heretofore we have been dealing entirely with the price of crude oil. ECA and the oil companies also became involved in a controversy over product prices, though the government did not take this dispute to the courts and seek refunds of dollars which had been paid out.

7. The Price of Products

As in crude oil so in products ECA was primarily concerned with geographical price discrimination. To be sure, at times in its attack on product prices ECA expressed doubts about the relationship between product prices and crude prices and about the resulting margins of refinery profit. Crude oil prices had declined without a corresponding reduction in product prices, which were still equal to those at the U.S. Gulf Coast. But these attacks were never pressed home.

Primary attention was given to geographical price discrimination. The watershed for products was clearly somewhere in Europe and not about to cross the Atlantic like the crude oil watershed. No "high and low of the range" theory applied. The problem was simply one of the determining as nearly as possible where in Europe the watershed, or point of maximum delivered prices, was or should be located. ECA alleged that the watershed should be in northwest Europe, that oil companies were making sales into this area from the Middle East, and that netbacks on these sales should set prices for all Europe. It argued that the companies actually were realizing much more on their sales to southern Europe than on their deliveries into the Northwest and that this constituted geographical price discrimination. ECA claimed, for example, that Greece was charged for fuel oil an f.o.b. price of $8.30 per ton, which was the U.S. Gulf price (the "low of Platt's"), although the United Kingdom paid an f.o.b. price of only $3.95 a ton ($8.30 minus a "freight allowance" of $4.35).[19] In effect ECA was suggesting that failure to cut prices in southern Europe constituted an illegal divergence from the pattern of competitive behavior.

The oil companies demurred. They contended that shipments of products from the Middle East into western Europe were temporary and declining and that they would be eliminated altogether when projected refineries in the area were completed. They suggested that they were absorbing freight into western Europe in order to "meet the competition," the competition of Caribbean oil. They went on to contend that the true watershed was in the Mediterranean and that if they were not permitted to absorb freight to Great Britain, Scandinavia, and other countries, they would, rather than reduce prices in the nearby markets of southern Europe, eliminate discrimination by ceasing to ship products from the Middle East into western European markets, supplying them instead from the Caribbean. Such actions, they argued, would reduce competition in western Europe.

[19] Petroleum Branch, Industry Division, Mutual Security Agency, *Statement on ECA/MSA Petroleum Price History*, submitted to Monopoly Subcommittee, Senate Small Business Committee, August 15, 1952, pp. 12–13.

ECA, after determining the magnitudes involved, in effect had to decide how much weight to give to stability and how much to change; it had to decide how large western European shipments would have to be and how long they would have to take place before the area should be considered a part of the Middle Eastern market basin. Moreover, the threat of the companies to cease shipments from the Middle East into western Europe rather than reduce prices in southern Europe placed a serious obstacle before ECA in its attempts to control prices and eliminate geographical price discrimination. The companies might really have pulled their Middle East oil out of western Europe rather than reduce prices on large volumes in the South. And the higher marginal costs of substitute products delivered into western Europe from the Caribbean would have moderated the tendency to compete through reductions in price. (If these marginal costs had not been higher, western Europe probably would have been supplied from this area all along.) Nor is it certain that Middle East oil taken out of western Europe would have been pushed into southern Europe, for it is quite possible that the oil companies had been forgoing the higher realizations obtainable on nearby sales to protect the price structure in these markets and that as oligopolists they would have continued to respond to such motives. When ECA, then, attempted to eliminate geographical price discrimination in oil products, it ran the risk of reducing competition in, say, England or Sweden without providing any real gains for buyers in Italy, Greece, or Turkey.

8. The Power of ECA to Control Prices

We will find it of value to consider in some detail and to analyze carefully the efforts of ECA to control prices and thereby to eliminate geographical price discrimination. At the outset we might look at the sequence of events, first in crude oil and then in products. Dates, governmental actions, and crude price changes follow:

Dates	Governmental actions	Crude price changes in the Persian Gulf
April 3, 1948	ECA Act becomes law	
June 15, 1948		Socony lowers Saudi Arabian price from $2.22 per bbl. to $2.08 and Caltex from $2.22 to $2.03
June 26, 1948	Sen. O'Mahoney sends telegram to Eugene Holman, president of Jersey Standard, criticizing Middle East oil prices charged on ECA-financed purchases	
July 1, 1948	Holman replies to Sen. O'Mahoney explaining and defending Jersey's prices	Jersey reduces Saudi Arabian price from $2.22 to $2.07; Gulf reduces price at Kuwait from $2.15 to $2.02
Aug. 1–Nov. 1, 1948		Further price adjustments with Saudi price settling at $2.03 and Kuwait price at $1.97
Feb. 14, 1949	ECA sends letter to companies noting shipments to Western Hemisphere and questioning prices	
March 22–23, 1949	ECA's panel of consultants meets and sug-	

143

Dates (cont.)	Governmental actions (cont.)	Crude price changes in the Persian Gulf (cont.)
	gests that price adjustments "may well have lagged behind the emerging supply situation"	
April 1, 1949		Caltex and Jersey Standard reduce Saudi Arabian price to $1.88; Gulf at Kuwait reduces price to $1.82
April 22, 1949		Socony reduces Saudi price to $1.88
July 15, 1949		Gulf reduces price at Kuwait to $1.75
Sept. 7– Oct. 1, 1949		Remaining companies reduce Saudi Arabian and Kuwait prices to $1.75
Nov. 2, 1949	ECA's panel of consultants meets for the second time and "notes with approval" the recent price reductions	

ECA accepted the $1.75 price for many months until the spot tanker rate began to rise in the latter half of 1950; it then tried without success to get the price lowered further. (Actually it is possible, as we shall see, that by the very nature of its operations ECA had put a floor under the price.) ECA continued to finance shipments at $1.75 until 1952; early in the year it turned refund claims over to the Justice Department for collection, and

144

on June 21 it decided (effective August 31, 1952) to cease financing nonspecialty crude, which was the type produced in the Middle East.

Of course, the sequence of events here described does not prove that the price of Middle East crude oil declined in 1948 and 1949 because of ECA pressure (reinforced by Senator O'Mahoney's telegram). These price reductions might have occurred without ECA. But it is difficult not to believe that, at the very least, pressure from ECA accelerated the decline (and as a consequence saved European consumers many millions of dollars).

ECA did not have even an appearance of success in its efforts, either earlier or later, to get product prices in the Middle East reduced. As we have noted, when it raised questions about these prices, the oil companies said that they would stop shipping products from the Middle East to western Europe before they would reduce prices to southern Europe. The subsequent efforts of ECA to obtain compliance are very interesting. At its second meeting on November 2, 1949, the panel of consultants supported ECA in its criticism of geographical price discrimination in products. It said:

ECA's present policy of financing sales of Middle East petroleum products from the Persian Gulf for delivery to the Eastern Mediterranean at a netback price higher than that realized on sales to Western Europe is difficult to justify and steps should be taken for discontinuing it.[20]

But upon strong protests by the oil companies concerned, ECA arranged for them to present their views directly to the consultants on December 6, 1949, after which the panel modified its statement to read:

ECA's present policy of financing sales of Middle East petroleum products from the Persian Gulf for delivery to the Eastern Mediterranean at a netback price *substantially* higher than that realized

[20] *Ibid.*, p. 14.

on sales to Western Europe is difficult to justify and steps should be taken for discontinuing it.[21]

There is reason to believe that the consultants feared that insistence upon complete elimination of freight absorption would cause the companies to withdraw from western Europe and that this would check competition in distant markets. Apparently they hoped that if only substantial discrimination was forbidden and moderate discrimination was permitted, the companies would lower prices to southern Europe without pulling out of western Europe. Whether or not their hopes could be realized would depend on the relative magnitudes of sales to nearby and distant markets. It is difficult to imagine the companies agreeing to even a small reduction in price on large sales to nearby markets if they could eliminate pressure directed toward such action by removing small volumes from distant markets. In reality, however, sales to Greece and Turkey were very small[22] so that it was reasonable for the consultants to hope that the oil firms might reduce prices in this area, continue to ship into western Europe, and thereby eliminate substantial price discrimination.

Nevertheless, the companies continued to resist reductions in product prices. In September, 1950, therefore, ECA published Amendment 5 to its Regulation 1. The unique feature of this amendment was an actual schedule of prices for shipments of Middle East oil products to various destinations in Europe; it asserted that no prices higher than these would be eligible for ECA financing.[23] The published schedule of prices was interesting. It placed the watershed at Gibraltar (strictly speaking at the so-called "Portugal, Gibraltar, Casablanca range"), eliminated geographical price discrimination east of the watershed, and permitted "historical" freight absorption west and north of this point.[24] In other words, it left prices to northwest Europe as

[21] Ibid.   [22] Journal of Commerce, January 18, 1950.
[23] ECA/MSA Petroleum Price History, p. 15.
[24] Economic Co-operation Administration, PMCS Bulletin No. 36, September 6, 1950.

146

they were and sought to lower prices on shipments into southern Europe. Under the schedule sellers would have obtained identical realizations on all deliveries up to Gibraltar (realizations lower than they had been getting), but they would have continued to absorb freight on shipments to Britain, Sweden, and other distant countries (and hence continued to realize less on these shipments than on shipments to nearby markets). In working out the scheduled prices, ECA rather cleverly used the "freight allowance" which had been "historically applied" by the supplying firms; this selection of freight rates of course eliminated one possible basis for dispute between the government and the companies concerned. Naturally the ECA price schedule had all the disadvantages of any attempt at price control; in a dynamic economy it was certain to get out of date fairly soon.

At all events, the companies objected strongly; Caltex in particular said it would not supply products at the scheduled prices. And, with one exception, no petroleum products were financed by ECA from the effective date of Amendment 5. The exception occurred in shipments of fuel oil to Athens for the generation of electricity; the city was in danger of a cutoff in electric power because it could not acquire oil for nondollar payment. ECA then felt that it had to grant waivers of Amendment 5, and Caltex supplied the oil at its old price,[25] the price which ECA believed to be discriminatory!

How can we explain what appears to have been early ECA successes in getting crude prices reduced followed by later failures to obtain reductions in either crude or products? We have already suggested that the reductions in crude prices may not have been a consequence of ECA pressure, that the companies might have reduced these prices in the absence of ECA representations, but then we went on to suggest a likelihood that pressure from ECA at least accelerated the price decline. Perhaps, then, ECA owed its early successes to oil company recognition of the essential justice of its claims. But we must also observe

[25] ECA/MSA Petroleum Price History, p. 16.

that in this early period ECA was in a strong position: Europe was very short of dollars and ECA was a major source of this currency.[26] ECA dollars were particularly valued at this time because of the difficulties American companies were beginning to experience in selling for sterling. Britain's dollar position was deteriorating in the first three quarters of 1949 and plans were afoot to substitute "sterling oil" for "dollar oil" in many markets.

Later ECA lost some of its power. European countries had more "free dollars" (i.e., non-ECA dollars) available for the purchase of oil which was not in compliance with ECA regulations (and they did not lose ECA dollars by doing so, since ECA felt obliged to finance other items with its funds). Moreover, the oil companies were less interested in dollars, since they found themselves in a better position to sell for soft currencies as their programs for the purchase of equipment, tankers, and supplies in Europe developed. ECA dollars had lost some of their appeal, and consequently ECA appears to have lost any power it had had to influence prices.

ECA may never have had as much power as some people, perhaps even some oil men, had thought. Once the oil companies chose to make a stand, ECA faced the basic difficulty that there would be much opposition to a "strike" (a refusal to finance oil shipments). The countries concerned would dislike the consequent unemployment and the interruption of development as well as rearmament programs, and the U.S. Departments of State and Defense would oppose anything that threatened to check European rearmament. When ECA refused to finance, there would be a strong inclination to spend free dollars on oil and, if these were lacking, a tendency to put pressure on ECA to waive its requirements and finance shipments at prices higher than it considered proper. ECA waivers of its Amendment 5,

[26] From April, 1948, to December, 1951, ECA financed 56 percent of the sales made by U.S. oil companies in European countries receiving Marshall Plan aid. During the earlier months the percentage may have been higher (*ibid.*, p. 2).

granted when Athens needed fuel oil for the generation of electricity, no doubt reflected such pressures.

ECA might have faced another source of pressure in its efforts to eliminate discrimination against nearby purchasers. Had the oil companies not refused to supply at scheduled prices but simply withdrawn supplies from distant markets—had they withdrawn crude from the U.S. East Coast or products from northwest Europe—purchasers at a distance might have protested. It is amusing to think that under some circumstances ECA might have caused the U.S. purchaser to pay more for petroleum products without having been successful in reducing the expenditure of his tax dollars on oil for Europe.

There is one other difficulty that characterized the operations of ECA. In its efforts to control prices and eliminate geographical price discrimination, it may really have installed a price floor, or made more rigid an already existing oligopolistic rigidity. In all the markets deemed comparable by ECA and accepted as such by the companies, the incentive of any one firm to reduce its price was checked.

The requirement of ECA that each firm observe the lowest competitive price at each crude source offered no incentive for a firm to risk a secret price cut in a particular market in order to gain additional outlet. Under the rules, all competitors would be immediately notified and with the prevailing oil supply and currency conditions in the market, it became a certainty (instead of a probability), that the lower price would be instantaneously matched. Therefore, nobody would benefit by cutting price.[27]

When an agency, using a criterion of comparable prices, places a ceiling on some prices, that is, on particular prices which it believes should be no higher than certain others, it tends at the same time to put a floor on all the prices in the region of comparable transactions.

[27] Vernon Herbert Grigg, "The International Price Structure of Crude Oil" (Ph.D. dissertation, Massachusetts Institute of Technology, Boston, June, 1954), p. 408.

9. The Lessons of ECA

Though there were other economic questions involved, the principal dispute between ECA and the oil companies was over the issue of geographical price discrimination.

Under competition such discrimination would be eliminated as sellers withdrew from low realization areas and entered areas yielding higher realizations, and, generally speaking, the more competitive the market the more quickly geographical price discrimination would be eliminated. But the competitive model gives no weight to the value of stability. Businessmen in reality are not interested in economy alone; with the approval of society, they seek security in the ties of custom and contract. They do not pull out of a market as soon as realizations from it decline. The desire for security, however, may become lethargy, and even though competition which is massive rather than hysterical slowly eliminates geographical price discrimination, buyers paying the higher prices in some markets may feel that the values of stability are better served than the values of change. ECA, effectively a purchaser, came to hold this view and as a consequence sought to obtain lower prices from the oil companies.

The writer will not attempt here to decide the ECA Case, primarily because he has discussed only the economic issues involved and has not dealt with its legal aspects. That some discrimination against crude oil buyers in Europe and product buyers in southern Europe occurred cannot be denied. Whether the oil companies were too much concerned with stability, too slow to switch supplies and adjust prices, is a matter of judgment. The writer's inclination is to believe that in international oil stability is given more emphasis than is socially desirable, so that the price of Middle East oil is less responsive to change than it should be. But the government is certainly not correct in using its netback formula to determine the competitive price, and hence, even if the case had been decided in favor of ECA, it would have been unjust to use the calculations made by the government when it sought to establish the size of the refund which the companies might be required to pay.

It is clear that ECA attempts to control prices had but limited success. The experience of ECA would appear to indicate, therefore, that a governmental agency which chooses to attack geographical price discrimination might hope to eliminate only major and prolonged discrimination of this sort. Difficulties in comparing f.o.b. and c.i.f. prices may arise, and it would have to recognize some value in stability; it could not expect frequent shifts in supply patterns or frequent price adjustments. But even if an agency was very self-denying and sought only to eliminate large and enduring geographical price discrimination, it would run into many difficulties. The companies might withdraw small supplies from distant markets rather than reduce prices in those nearby; this could check competition at a distance without helping purchasers nearer the center of production. The companies, if they have alternative markets, may simply refuse to sell at scheduled or official prices in nearby markets, and an interruption of supply there may cause trouble. A simple criterion of comparable prices tends to put a floor under the prices of all transactions considered to be comparable, since every seller is notified of reductions made by any one and a firm cannot hope to gain additional sales by secret price cuts.

It appears, then, that an effective check on geographical price discrimination could only be obtained as part of a fairly comprehensive program of price control. If society concludes that the rigidities of oligopoly have become serious in a sector of the economy, if it concludes, that is, that the number of firms is too few, the threat of entry of outsiders too remote, the competition of substitutes too distant, and the rivalry occurring through regular innovation not impressive, then it may choose to undertake a comprehensive program of price control, one phase of which might involve the elimination of serious and prolonged geographical price discrimination. Such a program would, of course, have to cover most of the transactions in the product and would have to consider costs, profit margins, rates of return on investment, and the like. That a program of this sort would be wise, and if wise, feasible, for Middle East oil, which is produced and marketed in many independent political jurisdictions, is very doubtful.

VI

Middle East Oil in the Alleged International Petroleum Cartel

FREQUENTLY it is alleged that an international cartel has existed in the oil industry, and sometimes it is said that there is still a cartel in oil. The first really serious attempt to establish the past and present existence of a cartel in world oil was made by the staff of the Federal Trade Commission and published in a long report entitled *The International Petroleum Cartel*.[1] The report was never accepted by the FTC itself but received a great deal of attention in the press. In 1953 the federal government instituted a civil suit against the five American companies generally classed as international majors, charging "an unlawful combination and conspiracy," the unlawful monopolizing of trade and commerce in petroleum, and "a continuing agreement and concert of action among the defendants."[2] This government suit has become known as the Cartel Case. It has not been brought to

[1] Washington, D.C., August 22, 1952. This is being cited as the "FTC Report."

[2] Complaint, U.S. vs. Standard Oil Company (New Jersey), Socony-Vacuum Oil Company, Inc., Standard Oil Company of California, The Texas Company, Gulf Oil Corporation, Defendants, Civil Action No. 86–27, published in *Emergency Oil Lift Program*, Part 3, p. 1594.

trial, although two of the defendants, Jersey Standard and Gulf Oil, have entered into consent decrees (November, 1960); Jersey has agreed to the split-up of Standard-Vacuum (see pp. 30–31); and Gulf has modified in some respects its marketing of Kuwait oil.

In the pages which follow, we shall limit the range of our discussion severely. We will not attempt to decide the broad question of whether or not a *world* oil cartel exists; we will simply see whether a cartel can be detected in Middle East oil. And we will use the word "cartel" in a restricted sense as a group of firms systematically united by a fairly elaborate set of formal agreements to limit output, divide up markets, and control prices. (The broader question of monopoly in general, or rather oligopoly, in the market for Middle East oil has been treated in earlier chapters.) The reader should keep in mind that the following treatment of Middle East oil in the alleged world cartel is based on incomplete information, on much less information than probably would come to light should the Cartel Case be brought to trial. The principal source of the material which follows is the FTC Report. Oil men tend to admit privately that this report is factually correct even when they, quite rightly, observe that its interpretations are often most dubious.

1. The Red-Line Agreement of 1928

After the First World War when Americans became interested in entering the Middle East, they found that the most promising areas were already under the control of British, British-Dutch, and French companies. With the support of the State Department, a number of American companies in 1928 finally persuaded—or, more probably, forced—the Europeans to sell them a share (23.75 percent) in the Turkish Petroleum Company (later to become the Iraq Petroleum Company).[3] The American

[3] FTC Report, pp. 51–61; Stephen Hemsley Longrigg, *Oil in the Middle East: Its Discovery and Development* (London: Oxford University Press,

companies, however, obtained their participation only by accepting in the purchase contract, apparently with great reluctance, certain restrictions on their behavior, restrictions which were applicable to all of the several shareholders in TPC and which together became known as the "Red-Line Agreement." A "defined area," comprising most of the old Ottoman Empire, was outlined in red on a map and attached to the purchase contract and, with some exceptions that proved unimportant in practice, the companies in ownership of TPC agreed that TPC alone might hold concessions in this area; they agreed that the owners of TPC as well as their subsidiaries were not to be interested, directly or indirectly, in the production or purchase of oil in the area except through TPC.[4] At least one of the American companies concerned, Socony, in a plea for dismissal of the Cartel Case, has contended that "the transaction was entered into with the approval of the United States, expressed through the Department of State," a contention which is supported by a State Department letter of the time quoted in Shwadran.[5]

Clearly, to the extent that the Red-Line Agreement was enforced, it restricted competition for concessions among the several firms owning the Iraq Petroleum Company. In dealing with governments in the Middle East, these firms acted as a unit and presumably obtained better terms as a result. Moreover, to the extent enforced, the agreement restrained competition in the demand for any oil in the defined area which was being sold by companies not in the IPC group. There is evidence that the Red-Line Agreement did in fact restrict competition for the Saudi

---

1954), pp. 45–46, 67–70. Originally five companies participated in the American holding, but eventually Jersey Standard and Socony bought out the others.

[4] FTC Report, p. 66.

[5] U.S. vs. Standard Oil Company (New Jersey), et al., answer of Defendant Socony-Vacuum Oil Company, Inc., p. 32; Benjamin Shwadran, The Middle East, Oil and the Great Powers, 2d ed., rev. (New York: Council for Middle Eastern Affairs Press, 1959), p. 246n.

Arabian concession in 1933 and possibly restricted competition in the purchase of Bahrein crude and products in the late thirties.[6] The Red-Line Agreement in essence served to promote what economists call "monopsony," a buyer's monopoly, in the purchase of concessions and in the purchase of oil.

In October, 1946, the American companies in IPC, Jersey Standard and Socony, declared the Red-Line Agreement to be dissolved; there were suits and countersuits with the American companies declaring that the agreement "was in restraint of trade and contrary to public policy and void and unenforcible in law."[7] After lengthy negotiations, settlement was reached out of court on November 3, 1948: the Red-Line Agreement was canceled and a new agreement, which eliminated most of the restrictive provisions, took its place. The companies owning IPC were henceforth free to acquire concessions independently in the Red-Line area and free to purchase crude and products independently in the area.

2. The Establishment of Caltex

In 1936 the Standard Oil Company of California and the Texas Company (now Texaco Inc.) entered into an agreement under which Standard of California received a 50 percent interest in the Texas Company's marketing facilities East of Suez and the Texas Company received a 50 percent interest in the Bahrein and Saudi Arabian concessions of Standard of California. The jointly owned company (50 percent owned by each parent) which was formed to hold both the marketing and producing properties involved was named the California Texas Oil Company, Ltd., and became known as Caltex. Later, on January 1, 1947, the Texas Company sold its European marketing facilities to Caltex.[8] Standard of California had found oil on the island of

[6] FTC Report, pp. 74–81, esp. p. 81; Longrigg, op. cit., p. 107.
[7] Statement of Claim Filed in High Court of Justice, Chancery Division, June 9, 1947, quoted in FTC Report, p. 104.
[8] FTC Report, pp. 114–116, 121.

Bahrein in 1932, but at the time it had no marketing properties outside the United States; it had been depending on Socony to market its products in the Far East. The Texas Company had developed markets in Europe, Africa, Australasia, China, and other areas in the Far East, but, for lack of nearer production, had been supplying these markets from the United States. The ensuing union can be, and has been, interpreted in two ways.

The FTC Report suggests, without explicitly saying so, that the agreement between Standard of California and the Texas Company represents a significant move in the development of a world oil cartel. It points out that Standard of California had discussed earlier with Royal Dutch–Shell, Jersey Standard, and Anglo-Iranian the problem of disposing of Bahrein production. It quotes a statement made by the *Petroleum Times* when Caltex was set up, for which it supplies italics: "The advantage of this merger is that . . . Bahrein production, as well as any output that may eventually come from countries now being developed by Standard of California, *will have assured and regulated outlets and will so lessen any possible danger of upsetting the equilibrium of international markets.*" [9] But the suggestion that Caltex was created as one move in the development of a world cartel established to stabilize world markets is not the only way of looking at the agreement between Standard of California and the Texas Company. Many of the oil men involved in the formation of Caltex probably viewed it as a simple business arrangement (an arrangement which, to be sure, had the consequence of reducing competition below what it might have been) Standard of California had oil production, and the Texas Company had marketing facilities; the merger of these properties was an extremely economical vertical integration enabling Standard of California to avoid the duplication of Texas Company marketing installations and providing, through deliveries from the Middle East instead of from the United States, important economies in transport. In due course the writer will give reasons for believing

[9] *Petroleum Times*, July 4, 1936, p. 8, quoted in FTC Report, p. 116.

that the simple business view of this and most of the subsequent arrangements discussed in the chapter is closer to the truth than the view that they represent steps in the development of an international petroleum cartel.

3. Jersey and Socony Buy into Aramco

After the Second World War, Jersey Standard and Socony acquired an interest in the Arabian American Oil Company (and in the Trans-Arabian Pipeline Company). At first (March 12, 1947) they merely subscribed to stock in Aramco and Tapline and guaranteed certain bank loans to the companies, but later (December, 1948) they took up their shares and acquired full ownership. Then Standard of California, the Texas Company, and Jersey Standard each had a 30 percent share in Aramco while Socony had a 10 percent share. (The distribution of ownership in Tapline was the same.[10])

As in the case of the establishment of Caltex, the union of these several companies in Aramco can be looked at in two ways. One can see it through the eyes of the FTC Report as a step in the cartelization of world oil. Aramco had emerged from the war with a tremendous potential to produce crude oil and would have to produce in substantial quantities to increase royalty payments to the King of Saudi Arabia.

The owners of Aramco (Standard of California and the Texas Company) were apparently faced with the choice of either forcing their way by competitive means into markets which, before the war, had been closed to them because of international cartel arrangements, i.e., the "as is position," or permitting companies which did have marketing outlets and positions in areas west of Suez to acquire a proprietary interest in Aramco. . . .

The international oil companies decided to take the latter course of action. Texas and Standard of California would obtain additional markets for Aramco without having to compete for them, while Jersey and Socony, with their world-wide interests, could distribute

[10] Arabian American Oil Company, *Middle East Oil Development* (New York: The Company, 1956), pp. 32–33; FTC Report, pp. 119–125.

158

their shares of Aramco's output, with the result that world prices and markets would not be disturbed.[11]

The "as is" arrangements were a series of arrangements made by a number of oil companies during the late twenties and the thirties to divide up world markets, or particular local markets, and restrict competition. Indubitably a cartel, the "as is" arrangements had the support of many governments and were in line with prevailing opinion that competition ought to be more "orderly." In practice the "as is" group was not very effective in maintaining its position against outsiders and there is little evidence to support the view that the "as is" arrangements continued in effect after the Second World War. The authors of the FTC Report certainly do not supply evidence to support their veiled suggestion that the purchase of Aramco shares by Jersey and Socony represents a postwar extension of the "as is" arrangements, nor do they demonstrate that international majors other than the four American companies were involved in the decision to expand the ownership of Aramco, though they suggest as much.

The agreement for Jersey and Socony to buy into Aramco can be looked at simply as a business transaction (a transaction which did, however, reduce the degree of competition below what it might have been). Standard of California and the Texas Company had found a large quantity of oil, more than they could readily sell, and they needed large quantities of capital to build a pipeline, develop Saudi production, and enlarge their marketing network. Jersey and Socony had markets and needed additional Middle East oil to supply them. The arrangements may have avoided an uneconomic duplication by Standard of California and the Texas Company of marketing facilities owned by Jersey and Socony.

4. The Kuwait Agreement of Anglo-Persian and Gulf Oil

In the early thirties Gulf Oil Corporation, an American firm, had, through a subsidiary, an option on an oil concession in the

[11] FTC Report, p. 121.

Sheikhdom of Kuwait. When Gulf Oil sought to exercise the option in this British protectorate, opposition arose from British oil interests and the British government; it had been general British policy that only British firms should be given concessions in British territories. And as a rival to Gulf, Anglo-Persian Oil Company, Ltd. (now British Petroleum Company), was negotiating with the Sheikh for a Kuwait concession. The U.S. Department of State supported the claims of Gulf Oil, and a deadlock developed. It was broken only in 1933 when Gulf Oil and Anglo-Persian decided to make common cause, to seek a concession together, and if one was obtained to operate it jointly.[12] Besides an agreement to organize an operating company (the Kuwait Oil Company), to be owned and financed equally by the two corporations, the contract (which was signed December 14, 1933) included some provisions restrictive of competition (provisions which Gulf has since declared were always objectionable to it and were accepted only at the insistence of Anglo-Persian).[13]

It was agreed that Anglo-Persian, if it chose, could supply Gulf Oil with crude from Iraq or Iran, such crude to take the place of crude which Gulf might otherwise require Kuwait Oil Company to produce in Kuwait. By reserving the right to supply the requirements of Gulf from alternative sources, Anglo-Persian gained a certain control over total output, and hence over price, in the Middle East. If it had difficulty in cutting back output in Iraq or Iran, because of the desires of its partners in the Iraq Petroleum Company or because of pressure from the Arabs or Iranians, it might in effect cut back the Kuwait output for Gulf by supplying Gulf from these other areas. In addition to giving Anglo-Persian some control over the total supply of Middle East oil, the agreement between Anglo-Persian and Gulf Oil included restrictions on marketing. The two companies agreed that Kuwait oil would not be used to "upset or injure" the other's "trade

[12] Ibid., pp. 129–131; Longrigg, op. cit., pp. 110–111.
[13] FTC Report, pp. 131–134.

or marketing position directly or indirectly at any time or place."
Anglo-Persian's position in India was particularly noted. Moreover, each party agreed "to confer from time to time as either
party may desire and mutually settle in accordance with such
principles any question that may arise between them regarding
the marketing of Kuwait oil and products therefrom." [14]

A large quantity of oil was discovered in Kuwait in 1938, but
production did not begin until after the war. On November 30,
1951, Anglo-Iranian Oil Company and Gulf Oil agreed to cancel
the 1933 contract between Anglo-Persian and Gulf Oil.[15] There
is reason to believe, as we shall see, that some of its restrictive consequences were preserved in a contract Gulf made with Shell in
1947.

5. The Gulf-Shell Contract

Gulf Oil Corporation in May, 1947, acting through a subsidiary, entered into a long-term contract with Shell Petroleum
Company, Ltd. It agreed to sell to Shell over a period of years a
considerable part of its share of Kuwait crude oil. Originally
deliveries were to be through December 31, 1956; later the agreement was extended to December 31, 1969, and beyond, and now
it runs to the year 2026.[16] The quantities of oil involved in the
agreement started in 1947 at 15,000 barrels per day; in 1958 under
the contract Gulf sold an average of 413,000 barrels a day of
Kuwait oil to Shell, or 58 percent of its 713,952-barrel average
Kuwait output and 9.7 percent of average daily output in the
entire Middle East, certainly one of the grand commercial transactions of our day.[17]

[14] Ibid., p. 131.
[15] Ibid., p. 144n. Anglo-Iranian was successor to Anglo-Persian and of
course predecessor to the British Petroleum Company.
[16] FTC Report, p. 138; Preliminary Prospectus of Royal Dutch Petroleum Company and "Shell" Transport and Trading Company, Ltd. (concerning the purchase of Canadian Eagle Oil Company), May 27, 1959,
p. 13.
[17] Preliminary Prospectus, p. 14; Gulf Oil Corporation, *Annual Report*,

Rather than sell the oil outright to Shell at a stated price, Gulf agreed to share equally with Shell the total profits on the production, transportation, refining, and marketing of this crude. From an estimate of Shell's total receipts for the oil is subtracted an estimate of Shell's costs of transporting, refining, and marketing it as well as an estimate of Gulf's costs of producing it. The resulting annual profit, or loss, is shared equally by Gulf and Shell.[18] With this agreement, Gulf and Shell in effect became partners in the production and distribution of the oil covered by the contract, with Gulf through its holding in Kuwait Oil Company (and of course in partnership with Anglo-Iranian) undertaking the task of producing the oil while Shell undertook to refine it and carry it to market. (Basically the Gulf-Shell contract resembles the Standard of California–Texas Company establishment of Caltex, in which Standard of California production was united with Texas Company marketing.)

Finally, Gulf and Shell agreed that if it could be established that Gulf had increased its proportion of business at the expense of Shell in any of a number of "listed territories," territories comprising much of the Eastern Hemisphere, Shell would have the right to reduce its purchases under the contract.[19]

The Gulf-Shell contract enabled Gulf to find an outlet in the Eastern Hemisphere for its Kuwait oil without the necessity of fighting (competing) for a position, or an improved position, in that market. Moreover, having obtained the Shell outlet, Gulf under the contract is disinclined to go out in most of the Eastern Hemisphere and develop independent outlets of its own. The terms of the agreement clearly reduce its incentive to compete with Shell in the territories in which the contract assumes the

---

1958, p. 25; *World Oil*, August 15, 1959, p. 102. Gulf announced that under the contract Shell would buy 560,000 barrels per day during 1960 (*Petroleum Week*, May 16, 1960, p. 88).

18 FTC Report, p. 139. Estimates of Shell's costs and receipts are based on an assumed pattern of distribution in certain "listed territories," which, however, Shell is not obliged to follow in practice.

19 *Ibid.*, pp. 139–140.

Kuwait oil will be sold. If Gulf invades these areas, it will have to subtract from any gains it makes one-half of the reduction in profits, or even half of the losses, which the Gulf-Shell partnership in production and distribution suffers as a consequence. The contract we are considering not only protects Shell in many markets from the competition of Gulf but also gives the British Petroleum Company (formerly Anglo-Iranian) considerable protection. Since British Petroleum and Shell have joint-marketing arrangements in many of the territories covered by the agreement, the profit-sharing arrangements, which disincline Gulf to enter particular markets served by Shell, act to protect the trading position of British Petroleum in numerous areas where it is a Shell associate. For this reason the authors of the FTC Report contend that the Gulf-Shell sale-of-oil contract of 1947 took the place of the restrictive provisions of the Anglo-Persian–Gulf Oil agreement of 1933 (concerning Kuwait), so that these restrictive provisions could then be readily canceled in 1951.[20]

Although the Gulf-Shell contract checks competition between the two firms, Gulf Oil can enter Shell territory. Indeed, the contract may make Gulf entry easier, for Gulf, through the profit-sharing arrangement with Shell, almost certainly has information unknown to outsiders about distribution costs in the listed territories. But though Gulf entry is possible, it may not lead to more competition. Shell may withdraw as Gulf enters; the Gulf-Shell contract makes withdrawal easier by stating that should Gulf increase its sales at the expense of Shell in the listed territories, Shell has the right to reduce its purchases under the contract.

It seems scarcely debatable that on the whole the Gulf-Shell contract reduces competition. Gulf is certainly disinclined to compete with Shell in the listed territories when it is getting half of the profits which Shell gains in marketing there; at least it is disinclined to compete as long as it believes that Shell is operating economically. (And although society is interested in economical

[20] *Ibid.*, p. 144 and n.

163

activity, it need not be satisfied with economy alone; it can ask also for competition and competitive prices.) But to say that the Gulf-Shell contract moderates competition is not to say that it is part of a set of cartel agreements. Oil men tend to look at it simply as a commercial deal. Gulf Oil owned half of a tremendous reserve of oil in Kuwait. Anglo-Iranian, its partner there, was entitled to lift unlimited quantities of Kuwait oil and was likely to be lifting exceedingly large amounts in the postwar period. Gulf itself had a very small marketing position in the Eastern Hemisphere and could only expect to develop one slowly. Should it have set about to build up its own marketing operation, it would have watched, while doing so, its partner in Kuwait lift a great deal more than half of the oil. It is not surprising, then, that in 1947 Gulf Oil turned to Shell Petroleum, which had large markets in the Eastern Hemisphere but lacked a strong crude position in the Middle East.

As for the profit-sharing arrangements, a claim is made that they were adopted because Gulf and Shell could not agree on a set price for the oil or even on a pricing formula.[21] A very large quantity of oil was going to change hands over a long period of time; it was difficult for the parties to forecast its value, and if either side made a mistake, it could experience severe losses. A formula which tied the price of the Gulf-Shell trade to the price of the high-cost oil at the U.S. Gulf Coast was out of the question. A formula which tied the price of sale to some sort of average of Persian Gulf prices would have been better, but still not very satisfactory. An average of posted prices in the Persian Gulf would not be a good indicator of the value of Middle East oil, since these prices mostly represent the prices of sale to affiliates; they do not reflect arm's length bargaining. Prices placed on the 10 percent of Middle East oil which is sold in the open market to nonaffiliates are often discounted, hence usually not published, and in any case an average of these prices would seldom indicate

[21] Private interview with an oil company executive; FTC Report, p. 139n.

the real value of the 90 percent of Middle East oil which is sold, in large quantities, to affiliates. A cost-plus formula for pricing the oil sold under the Gulf-Shell contract would also run into difficulties: How is the plus element, the profit element, to be established? If it is set at a fixed profit per barrel, it rests in effect on a forecast of the market value of the oil, on a forecast of the amount by which the sale value of the oil would exceed costs. The parties would have difficulty in agreeing upon this forecast, and errors could be costly to the side which made them. If it is suggested that the profit element in the cost-plus formula be related to the average open-market value of the oil, we are back to the problems associated with the fact that only about 10 percent of Middle East oil is sold in the open market.

The Gulf-Shell contract, then, may be viewed as simply a solution adopted by businessmen to cope with the difficulties which arise in an exceedingly large commercial transaction, rather than part of a carefully calculated plan for cartelization of world oil.

6. The Anglo-Iranian Contracts with Jersey Standard and Socony

In 1947 and 1948 Anglo-Iranian Oil Company (now British Petroleum) agreed to deliver large quantities of oil to Standard Oil Company (New Jersey) and to Socony-Vacuum Oil Company (now Socony Mobil) over a twenty-year period. The contract with Jersey called for deliveries at an average rate of 90,000 barrels per day during the first three years and 114,000 barrels a day during the succeeding seven years; the rate of delivery for the last ten years was to be determined at a later date. Two contracts with Socony were signed calling for delivery of 70,000 barrels per day during the first ten years of the agreements (with the rate of delivery for the last ten years to be set later).[22] The price of the oil delivered under these contracts was to be calculated on a cost-plus principle, the cost to include all costs

[22] FTC Report, pp. 145–157.

165

of production and delivery (it turned out to be delivery "f.o.b. tankship") and the plus element to be a profit figure per ton. Under the Jersey contract and one of the Socony contracts this profit payable to Anglo-Iranian was an agreed *fixed* money profit per ton applicable throughout the twenty-year period of the agreements and completely independent of the sale price of the oil. Under the second Socony contract the profit per ton payable to Anglo-Iranian was variable, being equal to one-third of the difference between, on the one hand, the average costs of production and delivery and, on the other, the average open-market value of the oil. This "differential" or plus element added to cost in the second Socony contract, however, was free to fluctuate only within maximum and minimum figures which were stated in the contract. It is of significance that the profit received by Anglo-Iranian under this second contract was in some degree tied to the prevailing sale price of oil in the Middle East. All of the contracts observed that Anglo-Iranian, at its pleasure, might deliver the oil to Jersey and Socony from either Kuwait or Iran.

Jersey and Socony both asserted in the agreements that they intended to use the oil in supplying certain stated markets—such as Europe, North Africa, West Africa, the United States—all of which were "West of Suez." It was agreed, in supplementary contracts signed April 5, 1949, that any excess over 5 percent shipped East of Suez would be paid for at Anglo-Iranian's established f.o.b. spot cargo price, which of course would be higher than the cost-plus price.

The contracts between Anglo-Iranian (British Petroleum), on the one hand, and Jersey Standard and Socony, on the other, definitely have features restricting competition. The mere fact that Jersey and Socony state in a contract that they intend to market the oil West of Suez no doubt puts them under some obligation to behave accordingly, hence limits their freedom to compete in markets East of Suez. And the higher price paid for oil shipped East of Suez (oil in excess of 5 percent of the amounts deliverable under the contracts) very clearly checks competition in eastern

166

markets. It has been suggested that lower prices on shipments West of Suez may be defended by pointing to the distant markets which the purchaser is trying to reach or the tariff the purchaser must pay in taking the oil into particular political jurisdictions; only if British Petroleum cuts prices for firms selling in such markets can it expect to win this trade. But a differential netback, lower on sales West of Suez than on sales east of the Canal, would not endure in a highly competitive market of numerous sellers. Traders would withdraw supplies from the low netback markets of the west and ship them to the east until netbacks on sales in all directions were equalized. (Each trader would switch supplies because he would not expect his individual small volume to reduce prices in the new market.) It is difficult to imagine British Petroleum contracting for twenty years to sell oil at a relatively low netback West of Suez (forgoing more attractive netbacks on shipments to the east), if it is not trying to protect the price structure east of the Canal. And the higher prices charged Jersey and Socony on shipments East of Suez (charged of course on eastern shipments over 5 percent of the amounts deliverable under the contracts) clearly seem designed to ensure that these companies do not do what British Petroleum forgoes doing, namely, increase supplies substantially in eastern markets.

The device by which the profit earned by British Petroleum, on its second contract with Socony, is tied to the open-market price of oil could also serve to restrict competition. If British Petroleum were considering entry into a new market or an expanded volume through price reductions in an old market, it might have to subtract from anticipated gains on its new business a reduced return on its sales to Socony under its second contract with that company. Lower product prices consequent upon more competitive behavior and reflected back in lower open-market prices for crude in the Middle East could reduce the "differential" or profit which was added to costs in calculating the price of sale to Socony. Quite possibly, however, such considerations would have a negligible influence on British Petroleum, since there is a minimum figure stated in the contract below which the differential or profit charged cannot fall.

7. May We Infer the Existence of a Cartel in Middle East Oil?

All the arrangements we have discussed in this chapter tend to restrict competition in some degree—the Red-Line Agreement of 1928, the establishment of Caltex, the purchase of Aramco shares by Jersey and Socony, the Kuwait agreement of Anglo-Persian and Gulf Oil, the Gulf-Shell sale-of-oil contract, and the Anglo-Iranian sale-of-oil contracts with Jersey Standard and Socony. In the writer's view, the first of these, the Red-Line Agreement, was a cartel measure; it was one measure in a set of agreements which included the "as is" arrangements and which clearly made up a pre-Second-World-War cartel in international oil. But it seems doubtful that the remaining arrangements discussed in the chapter may be considered part of a petroleum cartel. Many of the people who made them were probably not thinking of market control but looked at them purely as commercial arrangements, as ways of getting large volumes of oil most expeditiously to market. If these people built a cartel, they did so unconsciously. More important, the arrangements we have been talking about are not a systematic, unified set of formal agreements to limit output, divide up markets, and seek control over price; they are not arrangements such as are discovered in what is usually called a cartel. Rather we have here a loose collection of more or less unrelated agreements.

The reader then may suggest that there is a secret agreement, or secret set of agreements, which tie the known arrangements together; the unifying compact, he may suggest, though not observed, can be inferred from the agreements which have been published. But it is unlikely that secret agreements of great significance exist. There is no real need for them. The international majors, as oligopolists, have accommodated themselves to one another and to circumstances well enough to obtain a degree of stability with which they can live. After discussing the Jersey and Socony purchase of Aramco shares, the Anglo-Iranian sale-of-oil contract with Jersey and Socony, and the Gulf-Shell contract, Dr. Frankel said:

To call the resulting set-up a Cartel is disingenuous. The simple fact is that such reasonably stable equilibrium made a cartel unnecessary. To say that there were some Secret Restrictive Covenants without which the situation would not have been as orderly as it was is on a par with a statement that there is no visible revolutionary movement in England or Switzerland because of its Repression By The Ruling Classes—whereas the truth is that there just is no revolutionary *situation*.[23]

[23] "A Turning Point."

VII

Government Roles in Consuming and Producing Countries

SO far we have observed in Middle East oil mostly the operations of the companies. But governments, both in producing countries and in consuming countries, influence oil prices in a number of ways. One of the most important governmental factors in oil markets of course is taxation.

1. The Influence of U.S. Protection on Middle East Oil Prices

Protection of the market in the United States from the competition of low-cost foreign oil has become an important factor in the international oil trade. Much of U.S. oil is high-cost oil; particularly so is the oil of the marginal, "stripper" wells, pumping only a few barrels a day but owned by the numerous, politically powerful, small oil men of the Southwest. In recent years American producers have been increasingly successful in winning protection for their domestic market.

The U.S. tariff on imported oil is relatively low, 10.5 cents per barrel for light crudes which are delivered on the East Coast at a price between $3.00 and $3.50. Hence by itself the tariff would provide little protection for domestic oil. Beginning in

GOVERNMENT ROLES

1955, however, the government sponsored a more or less voluntary import restraint program, and in March, 1959, the program was made definitely compulsory. The voluntary program limited imports to about 10 percent of total U.S. demand; the compulsory program limits imports of crude and products east of the Rockies to 9 percent of domestic requirements in the region plus export demand, but excluding ocean bunkers. (Permitted imports on the West Coast are calculated differently, and imports from Canada are exempt from control.)

Probably the voluntary program contributed to reduced prices abroad, in the Middle East and elsewhere, by shutting foreign oil out of the United States and forcing it into other markets. But in all likelihood the impact of the voluntary restraints was small. In fact, under the program U.S. imports *increased*, though perhaps not as much as they would have otherwise. In 1954, before the import restraints, U.S. imports from the Middle East (crude and products) averaged 214,000 barrels per day and from Venezuela and the Netherlands West Indies 689,000 barrels a day. In the last three quarters of 1958, the United States imported from the Middle East an average of 350,000 barrels a day and from Venezuela and the Netherlands West Indies an average of 943,000 barrels daily.[1] It is difficult to believe that the voluntary restraints did much to change prices outside the United States.

The compulsory quotas instituted in March, 1959, probably had a larger impact on oil prices. Imports into the United States from Venezuela did not decrease after quotas were imposed, but the expected rate of increase failed to occur. And U.S. imports from the Middle East apparently declined by about 5 percent.[2] Investments had been made in Venezuela and in the Middle East in anticipation of a rise in U.S. imports. The variable costs of producing this new capacity were and are low, and there has been

[1] Petroleum Industry Research Foundation, *United States Oil Imports: A Case Study in International Trade* (New York: The Foundation, 1958), p. 94; *Petroleum Press Service*, April, 1960, p. 149.
[2] *Ibid.*

171

a certain inclination to seek an early recovery of invested funds by operating the facilities, while pushing the oil produced into markets outside the United States. Such activity threatens to undermine prices in these markets. The international majors, of course, have a strong interest in stable prices and they have long pocketbooks (they can afford to wait); hence they are likely to market with restraint. The nonaffiliated firms, the independents with newly discovered oil, have a lesser interest in stability and often command smaller resources. When shut out of the United States, their oil more seriously threatens prices in non-U.S. markets.

Even displaced independent oil may not have the impact on prices which some oil men anticipate. The majors may check their own production and step aside for the independents' oil, acting either on their own initiative or at the insistence of producing-country governments. These governments have a strong interest in price stability; indeed the governments may defend prices by controlling the output of independents. Venezuela already has stopped three independents from selling some of their production at large discounts off posted price.[3]

U.S. import quotas probably put some pressure on oil prices outside the United States, but actual declines as a consequence of these quotas probably have not been great.

2. Protection in Western Europe and West European Excise Taxes on Gasoline

The pattern of protection in western Europe varies a great deal from country to country. Germany protects her indigenous oil with a high tariff on imported crude oil; net protection after certain duty refunds amounts to about $2.58 per barrel. France subsidizes domestic crude production, and many European countries have small duties on petroleum products.[4] In addition, ap-

---

[3] *Petroleum Press Service*, April, 1960, p. 142; *Petroleum Week*, March 18, 1960, p. 18.
[4] *Petroleum Press Service*, November, 1957, p. 405.

parently, Europe exercises a considerable amount of administrative protection of crude oil, products, and coal through exchange controls and import licenses, through the purchasing activities of nationalized industries, and recently in Germany through a governmentally prompted "crisis cartel" established to check the competition of fuel oil with indigenous coal.[5] Finally, excise taxes on fuel oil in western Europe serve to protect domestic coal and perhaps in some cases natural gas or hydroelectric power, but they do not protect indigenous oil so long as they are paid on all fuel oil sold, domestic as well as imported. In any case, European excise taxes on fuel oil, generally speaking, are relatively low. On the whole one can say that protection in western Europe is a comparatively minor factor in the price of Middle East oil. Although most production in the area probably takes place behind trade barriers, total 1959 production in western Europe amounted to only 5.7 percent of 1959 production in the Middle East.[6]

Of greater interest are the extremely high west European excise taxes on gasoline. They probably do not provide a great deal of protection—unless it is in small measure to the boot and shoe industry, the bicycle and scooter industries, the motor coach industry, or the production of indigenous donkeys. But because of their magnitude the incidence of these taxes on gasoline is a matter of great importance. At the end of 1958 in England, France, West Germany, and Italy, taxes and duties (apparently mostly excise taxes) amounted to 59, 78, 54, and 73 percent, respectively, of the sale price of gasoline.[7] On whom do European excise taxes on gasoline fall, on the sellers of Middle East oil, on the factors which produce it, or on the consumers who use it? Probably on the latter; it is likely that the tax is shifted to consumers through higher prices.

When excise taxes are imposed on the sellers of oil products,

---

[5] The establishment of this cartel is discussed in *ibid.*, January, 1959, p. 29, and its collapse in *ibid.*, September, 1959, p. 352.
[6] *Ibid.*, January, 1960, p. 5.
[7] Calculated from data in *ibid.*, January, 1959, p. 17.

their costs are increased and profits initially reduced. It is entirely possible that as oligopolists the sellers will have been able immediately to increase prices by the amount of the tax. Perhaps a price leader raised the price and other firms followed. A uniform response will have been facilitated by the fact that average costs were increased for all firms equally, and by definite, known amounts. If sellers use a system with a standard percentage mark-up over direct costs of labor, materials, and inventory, as they might very well do in Europe where competition is not greatly admired, then price increases by the amount of the tax will have been easier.[8]

Should the oligopoly not have been strong enough to shift the taxes immediately, part of them may have been absorbed by the sellers, through a reduction in excess, oligopolistic, profits. It is, however, most doubtful that oligopoly profits in Middle East oil have been great enough to absorb a substantial part of excise taxes which range from 50 to 80 percent of product sale prices.

In the event that excise taxes were not shifted to consumers immediately in higher prices or absorbed in excess profits, they will have impinged on necessary profits or have produced losses. Then as time passed, investment in the industry will have been checked or reduced, and the supply of petroleum products will have increased more slowly or have actually declined. The impact of a slower increase or a decline in supply upon factor prices and prices of sale depends upon the elasticities of supply and demand for the product. Were the supply of Middle East oil perfectly elastic, were it produced under conditions of constant cost, then prices to consumers would have risen by exactly the amount of the tax: factors of production would have left the industry until prices increased just enough to cover the new, higher costs and restored profits. (In this case the result is independent of the elasticity of demand.) [9]

[8] John F. Due, *Government Finance: An Economic Analysis* (Homewood, Ill.: R. D. Irwin, 1954), p. 288.
[9] *Ibid.*, p. 283.

If, however, Middle East oil has been produced under conditions of decreasing costs, which seems more likely to have been the case (and seems likely to be the case in the foreseeable future), then the price to consumers will have risen by more than the tax. After the taxes were imposed and the supply of oil reduced, costs will have been higher (1) because of the tax and (2) because of the higher costs associated with a smaller volume. Factors of production will have left the industry until prices rose enough to cover both the tax and the increased costs which accompanied the smaller volume.

Only if Middle East oil were produced under conditions of increasing costs, and this seems most unlikely to be the case, would excise taxes not have been shifted entirely to consumers. After the tax had been imposed, in this unlikely case, and the supply of oil reduced, production costs (associated with the smaller volume) would have been lower, offsetting at least part of the cost increase attributable to the tax itself. When supply had been reduced enough to restore profits, prices would have risen by less than the amount of the tax (because total costs would not have gone up by the amount of the tax), and part of the tax burden would have rested on the immobile factors of production, perhaps in the Middle East on the owners of the oil, that is, on the governments.[10]

It seems reasonable to conclude that none of the burden of excise taxes on petroleum products rests on the factors of production in the Middle East (including here under the heading of factor the governments which own the oil). These taxes are paid by consumers in higher prices.

Oil men are very much inclined to believe that high European excise taxes contribute to the rigidity of Middle East oil prices. With taxes on gasoline so high, a given percentage cut in the companies' delivered prices of gasoline will be followed by a much smaller percentage reduction in the prices paid by con-

[10] John F. Due, *The Theory of Incidence of Sales Taxation* (New York: King's Crown Press, 1942), p. 22.

sumers. And if the governments *increase* taxes when oil companies reduce prices, as they are wont to do, consumers receive no benefits at all from the price cut. Oil men argue, then, that high excise taxes and the inclination of governments to increase them eliminate most of their incentives to lower prices; the companies expect a price reduction to sell little additional oil.

The precise significance of this argument should be seen. Oil men here presumably are not contending simply that excise taxes raise prices to consumers because they are shifted. Few would dispute this contention. They are saying that prices are higher by *more* than the amount of the tax (and by more than any increases in costs associated with a smaller, taxed volume). In effect oil men are saying that excise taxes contribute to the rigidity of oligopoly prices and the collection by the companies of oligopoly profits, that oligopoly prices and profits are higher than they would be in the absence of these taxes. In their discussions of this subject, oil people *must* be thinking of oligopolistic rigidity and alleging that taxes make it more serious. Certainly in a market of numerous sellers competition would drive prices down to costs—excise taxes (and necessary profits) being included in costs—and no one would speak of a tax contribution to price rigidity. A large number of sellers, each so small that no one of them felt its output had an appreciable influence on price, would expand until price declines eliminated all excess profits.

Excise taxes may contribute to the rigidity of oligopoly prices, but the writer inclines to believe that the contribution is small. Suppose these taxes were eliminated and suppose governments lost their inclination to clap on a new tax whenever oil companies reduced prices. Would not the few international majors as oligopolists still act in accordance with "oligopolistic rationality" and hesitate to cut prices knowing that their rivals would meet the cut and that as a consequence they would sell only a small additional volume? It seems doubtful that European excise taxes add very much to the rigidity of prices in the market for Middle East oil.

We have suggested that protectionist policies in the United States and Europe have done comparatively little to lower the price of Middle East oil. And we have observed that high European excise taxes on oil are paid mostly by consumers. People in the Middle East have only one basis for complaint concerning these measures: they are measures which probably have checked the growth of Middle East production. Almost certainly, sales of Middle East oil in the United States and Europe would have been a good deal larger if the United States had not introduced quotas and if Europe had not established such high excise taxes. (Demand for gasoline is inelastic, but, even so, excise taxes which are so high as to double or treble prices will have a substantial effect on the amount purchased.)

3. The Concern of European Governments with Oil Storage

The previously considered actions of governments in countries which consume oil have had their greatest impact on people in the consuming countries themselves. Now we want to consider some governmental actions in consuming countries which may be felt more in the countries where oil is produced.

After the Suez Canal was blocked in 1956, Europeans became much more interested in holding reserve stocks of oil. The desire for larger inventories in some cases no doubt reflected a desire to hold strategic stocks against the possibility of war; such motivation might have been particularly important in neutral countries. More often, it seems likely, stocks were sought which could be used to tide consumers over a period during which new sources of supply were being developed to replace interrupted Middle Eastern supplies. Perhaps a few men, to improve European bargaining power, tried to put Europe in a stronger position for dealing with producing countries which sought to obtain better terms by withholding supplies.

The cost of carrying inventories is high, and only modest increases in European reserve stocks have been attained. One estimate is that for the OEEC countries as a whole an extra three-month supply beyond normal working stocks at 1957 rates of consumption, if held as crude, would cost almost $1,400,000,000 (counting the value of the oil itself, investment in tankage, associated pipelines, land, the cost of maintaining storage facilities, periodical rotation of oil in storage, and the like).[11] Some countries—France, Italy, Finland, Sweden, probably others—require oil companies to hold certain minimum stocks, say 15 or 25 percent of annual sales or similar percentages of refinery capacity. Sweden has appropriated state funds for an additional stockpile.[12]

Apart from the strategic advantages in large stocks or, with ample reserves to draw on, the reduced economic disruption that might follow upon an interruption of regular supplies, there is a real bargaining advantage in the possession of large inventories. Should Middle Eastern countries by withholding supplies seek to improve the terms on which they supply oil, Europeans would be in a better position to resist. Certainly if a pattern of bilateral governmental oligopoly emerged—a group of Middle Eastern governments controlling output, on the one side, and a group of governmental trading agencies engaged in purchasing, on the other—the essentially indeterminate outcome would be much influenced by the magnitude of reserve stocks in the consuming countries.

4. Price Controls and State Trading in Consuming Countries

While price controls may do something to limit profits in transportation, marketing, and the refining which takes place in consuming areas, it is doubtful that they do much, as they are now set up in the countries which have them, to check oligopoly profits in production or in the refining which is done in producing regions. Most price-control formulae start from posted prices

[11] *Petroleum Press Service,* December, 1957, p. 449.
[12] *Ibid.,* pp. 449, 450.

in producing areas, usually posted prices for products, and add to them the cost of shipment to areas of consumption, using an average freight rate. Italy and nations to her east in Europe add freight to Persian Gulf product postings; nations controlling prices to the west and north of Italy add freight to U.S. Gulf Coast and Caribbean posted prices. In India the price formula adds freight to prices posted at Abadan in the Persian Gulf, and apparently these are product postings.[13] It seems clear that price-control formulae which start out with posted prices do little to eliminate any oligopoly profits in Middle East refining or production—when these posted prices are set by the firms which constitute the oligopoly. Price controls, however, as we shall indicate shortly, probably could be more effective than these seem to be. But in years to come many countries which consume Middle East oil will try to obtain it at lower prices by setting up governmental agencies to trade in oil. Such actions might be in response to the oligopolistic prices obtained by the oil companies or by the oil states through their control of output.

Undoubtedly, under some circumstances a government which takes a monopoly of the oil trade in its territory can obtain oil on better terms than can a number of competing private oil traders. Independent private traders tend to raise prices as they compete with one another for supplies. A government agency purchasing oil for an entire territory stands back, asks for bids, and expects to see suppliers quote low prices to get a large order. Affiliates of major companies, to be sure, do not compete with one another for oil, since each of them regularly buys from its parent firm (or from other affiliates in its group), but even so, affiliates may make their purchases at relatively high prices. If the parent companies require them to pay such prices, they have no choice in the matter. There is evidence that in the second half of the fifties major-company marketing and refining affiliates in

[13] *Petroleum Week*, January 22, 1960, p. 18; *Petroleum Press Service*, December, 1959, p. 471.

the Eastern Hemisphere were paying exceptionally high prices for crude oil. (See Chapter III, Section 3.) State trading agencies might have been able to get better terms.

Actually state trading will improve substantially the terms of trade for a country only if the state agency is a major purchaser of oil—only, that is, if the agency purchases a large part of the total oil available for sale in the region.[14] A large country might obtain very much lower prices through state trading while a small country nearby with a similar program might improve its position scarcely at all. Moreover, state trading may bring no advantage if supplier countries retaliate by restricting production (to get higher prices).

In all likelihood countries at the periphery of a major supply basin such as the Middle East can hope to gain less by state trading than can countries nearby. Distant countries may be benefiting already from the competition of other areas, Venezuela perhaps, and they may be obtaining the benefits of freight absorption. Should they introduce state trading, they may simply drive out Middle Eastern firms, which have been receiving relatively low netbacks on this distant trade. Nearby countries, on the other hand, represent attractive markets which yield the companies high netbacks; suppliers may accept considerably lower prices from a state trading agency rather than give up this business.

Should several state agencies combine together in a common buying program, not a probable development, they would control a larger part of total demand and could expect the combination to improve still more the terms on which they purchase oil.

An alternative to state trading open to a country seeking to improve its terms of trade is for the country to limit imports, then bargain with suppliers concerning the amount of imports

---

[14] Jacob Viner, *Trade Relations between Free-Market and Controlled Economies* (Geneva: League of Nations, 1943), p. 70n; Lorie Tarshis, *Introduction to International Trade and Finance* (New York: John Wiley and Sons, 1955), p. 416.

that will be permitted and the prices at which suppliers will offer oil to purchasers in the country (price controls perhaps more effective than the ones discussed earlier). Or the country may bargain with producing countries concerning the level of oil imports which it will permit and the level of exports (or production) which they will allow. The use of import quotas in bargaining with oil companies or producing countries should obtain substantially the same results as state trading.[15] The ECA experience, discussed in Chapter V, may have demonstrated how import controls, when exercised over a large area, can be used to obtain lower prices. ECA by its allocation of scarce dollars for the purchase of oil had in effect the power to control imports into many European countries. (At least it had this power in its early days when dollars were very scarce and the companies poorly situated to sell against soft currencies.) Following ECA pressure on the oil companies, Middle East prices fell in 1948 and 1949 by large amounts. (See Chapter V, Section 8.)

People in the industry who follow oil prices closely assert that in recent years Argentina has used state trading very successfully to obtain its oil at low prices.

J. A. van den Heuval, head of the energy division of the Organization for European Economic Co-operation, said late in 1959 that Europe ought to integrate in the field of energy and that among other things European countries might try to obtain a rational joint import policy which would strengthen their bargaining power in negotiating import contracts (and in negotiating search, exploitation, and transit rights with third countries). There seems to be a suggestion here that Europeans should engage in supranational state trading in order to get oil on better terms, or perhaps the suggestion is only that they jointly control imports for bargaining purposes.[16]

Except as a response to serious industry oligopoly or as a reply

[15] Stephen Enke and Virgil Salera, *International Economics* (New York: Prentice-Hall, 1947), p. 476.
[16] Reported in *Petroleum Press Service*, December, 1959, pp. 472–473.

to stringent control of output by producing countries, both state trading and import quotas, established for purposes of obtaining lower prices, are most difficult to defend. Almost inevitably they will, if widely adopted, provoke the producing countries into output control. The result would be bilateral oligopoly, indeterminate prices, and serious strains as the two sides sought to negotiate their differences. Jacob Viner has shown clearly what happens when private trading is converted into state trading:

The process of competition—provided, as is generally the case, the competition is not completely "free" in the technical sense—will in the normal course of events give rise to a constant stream of allegations of chicanery, misrepresentation, gouging, unfair discrimination, and others of the less attractive manifestations of the mercantile art. If the alleged perpetrators of such practices in the international field, as also those who feel themselves injured thereby, are private individuals or firms, the resultant ill-feeling may put a strain on the maintenance of friendly relations, and if the individuals or groups concerned are influential may find expression in diplomatic complaints by the government of the aggrieved individuals. Where either perpetrators or victims are governments, however, and even more so if both parties are governments, the sense of grievance will result much more directly in an issue between governments, and the fact that a government, or governments, is involved will give the incident a much greater potency in inflaming public opinion in the countries concerned. The process of substitution of government business for private business is in the international field, therefore, also a process of transformation of private quarrels into intergovernmental quarrels.[17]

State trading, in the writer's opinion, ought to be looked at by western governments as a measure of last resort, to be used only in the event of seriously oppressive behavior by oil company

[17] Jacob Viner, "International Relations between State-controlled National Economies," *American Economic Review*, Supplement (March, 1944), p. 318; reprinted in *International Economics: Studies by Jacob Viner* (Glencoe, Ill.: The Free Press, 1951), p. 219. Quoted by permission.

oligopolists or tight control of output by producing-country governments.

5. General Support by Western Governments of Oil Companies in the Middle East

It seems probable that the terms of some Middle East concessions have been influenced by activities of the British government on behalf of oil companies, or at least on behalf of one firm, the British Petroleum Company. Certainly in the past Britain exercised considerable power in the Middle East. For years the oil regions in the south of Iran were in the British sphere of influence, Iraq was a British mandate, and Kuwait, Qatar, and Bahrein Island were, and still are, British protectorates. The British government owns a controlling interest in the British Petroleum Company, which at one time held all the Iranian oil and today owns 40 percent of the Iranian Consortium, along with 50 percent of the Kuwait Oil Company, 23.75 percent of the Iraq Petroleum Company, and 23.75 percent of the Qatar Petroleum Company. To be sure, though two British government representatives sit on the board of British Petroleum, the British government alleges that it does not participate in the management of the company. Almost certainly this is true of day-to-day commercial operations, but it is extremely doubtful that the broad policy decisions of British Petroleum are made without informal consultation with, and approval of, the government of the day. In any case, Great Britain has a tradition of vigorous diplomatic support of British companies operating abroad, and such support probably at times enabled firms in which British Petroleum had an interest to obtain more satisfactory concession terms than they would have otherwise. It is doubtful that the Iranian and Iraqi concessions of earlier years or the present-day Qatar and Kuwait concessions reflected or reflect real arms-length bargaining.

The observation is sometimes made that states under the protection of Great Britain always receive terms as good as those given other states in the Middle East, Saudi Arabia, for example, but this observation does not provide a complete answer to allegations that oil companies in areas of British power have gained in bargaining for concessions as a consequence of British governmental action. In at least one case, Kuwait, the country should probably by now have received much *better* terms than were granted anywhere else—because of its greatly superior oil deposits. (This point will be discussed later.)

It would certainly be possible to exaggerate the interested influence of the British government on concession terms. British officials abroad often have made every effort to serve the interests of the people in the areas they control, and in any case British power in the Middle East has declined in recent years. On the other hand, it must be recognized that when conflicts of interest arise, it is exceedingly difficult for an official on foreign service to be quite disinterested and forget completely his country of origin. And while British power has declined, Britain still controls Kuwait, Qatar, and Bahrein Island.

One is inclined to doubt that easier terms obtained in any concession as a consequence of the power of the British authorities have led to lower oil prices. One thinks of the general tendency of oligopolistic prices to be rigid, of the fact that the easier concession terms reduced costs in some areas but not in others, and of the idea that payments for oil concessions, being in the nature of an economic rent, are probably price-determined rather than price-determining.

Nothing has been said up to now about the U.S. government in the Middle East. It has been much less active in support of the oil companies. In the twenties and thirties the U.S. government made representations to the British on behalf of American companies (supporting an open-door policy) and thereby assisted them in obtaining a share of Iraq and Kuwait oil. In the early fifties it virtually presided over the Iranian settlement after the oil industry in Iran had been nationalized. But, generally speaking, American companies have been on their own in the Middle East. Indeed, oil men note with some bitterness that U.S. congressmen and agencies of the U.S. government frequently attack the oil companies publicly, accuse them of participation in a world oil cartel and the like, increase foreign suspicions of the companies, and hence reduce rather than increase their bargaining power abroad. Although the U.S. government definitely has been slow to support its nationals in business abroad, recent developments in the cold war have tended to make the United States more active in foreign countries, and there is a possibility that U.S. authorities will support the oil companies more strongly in the future. This approach to international business, as we shall see, probably would not be in the interests of either the companies or the United States.

For the present we want to turn from the activities of the governments of consuming countries to the activities of the governments of the producing areas.

6. Middle Eastern Governments: Receipt of Royalties and Participation in Net Income

Governments in the Middle East receive two kinds of payments from oil companies: (1) royalties (in Iran called "stated payments") and (2) income taxes on "profits." The royalties usually are taken in cash, though in Iraq and Iran the governments are entitled to take them in kind, in crude oil. Often the royalties are the traditional 12.5 percent of the value of the crude produced (traditional in the United States) though apparently at times the royalty is stated in terms of a definite sum of money per ton. From the new offshore Japanese concession in the Neutral Zone, the Saudi and Kuwait governments are to receive a 20 percent royalty if oil is discovered in commercial quantities.

Apart from the possibility of receiving royalty in kind,[18] the right to receive royalty amounts simply to the right to receive a minimum amount of money per ton or barrel produced without regard to the profit (or lack of profit) in its production. Since

[18] This possibility will be discussed shortly in a section dealing with the sale of oil by Middle Eastern governments.

profits in Middle East oil in recent years have been high, governmental receipts have far exceeded royalty minima, and consequently royalty provisions of concession agreements have been of little significance.

Income taxes collected by governments in the Middle East are more important. Through these levies Middle Eastern governments collect sums which, added to royalties, give them approximately 50 percent of the net income arising out of production. Whether the exact share of governments is more or less than 50 percent is difficult to determine. Oil men contend that governments get more than half of the net income, since calculations of income for tax purposes assume that oil is sold at posted prices while in fact a certain amount of Middle East crude, possibly as much as 10 percent, is sold to nonaffiliated firms at discounts off posted prices. But most Arabs and Iranians believe that the governments are not getting 50 percent of the income, though their beliefs are often vaguely founded. We know that petroleum accountants find it difficult to obtain a really satisfactory calculation of net income, so that oil company accounts may possibly understate the income on which taxes are based. For one thing, in the Middle East current outlays on exploration and development are treated as expenses, though they create capital values, and this tends to reduce current book profits. All things considered—governmental tax revenues based on posted prices rather than discounted prices, current outlays on exploration and development counted as expenses rather than capitalized, the difficulties of calculating net income in oil—it seems doubtful that any positive statement can be made concerning the exact division of Middle East oil income.

Actually the question of whether or not income is divided precisely in half is not at all important, for there is no economic rationale in a fifty-fifty income split anyway. (The companies, to be sure, attach great importance to this formula, but shrewd oil men recognize that it is only a psychological device; it has a ring of fairness about it: "We will be partners; we will share and share alike.") In considering the division of income, it must be realized that the return collected by the Middle Eastern governments is not, in economic terms, a profit; it is not a reward for bearing risk. Producing-country income is more properly classified as an economic rent, a return to the possessor of natural resources. And there is no reason why this return should be equal to the profits earned by the entrepreneur: when oil prospects or oil deposits are poor or badly located a government must expect to get much less than the profits earned by the companies bearing the risks of exploration and development; when prospects are good, oil wells prolific, and oil of high quality or well located, governments in possession may expect to get much more than the companies earn in profits.[19]

Because there is no economic rationale in an equal division of the net income from oil production, we will not enter into an elaborate discussion of whether or not the fifty-fifty formula has been broken by recent arrangements made with independents in the Middle East. At first glance the deals with Ente Nazionale Idrocarburi (ENI, the Italian state oil company), Indiana Standard, and the Arabian Oil Company, Ltd. (a Japanese firm), appear to undermine the fifty-fifty principle. A $25-million bonus has been paid by Indiana Standard to Iran, the Iranian government is to receive 75 percent of the net income in the Indiana Standard and ENI arrangements, and the Saudi and Kuwaiti governments are to receive 56 and 57 percent respectively of the income arising out of their respective undivided one-half interests in Neutral Zone oil offshore. But the international majors, in the interest of preserving the fifty-fifty formula, have at-

[19] It is of interest to observe that in January, 1959, the Irish government signed an agreement with Ambassador Irish Oil which provides that in the event of commercial production the government will receive from the company a royalty, of 7.5 percent of the value of oil or gas marketed, plus an income tax, with total governmental receipts on the production not to exceed 30 percent of net income in the first five years of production or 40 percent thereafter. Oil prospects in Ireland have been regarded as poor (*Petroleum Press Service*, February, 1959, p. 73).

tempted to demonstrate that the new deals do not appreciably improve the terms received by Middle Eastern governments. They have pointed out that the Iranian government must share in development costs in order to get an extra 25 percent of the income, and they have observed that nonaffiliated firms lack the large and diversified markets of the international companies, and that consequently, despite their apparently more generous terms, the independents really offer less to the Arabs and Iranians. But whether or not fifty-fifty has been breached fundamentally in the Middle East is not an interesting question. Almost certainly as time passes this meaningless formula will be eroded away, with the governments obtaining more than 50 percent of income from production in the prolific areas and less in the poorer regions.

One more point needs to be made concerning governmental participation in net income. The receipts of producing-country governments at any given time have a certain tendency to become minimum receipts and virtually fixed costs to the oil companies. The governments become dependent on oil income, find it difficult to adjust expenditures downward when revenues threaten to decline, and put pressure on the companies to maintain payments at any given level once it is attained. It becomes politically difficult, some would say impossible, to reduce payments to governments. But one could exaggerate this fixed-cost element in oil company operations. Probably the companies have often bowed to governmental pressure for maintenance of payments because they had excess profits to play with. Once excess profits are completely eliminated, it seems likely that the companies will defend more vigorously the profits which remain (their "necessary" profits) and that the governments will be forced to accept occasional reductions in income from oil.

7. Middle Eastern Governments: Participation in Management

Governments in the Middle East have only a small formal participation in the management of oil operations. In Iran the government-owned National Iranian Oil Company may appoint two of the seven directors in each of the two operating companies of the Consortium. The government has no direct representation in the holding company, Iranian Oil Participants Ltd., which controls the operating companies, nor is it represented in the trading companies which the participating oil firms have set up to market their respective shares of Iranian oil. In the spring of 1959 it was announced that the Iraqi government had obtained the right to appoint an executive director of the Iraq Petroleum Company; apparently, however, this has not yet become a firm agreement. In May, 1959, the government of Saudi Arabia exercised its right to appoint two, out of eleven, directors of the Arabian American Oil Company.

The new concessions in the Middle East provide for larger governmental participation in management. The National Iranian Oil Company appoints as many directors of the operating company which it owns jointly with Ente Nazionale Idrocarburi as ENI appoints, and it designates the chairman of the board, but the Italians appoint the managing director. The National Iranian Oil Company has a similar position in management in its arrangements with Indiana Standard. The Saudi and Kuwaiti governments each may appoint one-sixth of the board of directors, or no fewer than two directors each, of the Arabian Oil Company, Ltd., the Japanese firm which obtained the concession offshore from the Neutral Zone.

Of course, apart from formal participation in management through positions on management bodies, Arabian and Iranian government people may participate informally in management through consultation with company officials. It is difficult for an outsider to discover how much consultation of this sort takes place and how often the wishes of the Arabs and Iranians are heeded by the companies. Some oil men have contended that it is virtually impossible to reduce output or prices against the opposition of Middle Eastern governments; there has even been talk of an "Arab floor" on oil prices. On the other hand, delegates attending the first Arab Oil Congress seemed to feel that consultation was insufficient; in their final resolution they said that "changes in the system of pricing, or any change in the price of crude and its products, should not take place prior to declaration by the producing companies of such prices, and discussion and study with the governments of the exporting countries concerned." [20] It should also be observed that the Arab floor was not strong enough to prevent a crude oil price decline in the spring of 1959.

Whatever may have been the case in earlier days, it appears that in recent years great efforts have been made by the oil companies to minimize friction and misunderstanding by consultation with Middle Eastern governments. No doubt from time to time the requests of these governments have been heeded. Nevertheless, it seems likely that the oil companies still retain the ultimate power of decision in matters such as output and price.

8. Sale of Oil by Middle Eastern Governments

The governments of two of the four large established producing regions in the Middle East are entitled to take payment partly in kind, in crude oil; these are the Iraqi and the Iranian governments. From time to time observers of the industry have feared that Iraqi or Iranian oil might appear in world markets and disorganize them. Moreover, the agreements signed recently with the new firms entering the Middle East may put more oil in the hands of governments, and the thought has been expressed that this oil might in the future "spoil" the market. It will be worth our while to review most of these arrangements.

In Iraq the government may take as royalty 12.5 percent of the crude oil produced. If it does not choose to exercise this right, the owners of the Iraq Petroleum Company automatically acquire the oil and pay the government for it at posted prices. In Iran the government also may receive in kind 12.5 percent of the oil produced, though this oil is not called a royalty. If the gov-

[20] Reported in *Petroleum Week*, May 1, 1959, p. 49.

ernment, strictly speaking the National Iranian Oil Company (NIOC), a government concern, does not exercise its right to receive oil in kind, the parent companies in the Consortium take it and make "stated payments" to NIOC of 12.5 percent of the posted price on the total quantity of oil which they lift. The Iraqi and Iranian agreements differ in form but amount to the same thing in practice. The governments have a choice of taking 12.5 percent of the oil produced or receiving from the parent companies in cash 12.5 percent of its total value. Either the value of the oil taken or the cash payment is subtracted from sums due the governments under the fifty-fifty profit-sharing arrangements.

We noted earlier that if the governments do not elect to receive oil in kind, the Iraqi cash royalty and the Iranian "stated payment" are in effect floors on government receipts, minimum payments by the companies without regard to whether or not they make profits on oil lifted. If the governments do exercise their rights to receive oil in kind, they have the problem of disposing of it, while at the same time they forgo attractive payments from the companies, payments equal to the quantity of oil they take times the posted price.

It is easy to see why the Iraqi and Iranian governments have seldom chosen to take oil in kind. Without a marketing organization, they have little chance of getting the posted price for their oil and getting it in currencies which are as good as those paid them by the oil companies. Particularly when the posted price is high and out of line with supply and demand will they find it difficult to sell oil at this price. Even if they succeed in selling crude at the posted price, they may net less after selling expenses are subtracted. It is possible, to be sure, for a government to establish a marketing organization, sell at delivered prices, and earn the profits of transportation, refining, and marketing, as well as the profits of production. It is of interest in this connection that NIOC has ordered four tankers, one of which was launched in 1958. But marketing ventures are fraught with risk and require skilled personnel, and since the mid-fifties high posted prices for crude have restricted profits in refining and marketing. It is easier for governments to sit back and collect cash royalties or stated payments. One may conclude that in paying to the governments sums equal to the market value of the oil the governments might have lifted, or in paying even more (when the posted price is above the market), the oil companies are doing the equivalent of purchasing distress oil from hard-pressed independents. Such payments make it much less likely that the oil will appear in the market and spoil it. Hence there has been little basis for past fears that government oil would disorganize world markets or even little likelihood that it would make those markets more competitive.

What of the new concessions? The Japanese concession off-shore from the Neutral Zone does not appear to change the situation. While the Saudi and Kuwaiti governments get a 20 percent royalty instead of 12.5 percent, they can elect to receive it in cash (20 percent of the posted price on all oil lifted). The temptation will be strong for them to take it that way rather than assume the burden of marketing royalty oil which is received in kind. It is true, however, that the concessionaire (the Arabian Oil Company, Ltd.) is required by its agreements with the two governments to integrate vertically, to hire many Arabs, and to train them in all aspects of the oil industry. As Arab personnel gain experience in marketing, the governments are more likely to venture into the distribution of royalty oil abroad. (Kuwait's first tanker made its maiden voyage in the spring of 1959.) Still it seems probable that the Iranian government will get into foreign distribution more rapidly. In the new agreements with ENI and Indiana Standard, NIOC has first option on half of the oil available for export and on any oil the other party to each agreement does not elect to lift. It will have the profits of distribution as incentive to take at least half of the oil; and it may possibly get some of the profits of production if any of the subsidiary operating companies offer oil to NIOC (and to the other parent—ENI or Indiana Standard) at a discount off posted price, which, with the agreement of NIOC and their other parent firm, they can do. There is evidence that NIOC is determined to get into distribution. We have already mentioned the four tankers it has ordered. And an Iranian is quoted by *Petroleum Week* as follows:

With the full cooperation of the West, we want to build up NIOC into an experienced oil company. The best way to start is by partnership with private companies having experience, knowhow, and capital, who will train us in the oil business. At the beginning, we can sell them our share of the joint production. But our ultimate aim is to build up our own markets and set up our own refineries abroad through partnership with local capital.[21]

Some concern has been expressed that the Arab governments or Iran, over the next few years, might enter into a series of barter agreements with China, India, and other underdeveloped countries; presumably these would involve state trading on both sides.[22] If such exchanges displaced oil sold by Middle East firms, they might simply provide additional competition, but they could disorganize world markets. Though it is difficult to be certain, it seems doubtful that they will do either. Governments in the producing countries have a great deal at stake in stable, even oligopolistic, prices, and along with controlling the production of independents they probably will learn to restrain themselves in their own marketing activities. On the other hand, in the interest of getting out from under the control of the majors through development of separate routes to market, the governments in the Middle East might be prepared to risk lower prices.

We may conclude that royalty oil in Iraq and the oil receivable in lieu of stated payments in Iran have never seriously threatened

[21] March 15, 1957, p. 46.
[22] G. Tugendhat, *Petroleum Times*, quoted in the *Observer*, September 28, 1958, p. 2. Recently Iraq concluded a barter agreement with North Vietnam, an exchange of crude oil and products for rice, sugar, silk, and machinery (*Petroleum Week*, July 24, 1959, p. 48).

to disorganize world markets nor promised to make them more competitive, since the governments could always elect to receive attractive cash payments from the companies instead of oil. Royalty oil receivable by the Saudi and Kuwaiti governments from the Japanese offshore concession is not apt to become a significant factor in the market inasmuch as these governments have the option of receiving a cash royalty instead of a royalty in kind, though as Saudi and Kuwaiti Arabs become trained in marketing, the governments may venture into distribution. It would seem that the Iranians are more likely to enter marketing seriously, with the half of the oil they are entitled to take from their new arrangements with ENI and Indiana Standard, particularly if they receive it at a discount off posted price. Barter transactions between Middle Eastern governments and governments of underdeveloped countries are not likely substantially to increase competition in Middle East oil, since governments in the producing countries have a great deal at stake in market stability, though it is possible that they would take a chance on undermining that stability in order to become more independent of the international majors.

VIII

Middle East Prices:
A General Appraisal

BEFORE going on to consider likely future developments, we will find it helpful to draw together the various strands in our analysis.

1. Market Structure, Output, Profits, and Middle East Prices in the Pattern of World Oil Prices

Orderly advance probably would be quite generally accepted as a suitable goal for a modern economy. Ideally we should have short-run restraints on entry and long-run freedom to enter, short-run stability in price and long-run flexibility.

In Middle East oil order and stability are well served, probably too well served. Much of the time competition is attenuated, with prices rigid and slow to decline.

Excluding the small interests, we find eight sellers of crude oil and oil products on the Persian Gulf and seven sellers of crude oil on the eastern Mediterranean. These few sellers form an oligopoly and almost certainly tend to behave as oligopolists, hesitating to lower prices in the expectation that reductions will be matched, reluctant to raise them for fear that rivals will not follow, yet inclining over the long run to move toward relatively high prices and "comfortable" profit margins. Competition is further reduced by major company participation in various joint enterprises, many of which interlock—joint production, jointly used pipelines and terminals, joint refining and marketing. Over the long run joint enterprises are likely to be developed more slowly than individual, separate firms; the reluctance of conservative owners to invest in a rapid development of any given operation often limits the quantity of oil which dynamic companies can obtain and push into the market. Costs common to the several firms in a joint enterprise provide a basis for possible tacit or explicit concerted action on prices, and of course regular consultation between the participating firms provides a means for obtaining uniformity of behavior. Joint marketing reduces the number of independent sellers in a given market. And then the outsider, the independent, without the economies of large-scale operation associated with joint enterprises, is at a competitive disadvantage.

There is a possibility that the new independents in the Middle East, and in Venezuela, will disorganize world markets for oil in the next few years and over the long run make them more competitive. Having paid very large sums for their concessions, they are going to want to develop them rapidly; at the same time they lack marketing outlets abroad, and import controls often prevent them from selling the oil in the United States. But disorganization of world markets probably will be checked by several factors. Governments in consuming countries may give preference to independent oil produced by their nationals, and the majors may not push displaced oil into other markets. The majors may step aside to make room for independent oil, purchase independent oil, or purchase the independents themselves. The amount of disorganization depends in large degree on the magnitude of oil seeking markets; there is a limit to the amount of independent oil which the majors can make room for or can purchase. In any case disorganization will disappear as time passes:

more independent refineries and marketers will come into existence and absorb independently produced crude; some independent producers will integrate vertically themselves; others will sell out to the majors. Because the independents tend to pay very large sums for their concessions while their operations often are small, they are not very likely to obtain low-cost, competitive oil. We have spoken of a *natural* oligopoly. Any independent firms which do develop low-cost supplies and which remain unaffiliated probably will find the Arabian governments and Iran controlling their production in the interest of stability and following the precedent of Texas, Oklahoma, and Louisiana. So it is doubtful that over the long run the entry of independents will make Middle East oil a great deal more competitive.

The sale of government oil is not likely to disorganize markets or add a serious element of competition. Much government oil is, and will be, purchased by the majors at attractive prices, and the remainder will be sold by governments which themselves have a strong interest in stability, perhaps even an interest in high oligopoly prices. There is a possibility, however, that the governments of the producing countries will take a chance on disorganizing the world oil trade, when seeking independent routes to market, in order to become free of control by the international majors.

Middle East oil does not experience serious competition from the smaller producing areas. Much of this oil, high in cost and small in magnitude, shelters under an umbrella of world oil prices established in the major producing centers or seeks the protection of tariffs, import quotas, and exchange controls. In other areas where magnitudes are larger, the oil is not low-cost or is under the control of the international majors. North African oil is likely to increase competition West of Suez, and Soviet oil may be a factor in some markets. Middle East oil meets the competition of major producing regions on the periphery of its marketing area, perhaps most seriously in South America.

Fuel oil processed from Middle East crude has encountered

or will encounter in particular markets the competition of coal, natural gas, water power, and nuclear energy. None of these sources of energy compete effectively with gasoline.

Sellers of Middle East oil engage in nonprice competition which probably increases the rate of product development, improves service, and increases the number of service stations. It is possible, however, that the consumer would prefer an opportunity to choose lower quality, less service, less convenience in location, less advertising, and lower prices.

Although the situation is in general an oligopolistic one, with some additional restrictions on competition arising out of numerous interlocking joint enterprises, the degree of competition varies a great deal from one region to another and from one product to another.

Italy, Switzerland, Sweden, West Germany, and Japan are rather competitive markets, each with a number of independent sellers. France and England, on the other hand, are much less competitive, France because of governmental controls over imports, England because there are only four major distributors—Shell-Mex and BP, Esso (Jersey Standard), Regent (Caltex), and Socony Mobil—along with a small fringe of independents.[1] Though there are exceptions, markets East of Suez tend to be considerably less competitive than markets West of Suez. In many territories east of the Canal there are only three sellers, Royal Dutch–Shell (often associated with BP), Stanvac (Jersey Standard and Socony), and Caltex (Standard of California and Texaco).[2] When in 1947 and 1948 Jersey Standard and Socony Mobil entered into contracts with British Petroleum to purchase large volumes of oil on attractive terms over a period of years, each stated that it was its intent to supply with the oil certain specified countries, none of them East of Suez. In supplementary

---

[1] *Economist*, December 7, 1957, p. 885; January 23, 1960, p. 333.

[2] In 1960 Jersey and Socony agreed to break up Stanvac, and in time the degree of competition in eastern markets may increase as a consequence.

contracts signed in 1949 it was agreed that Jersey and Socony might ship East of Suez 5 percent of the amounts deliverable under the contracts and pay for this oil at the low contract price but that any excess over 5 percent would be paid for at British Petroleum's established spot cargo price.[3] Contract provisions limiting the entry of low-cost oil into markets East of Suez almost certainly make them less competitive. (We have already observed that North African oil is not likely to increase competition in markets east of the Canal.)

Finally, the degree of competition varies considerably between products. The market for fuel oil sold under long-term contract is very competitive. Oligopolists are not so reluctant to cut price when they know that by doing so they can win a one- or two-year supply contract. The market for gasoline, on the other hand, is not very competitive, though the motorist who settles his account monthly often can get a discount at the service station.

It is probably the private operator of an automobile, and particularly the motorist East of Suez, who most often pays oligopoly prices for the products of Middle East oil.

Frequently critics of the oil industry have alleged that the development and production of Middle East oil has been held back by the international majors in order to protect their high-cost holdings in the Western Hemisphere.

The majors have in fact developed the Middle East very rapidly: crude oil production there amounted to about 9 percent of the world total in 1946 and 24 percent of the world total in 1959.[4] Nevertheless, oil firms without holdings in other areas might have developed Middle East oil still more rapidly. The majors may have checked the development of Middle East oil in order to defend world prices, ensure profitable production of their Western Hemisphere properties, and thereby protect their

[3] FTC Report, pp. 151–152, 157.
[4] Calculated from statistics in *World Oil*, August 15, 1958, pp. 129, 130; February 15, 1960, p. 95.

earlier investment in the Western Hemisphere. They might feel that they could maximize their total profits by producing their Western Hemisphere oil before they went all out to develop the Middle East. Speaking of production control by the international majors, Dr. P. H. Frankel wrote:

We have seen that the United States price level—that of a high-cost producer—was maintained with the assistance . . . of low-cost producers who, at the same time acted in accordance with their own interest. . . . The *sine qua non* of a satisfactory price level was . . . a reasonable control of output *everywhere*. . . . *There was an invisible hedge round the American market formed by the deliberate policy of big foreign producers.*[5]

Dr. Frankel also quoted Col. Harry T. Klein, at the time president of the Texas Company, who said: "Would it not be asinine for the Texas Company, whose assets abroad were but one-third of those within the U.S., to act in any way which would impair the value and earning powers of its domestic investments?"[6]

It is possible, however, that the oil companies would consider it uneconomic to develop their Western Hemisphere holdings ahead of their Middle Eastern properties. If an international oil company had found very large quantities of oil in the Middle East, so large as to be for practical purposes virtually unlimited, if the total costs of producing and transporting this oil to most of its markets were below the variable costs of producing and transporting Western Hemisphere oil, then the company would find it most profitable to develop its Middle East oil rather than its Western Hemisphere holdings. This is very nearly the position of the Gulf Oil Corporation in Kuwait (and it is interesting to observe that Kuwait oil has been developed with extraordinary rapidity). Or, if an international oil company were fearful of being expropriated in the Middle East, it might choose to

[5] *Essentials of Petroleum*, p. 117, italics in the original.
[6] "The State of the American Oil Industry," p. 23n.

develop and produce its Middle East concessions rapidly and save its Western Hemisphere reserves.

It is difficult to say whether or not the international majors have checked the development of low-cost Middle East oil to protect their investments elsewhere in the world. In general, an international company probably prefers a balanced development of its holdings in various parts of the world in order to protect itself against adverse developments in any one area. It is entirely possible, then, that firms producing exclusively in the Middle East would have developed the oil in this area more rapidly than the majors have done, would have shipped more of it into world markets, and would have lowered thereby the structure of world prices. (At the same time it should be recognized that oil company hesitation about developing Middle East oil may have arisen, not out of a desire to protect Western Hemisphere investments, but out of knowledge that efforts to import larger quantities of foreign oil into the United States or certain European countries would result in the erection of more serious formal barriers to trade.)

Our analysis of costs and profits in Chapter III left us with the impression of unusually large profits in Middle East oil, profits which endured for a long period of time. Large, enduring profits of this sort lend support to the view that the structure of the market is oligopoly and that prices have been rigid and high, with output lower than it would have been in a more competitive situation.

Though Middle East prices are not as closely tied to prices at the U.S. Gulf Coast as critics of the industry have alleged, it seems likely that the former have declined relative to the latter more slowly and less far than they would have done in a market with a higher degree of competition. Moreover, in establishing prices on sales to different geographical areas, the companies without doubt realized more on sales to some areas than others; they discriminated against crude oil buyers in Europe and product buyers in southern Europe. (See Chapter V.) The writer inclines to the view that the companies were too much concerned with stability in these markets: they were too slow in switching supplies to areas of high realizations and too slow in adjusting prices.

That the price of Middle East oil has been too high can, in the opinion of the writer, scarcely be denied. But how much lower its price would have been in the absence of oligopoly cannot be estimated with any precision without more information on costs and returns than has been published. The writer's guess—based on numerous interviews with oil men, the scanty cost and profit data discussed in Chapter III, and reflection—is that price reductions in Middle East oil should be substantial.

2. The Influence of Governments on Prices

The compulsory import quotas established by the United States in March, 1959, probably have had some tendency to depress oil prices outside the United States. Investments had been made in Venezuela and in the Middle East in anticipation of a rate of increase in U.S. imports which could not materialize after the quotas were imposed. The variable costs of producing this new capacity are low, and there has been an inclination to operate the facilities and push the oil produced into markets outside the United States. On the other hand, the majors, with a strong interest in stability, are inclined to market with restraint and perhaps make room for independent oil, while the producing-country governments are strongly motivated to limit the sales of independent firms which threaten to undermine prices. Hence the impact of U.S. import quotas on prices outside the United States probably has not been great.

With total 1959 oil production in western Europe only 5.7 percent of 1959 production in the Middle East, it is doubtful that European protection has had a substantial effect on Middle East prices. It is also doubtful that any very substantial part of the burden of high European excise taxes on petroleum products rests on the factors of production in the Middle East or on

Middle East governments. It seems quite certain that these taxes are paid by consumers in higher prices.

Large markets not too far from a center of production like the Middle East might obtain considerably lower prices through state trading. A large purchaser is likely to have some influence on prices, and the attractive netbacks obtained from nearby sales make the oil companies reluctant to lose such business. Of course state trading would bring no advantage if supplier countries retaliated by restricting production.

The sale of oil by Middle Eastern governments has never seriously threatened to disorganize world markets, nor has it promised to make them more competitive. The governments entitled to royalty oil could always elect to take attractive cash payments instead, and the Saudi and Kuwaiti governments have the same alternative open to them under the agreement with the Japanese company operating offshore from the Neutral Zone. The growing interest of Middle Eastern governments in price stability makes it almost certain that they will not market any oil they acquire in such a way as to undermine prices.

We may conclude that governments have had little influence on the price of Middle East oil. Should producing-country governments in the future succeed in controlling output as a group, through their newly established Organization of Petroleum Exporting Countries (discussed later, in Chapter IX) or should consuming-country governments become involved in state trading on a large scale (or in bargaining over prices and the magnitude of permitted imports), the influence of governments on Middle East prices could become a very important matter.

3. Stability in Oil Prices

The concentrated ownership of Middle East oil has often been defended with the argument that such concentration assists in the maintenance of price stability in world markets. There are, it is suggested, factors which, in the absence of market control by the international majors, would make for serious instability.

Chance plays a large part in the search for oil. Discoveries, particularly large discoveries, are likely to be irregular. Sudden increases in reserves available for exploitation occur and tend to exert a downward pressure on prices. Moreover, demand, in the short run at least, is inelastic, so that abrupt additions to supplies are not readily absorbed by the market and the pressure on prices may be very great. Finally, the high proportion of fixed costs in production, pipeline transportation, terminal operation, and refining means that prices will have to fall very far before they reach variable costs, the level at which output is reduced and an oversupply corrected. Were relatively small, independent, nonaffiliated producers an important factor in Middle East oil, the full impact of irregular discoveries, inelastic demand, and large fixed costs probably would be felt on prices. Small independents tend to lack the motive for holding back production when, as is often the case, the output of no one of them is great enough to influence the price noticeably. And should they be inclined to withhold oil from the market, small firms rarely have the long pocketbooks which are required to do it.

In addition to suggesting that irregular discoveries, inelastic demand, and large fixed costs are potential sources of instability, some students of petroleum economics contend that increasing returns in production tend to cause unstable prices.

Crude-oil production is, in fact, an important example of the well-known theorem that industries enjoying increasing returns will, if composed of a large number of autonomous producers, operate at a loss. The early history of the East-Texas discovery, which at one point in the inter-war period drove down the price of oil to 10 U.S. cents a barrel and led to the employment of State forces to impose output control, provides a convincing illustration of the validity of the theorem.[7]

But this analysis certainly is faulty and overstates the case against a market of numerous competitive firms. An industry of increas-

[7] ECE Report, pp. 17–18.

ing returns with a large number of autonomous producers does not always operate at a loss. It does so when there is an over-supply, but so do industries of decreasing returns under such circumstances. In considering the impact of increasing returns on price, we encounter two possibilities. The authors of the ECE Report may have had reference to short-run increasing returns associated with the spreading of fixed costs over a large volume, or they may have referred to long-run increasing returns associated with the economies of large-scale production.

We have already discussed the first possibility, short-run increasing returns. When irregular discoveries or mistaken forecasts lead to an oversupply, prices in the short run tend to fall below average total unit costs and may decline to average variable costs, which in an industry with a high proportion of fixed costs can be very low. Hence with short-run increasing returns, sales at very substantial losses can take place—when there is an oversupply.

As for the second possibility, long-run increasing returns, sales at prices below average total unit costs occur—not always, however, but at times—when irregular discoveries or mistaken forecasts lead to an oversupply, or when an unduly large number of firms oversupply the market while jostling for position in an industry which will support only a smaller number of optimum-sized companies. And indeed we have here another possible source of price instability in Middle East oil: along with irregular discoveries, inelastic demand, and high fixed costs, there may be a struggle for position among firms seeking the high volume and low costs which alone will enable them to survive in an industry capable of supporting only a handful of firms of optimum size. In Chapter II, Section 10, we observed that the economies of scale in Middle East oil are great enough to make the market for Middle East oil a natural oligopoly. But it is doubtful that price instability is the most serious consequence of this situation. While the struggle for position among firms in a natural oligopoly can lead to great instability in price before equilibrium is obtained, a serious, probably more serious, problem arises at a later period when the oligopolists are firmly entrenched and prices become rigid or "sticky." An oligopolist hesitates to raise prices for fear his rivals will not follow, and once established he becomes reluctant to lower them because competitors (few in number and consequently sure to be hurt by his action) are certain to match his cut, with the result that after the price reduction he sells only a small additional volume. Hence though long-run increasing returns may temporarily cause serious instability in price (as emerging oligopolists struggle for position), over a period of time they are more significant as a source of price rigidity.

But in all cases, short-run or long-run increasing returns, firms operate at a loss only when there is an oversupply. The early history of the East Texas field may not validly be adduced in support of the notion that industries with a large number of producers and with increasing returns always perform at a loss. Ten-cent oil in east Texas reflected a very large discovery during the Great Depression under land with a great many owners each with subsurface rights defined by the law of capture; the result was naturally a mad scramble to produce oil, and very low prices. The history of the East Texas field established only that oil production takes place at a loss when there is an oversupply and numerous producers all are trying to extract the same deposit.

Nevertheless, we have found several reasons—irregular discoveries, inelastic demand, a high proportion of fixed costs, perhaps a struggle for position among emerging oligopolists—for believing that Middle East oil prices would be very unstable were there numerous small producers. How serious would such instability be? What advantages are there in the price stability which is undoubtedly provided by the dominance of the international majors?

It is often contended that stable prices are necessary if large investments are to be made in an industry. Only stable prices, oil men argue, will ensure a steady and continuous search for oil. The argument is not completely without merit. We have already discussed the Schumpeterian notion that short-run restraints on entry are necessary for innovation, that a firm would not undertake the risks of entering a new field if it knew that imitators could rush in immediately, depress prices, and eliminate the gains associated with doing something new. (See p. 7.) But while investors who innovate must be protected against immediate price declines which then become permanent and make impossible the recovery of a special premium for the risks of innovation, investors generally, whether in old fields or new, can cope with price fluctuations as such, with prices which decline but then rise again. As long as average prices over a period of time cover costs, including necessary profits, investments will be made. Businessmen expect to recover their capital over a period of years, and this may be accomplished even though prices fluctuate a good deal during the time of capital recovery. We know that investors in some products—copper, lead and zinc, sugar, cocoa—live with fluctuating prices most of the time, and there is no reason to doubt that oil men could do the same.

We do not want, however, to deny that price stability has advantages. Probably in most cases fluctuating prices increase uncertainty; uncertainty is a cost which must be covered by profits; hence price fluctuations no doubt often make larger profits necessary and promote a higher average level of prices than would otherwise occur. But, it is necessary to add, consumers may pay still higher prices if an oligopoly which stabilizes them does so at a level enabling the firms in it to collect oligopoly profits.

Perhaps the best defense of price stability rests in the assertion that stability is valuable as an end in itself. Adaptation to sudden price increases or decreases is very difficult. Price changes often reduce the value of factors of production—labor, capital, and land—or even make factors completely obsolescent, and they frequently force on producers and consumers hard adjustments to a reduced standard of life. People or firms without large resources cannot always wait for better times, and they may be required to liquidate their accumulated capital at a loss. In the Middle East, governments are exceedingly dependent on oil revenues; a sudden reduction in governmental receipts from oil is most serious.

Our goal probably should be, as we have observed earlier, the goal of orderly advance—prices stable in the short run and flexible over the long run, stability without rigidity. Administrators, judges, and scholars will have to form judgments in any given case as to whether a proper balance is being struck between the values of stability and the values which inhere in progressive change. It is the opinion of the writer that stability in the Middle East has been better served than change, that there has been an element of rigidity in prices which has permitted the oil companies to earn the profits of oligopoly. Though difficult to obtain, a higher degree of competition would appear to be desirable.

Those who, in the name of stability, oppose more competition might give some thought to alternative patterns likely to emerge. The continued existence of oligopoly and oligopoly pricing almost certainly will lead to intervention of one sort or another by the governments of consuming countries, the intervention in many cases taking the form of state trading. Such buyers' monopolies, perhaps a kind of world-wide buyers' oligopoly (oligopsony), probably would lead to increased intervention by the governments of producing countries; they would, in all likelihood, seek more vigorously to control output. The end result for much of the world oil trade would be what economists call bilateral monopoly, or, strictly speaking, bilateral oligopoly —an oligopoly of buyers facing an oligopoly of sellers. Prices would be negotiated by the governments of consuming and producing countries, and probably there would be long periods of extreme rigidity punctuated by intense struggles, struggles which occurred when some participants sought to improve their positions while others resisted change. The instability of a competitive market with numerous autonomous producers might be a great deal more satisfactory than the alternating rigidity and extreme instability of a market dominated by governments.

IX

Arab-Iranian Aspirations and Strategy; the Response of the West

IT is trite to say that the Middle East is in ferment. Above or below the surface revolutionary forces are at work in most of the countries. Oil cannot remain unaffected. And Arab and Iranian goals in the sphere of oil can only be understood fully in the larger context of the fundamental political objectives of people in the Middle East. So at the outset of this chapter we will address ourselves to the subject of Arab nationalism, and then look briefly at a currently quiescent Iranian nationalism.

1. The Meaning of Arab Nationalism

The goals of Arab nationalism, in its modern version, are three: independence, unity, and reform. (1) The Arabs want to be completely independent, want to eliminate the last vestige of western power from their lands while not falling under the control of other outsiders (though westerners incline to feel that some Arabs are insufficiently aware of the dangers of a new, Soviet domination). (2) The Arabs want to unify a number of the smaller Arab states into a larger Arab nation, though there is a good deal of disagreement as to which states should be united, how soon union should be or can be attained, and how firmly the union should be knit. Whether the Arab nation should comprise a Greater Syria of the Fertile Cresent lands alone, all the countries of the Middle East, or all the Arabs from the Persian Gulf to the Atlantic Ocean has been debated, as have been the relative merits of confederation, federation, and a unitary state. (3) The Arabs, the younger Arabs and the emerging middle classes, desire deep social, economic, and political reforms. They want to eliminate outdated monarchies and feudal regimes, modernize governments, promote land reform and economic development, and turn from a system which relies largely on private initiative to a system which puts a good deal of emphasis on socialism and co-operation. It is thought that political reforms will contribute to Arab unity by eliminating the western ties of the old regimes and by eliminating some of the local vested interests in a divided Arab world.

An outsider cannot easily decide how seriously to take Arab nationalism. Almost certainly those who say the Arabs will never unite, that they are parochial, selfish, and too much influenced by family and tribal loyalties, are wrong, as are those who think that unity will come overnight. The writer has been impressed by the ubiquity and force of the longing for independence, union, and reform, by the ability and determination of many young and middle-aged Arabs, by the striving for education and for the knowledge necessary to the creation of a modern Arab state. But he has also become aware of localism and provincialism, the remnants of tribalism, the opposition of minorities (Christians, Kurds, and others), internal and external vested interests in existing institutions, and a tendency among many Arabs to substitute emotions and dreams for hard thinking, hard study, and hard work. For the writer, Arab nationalism seems to be almost an irresistible force—but its timetable probably should be drawn up in years and decades rather than in weeks and months.

Iranian nationalism is not quite the same thing as Arab

nationalism. The Iranian nationalists seek independence from western control along with political, economic, and social reform, but the Iranian nation is one and the problem of unification does not arise. As they seek independence from the West, Iranian nationalists probably are more aware than the Arabs of the dangers of Soviet domination. Iran has a common border with the Soviet Union, and Soviet penetration of northern Iran was actually experienced during and after the Second World War. Since the surge of nationalism from 1951 to 1953 under the leadership of Mossadegh, the nationalists in Iran have been quiet. The Shah, with his belief in a close alliance with the West, is in power, and although an underground National Resistance Movement exists, or at least existed in 1958 when the writer was in Iran, publishing a paper called *The Way of Mossadegh*, it appears to be weak and confined in membership to students at the University of Tehran. But the oil companies would be unwise to count on an indefinite period of political stability in Iran. The power of the Shah is "narrowly based on the support of a few hundred land-owning families," [1] while the educated classes are bitterly unhappy with the old ways of feudalism and corruption and extremely dubious of the western alliance (promises of U.S. support of the government against "indirect aggression" being considered virtually a guarantee of the *status quo* in Iran). "Malevolent apathy" the *Economist* characterized the attitude of the Iranian nationalists five years after Mossadegh; by 1961 dissident elements seemed much less apathetic.

One thing is certain with regard to both Arab and Iranian nationalism: economic development and education will not reconcile the nationalists to existing arrangements. As development raises the standard of living, a higher level of education becomes possible. Educated Arabs and Iranians absorb western concepts of nationalism and independence, and apathy is replaced by the western notion that reform or revolution can remake human institutions so that they more effectively serve the needs of men. The belief of many oil men that the fruits of

[1] *Economist*, April 18, 1959, p. 241.

large-scale development projects—dams, roads, bridges, and the like, paid for out of governmental oil revenues—will lead the Arabs and Iranians to acquiesce in existing institutions is untenable. Such a "materialistic interpretation" of history does not recognize the immense appeal in modern times, in underdeveloped areas, of the goals of nationalism, independence, and reform.

What do the Arab and Iranian nationalists want with respect to oil? This is not an easy question to answer, for, as might be imagined, the nationalists are not in complete agreement on the subject. Nevertheless, a basic pattern can be detected. Fundamentally, the Arabs and Iranians want independence and reform: independence from the control of western oil firms and eventually the elimination of private enterprise in the exploitation of oil resources. Oil revenues make up a large part of the national income in several Middle Eastern countries, so that when an oil company changes its policy concerning production or price, it can have serious consequences for a national economy. Hence the exceedingly strong desire of Middle Eastern governments is to exercise control over, perhaps obtain ownership of, the companies. In addition the Arab nationalists, and perhaps some Iranians, want a unified oil policy (which might accompany, or promote, Arab unity), along with, possibly, some redistribution of oil revenues from the wealthier to the poorer Middle Eastern areas. Apart from basic goals, there are less fundamental ends which are sought and numerous possibilities in tactics and strategy by which various objectives may be pursued. We will find it useful at the beginning to look at the most controversial, the most emotion-laden, of the goals of the nationalists: the elimination of private enterprise in oil, in other words, the nationalization of the oil installations.

2. Nationalization

Though it is frequently denied, complete nationalization of oil in the Middle East is the dream of most Arabs and Iranians. Nominally Iranian oil has already been nationalized. The government-owned National Iranian Oil Company is said to be the "owner" of the fixed assets of the oil industry in southern Iran, while the Consortium operating companies have the unrestricted use of them during the forty-year period of the agreement.[2] But property is a "bundle of rights," and the rights in the Consortium bundle are so much greater than the rights in the NIOC bundle that the nationalization of the Iranian oil industry is pretty much a fiction put forth to make the Consortium agreement more palatable to Iranian public opinion. Complete nationalization remains a dream for both the Arabs and the Iranians. Of course oil men oppose nationalization; they contend that their concession contracts with the governments are sacred. Arabs and Iranians point out that these contracts often were negotiated in the past by inexperienced desert sheikhs or kings or by Middle Eastern governments which were under the domination of Western governments. They argue that, if it compensates the owners, a government may exercise its sovereignty and nationalize an industry.

The younger, less-knowledgeable Arabs and Iranians would like to see immediate nationalization. Older, more experienced individuals, particularly the Arab and Iranian oil experts who are emerging in the various countries of the Middle East, see the necessity of waiting. But even as they deny the existence of plans to nationalize oil, these experts reveal that nationalization is their ultimate goal. Abdulla Tariki, at the time director general of the Office of Petroleum and Mineral Affairs, Saudi Arabia, has been quoted as follows:

While I can't predict what might happen ten years from now, right now we couldn't succeed in nationalizing even if we tried. . . . If we nationalized Saudi Arabian oil now, Kuwait or Iran would merely fill the gap. . . . Also if we nationalized now, we'd end up merely run by another group of foreigners. [He refers to the Saudi

[2] *Iran*, a booklet published by Iranian Oil Participants Ltd. (London, 1956), p. 44; *The Iranian Oil Agreement*, published by Standard Oil Company (New Jersey), p. 6.

lack of engineers, technicians, and administrators.] The thing to do is to start small. Walk before you run. Form your own small company, get experience, and grow slowly; not jump on the existing industry.[3]

With so much emphasis in this statement on the *present-day* difficulties of nationalization, it is hard to imagine that Tariki really believes another assertion he made in the same interview to the effect that eventual nationalization "will hurt us, as well as the companies."

There are several reasons for Arab and Iranian belief in nationalization of oil. In the first place, most educated people in the underdeveloped regions of the world, and the Arabs and Iranians are no exceptions, believe in socialism, believe that elimination of the profit motive and its replacement with economic planning will lead to a better allocation of resources and a fairer distribution of income. In the second place, it is felt that a nationalized oil company would serve better the needs of people in the Middle East; its administrators and technicians would no longer represent owners with interests in holdings elsewhere in the world, and a higher proportion of its executives would be nationals of Middle Eastern countries. It is thought that Arab and Iranian administrators would be more willing to train and develop their fellow countrymen than are present foreign administrators; the latter, many believe, are fearful of being displaced by those they train.

There is reason, however, to doubt that as much can be gained by nationalization as many of its advocates believe. A scarcity of skilled administrators and technicians may cause difficulties, and political influences may undermine efficient management. Most important, nationalization will not give to Arabs and Iranians the independence from western oil companies which they desire. After nationalization, the international

[3] Wanda M. Jablonski, "Terms for New Saudi Concessions Spelled Out," *Petroleum Week*, June 20, 1958, p. 41. Tariki later became Minister of Petroleum, a position he still holds.

majors would still control over 90 percent of the markets out-side the United States, and the Arabs and Iranians would have to sell to these firms. While no longer disputing the division of profits with the oil companies, the Middle Eastern countries would have to negotiate a sale price with a buyers' oligopoly (oligopsony). They would also have to negotiate the quantity to be taken by the majors, and these negotiations would largely determine the volume of Arab and Iranian production. It is not surprising, under these circumstances, that Middle Eastern governments should seek to obtain independence from the inter-national majors by other means. But before we turn to other aspects of Arab and Iranian strategy, we should ask ourselves whether the Middle Eastern governments could succeed in nationalizing their oil installations if they made an attempt to do so.

Almost certainly they could not succeed at present. To quote Tariki again (we are in part repeating an earlier quotation):

Right now we couldn't succeed in nationalizing even if we tried. Right now we have to cooperate with the West because that's where our markets are.

If we nationalized Saudi Arabian oil now, Kuwait or Iran would merely fill the gap. You can nationalize all the Middle East to-gether, but you cannot nationalize just one Middle East country. Any one of the four main producers could supply all the Middle East oil needed.[4]

The Middle Eastern governments individually could not succeed in nationalization because the international majors control their markets and because surplus capacity has been developed in each of the principal concession areas. Only if the four large producing countries could agree to nationalize together and withhold oil from the West until the majors became willing to purchase from their nationalized enterprises would nationaliza-tion succeed. An agreement of this sort is not at all likely in the next few years. Indeed, it might be necessary to draw Venezuela

[4] *Ibid.*

216

into accord in order to keep the oil companies from supplying a large part of their markets from this source, and such an agreement would be very hard to obtain.

Iran's attempt to nationalize during the early fifties is worth some attention. The Iranians may have failed to nationalize successfully, may have failed, that is, to obtain more than token nationalization, (1) because they were unable to produce and refine their oil, (2) because of the solidarity of the international majors who supplied world markets from other sources and left Iranian oil without purchasers, or (3) because of the intervention of the British government (and perhaps other western governments) in consuming countries. Oil men in New York and London assert that the Iranians failed because they lacked the technicians to produce and refine the oil. But the Iranians, and many others, dispute this. An Iranian official in the National Iranian Oil Company told the writer, "Our own technicians could have operated the oil fields at about 200,000 barrels per day, or 30 percent of capacity, and the refinery at about 100,000 barrels daily, or 20 percent of capacity, and we could have hired technicians in Europe; we were successful in marketing, however, only a minute fraction of our potential output." And, indeed, we know that the half-dozen cargoes of oil which were all, apparently, that Iran marketed during the three-year dispute, four in Italy and two in Japan,[5] were sold in the face of a great deal of official harassment around the world by the British government. The *New York Times* reported on September 12, 1953 (p. 3), that the Japanese government had told the British authorities, informally, that it would not grant more foreign exchange for the purchase of Iranian oil.

Knowing the possibility of hiring foreign technicians and recalling the success of the Egyptians in operating the Suez Canal, the writer doubts that it was inability to produce and refine that caused the Iranian failure in nationalization. He believes that basically the Iranians were defeated by major-

[5] *New York Times*, May 12, 1953, p. 5; July 6, 1953, p. 3.

company control of world markets outside the United States, although the intervention of the British government (and other western governments) in consuming countries may have contributed to the failure.

In recognition of the difficulties of nationalization, perhaps in recognition of the limited gains to be obtained from it, the Arabs and Iranians in recent years have directed their attention to other objectives.

3. Higher Prices or a Larger Output

Of course people in the Middle East are interested in greater profits from their oil. Many Arabs and Iranians feel that they should have more than 50 percent of the net income. We have already suggested that there is no economic rationale in a fifty-fifty profit split; in prolific areas, it may very well be that governments can and should demand more than half of the net income. Some Arabs and Iranians feel that they are not yet getting 50 percent of the profits, that different accounting methods would give them a larger revenue even under the fifty-fifty rule. Certainly it is true that petroleum accounting is a relatively underdeveloped discipline.

In seeking higher revenues from oil, Arab and Iranian critics devote a great deal of attention to prices and output. Sometimes it is suggested that the posted price of Middle East oil is too low, and that governmental oil revenues calculated on this price are therefore too small. Such allegations are almost certainly incorrect. All the evidence is that in recent years the international majors, as oligopolists, have kept the posted price *high*, above discounted prices which nonaffiliates have been paying, and that Middle Eastern governments have been sharing in oligopoly profits. Governments in the Middle East, skeptical of company sale prices and entitled to take royalty in kind, can test the market with their royalty oil; it is revealing that these governments generally have preferred to sell this oil to the companies at posted prices rather than sell it in the open market.

218

A view sometimes expressed by Arabs which is more interesting, and more difficult to appraise, is that the oil companies have kept prices *too high* and that their volume of sales, along with government oil revenues, has suffered as a consequence. Indeed, it is widely believed that the development and production of Middle East oil has been held back by the international majors in order to protect their high-cost holdings in the Western Hemisphere; it is sometimes thought that the interests of the Arabs and Iranians would be served best by lower prices for Middle East oil with an accompanying larger volume of sales.

We have already discussed the rate of oil development in the Middle East (in Chapter VIII, Section 1). We recognized there that although oil in the area has been developed with extraordinary rapidity, the international majors may have developed it less rapidly than would have companies without interests elsewhere in the world. Arab governments likewise, had they made the decisions, might have developed and produced their oil more rapidly. The interests of the Arabs and Iranians, with oil only in the Middle East, and the interests of the international majors, with oil properties all over the world, may definitely diverge when it is a question of deciding upon the rate of development and production of Middle East oil.

Some Arabs and Iranians who believe that the development of Middle East oil has been held back by the oil companies contend that were the output of Middle East oil under the control of the Arabs and Iranians, it would be strikingly expanded. "After all," said one young Arab to the writer, "if low-cost Middle East oil were properly developed, it would supply the entire world." It is doubtful, however, that, even with its extremely low costs, Middle East oil under the control of the Arabs and Iranians would "sweep the board." If the Arabs and Iranians were to attempt a marked expansion of oil production and sales, they would have to sell at very low prices over a long period of time, for suppliers in other areas, with developed oil fields, would defend their markets by cutting prices, if necessary cutting them until they equaled variable costs. Since the actual lifting costs of developed oil properties are very low, the Arabs and Iranians probably would decide on a slower penetration of new markets in order to obtain better prices.

Moreover, an attempt to expand the output of Middle East oil markedly would run into protectionist feelings in Europe, Canada, and some other countries. Barriers to entry would be erected or strengthened in the interest of protecting indigenous oil, gas, and coal. Indeed, much oil company hesitation about developing Middle East oil may have arisen, not out of a desire to protect Western Hemisphere investments, but out of knowledge that efforts to import larger quantities of foreign oil into the United States or certain European countries would result in the erection of more serious formal barriers to trade. It is possible that western oil companies can get more Middle East oil into Europe and America than could purely Arab and Iranian oil firms which lacked a European or American partner to speak for them before governmental bodies. To this observation, Arabs and Iranians reply that Middle East oil is the lowest-cost oil in the world and that in due course the world will come to buy it from them. This statement is no doubt true, though there are circumstances under which a western partner might speed the sale, and the development, of Middle East oil.

The international majors, it must be recognized, may have checked the development of Middle East oil in order to protect their Western Hemisphere investments, but it is most unlikely that the Arabs and Iranians, even were they in complete control, would find it profitable, or possible, to expand production and sales by an extremely large amount. And there is no possibility at all that they could sweep the board and win the entire world market for their oil.

Whatever may be their beliefs concerning the desirability or feasibility of a faster rate of development and production in

Middle East oil *over the long run,* a number of Arabs and Iranians are beginning to recognize that during the current world oil surplus attention might be given to checking Middle East output in order to defend the present level of world oil prices. At the first Arab Oil Congress (spring, 1959) there was considerable interest in an informal Venezuelan proposal to control production and stabilize prices on a co-operative basis, and in September, 1960, an Organization of Petroleum Exporting Countries was set up with production control as one of its objectives. We shall have more to say later in the chapter on the growing Middle Eastern interest in governmental control of production.

4. Greater Participation in Management

One of the most insistent demands of the Arabs and Iranians is for greater participation in management; they want more places in oil company management for individual Arabs and Iranians, and they want Middle Eastern governments to have a larger voice in oil company affairs.

The problem of the training and advancement of Middle Eastern nationals is a thorny one. Many of the Arabs and Iranians who feel that they should advance more rapidly, say the companies, exaggerate their qualifications. Moreover, the companies contend, Arabs and Iranians frequently do not want to live out in the desert but prefer to take desk jobs in the cities, perhaps in government offices. One oil company executive in the Middle East put it this way: "Take five Arabs or Iranians who have studied petroleum engineering or geology abroad. Two probably just made their grades, just got by, exactly as do their counterparts among American students; one or two will be recruited by governments for their offices; we can hope, then, to get only one or two good men out of the five." An outsider is inclined to suspect that these observations of the oil companies have some validity. Most ambitious men, particularly young men, of whatever nationality, tend to exaggerate their qualifications and to feel, often mistakenly, that recognition comes too slowly. And it is common in underdeveloped countries for educated people to prefer comfortable berths in the cities to difficult positions in the field.

On the other hand, Middle East students of the oil industry point out, justly, that expatriate Europeans and Americans have vested interests in their jobs and that they may not support, or may even sabotage, a company policy of hiring Arabs and Iranians and advancing them to higher positions. And then, the companies themselves, desiring to earn the profits of production as long as possible, may lack enthusiasm for a program set up to train possible successors. Here is a genuine divergence of interest, both individual and corporate. Finally, the oil companies may not find ability because, being skeptical of its existence, they hesitate to give Arabs and Iranians the responsibilities which will enable them to develop. The full flowering of a people requires leaders who have confidence in it and who are ready and willing to give ability its chance. Quite possibly western oil men lack the necessary faith.

Arabs and Iranians who feel that their governments should have a larger voice in the management of oil operations in the Middle East are unhappy because the oil companies are largely run from the United States and England. The international majors, the parent companies, frequently occupy the position of absentee landlord; important decisions must be referred to them in New York or London, while local management often appears to be little more than a bailiff. Speaking of the Arabian American Oil Company, Abdulla Tariki has said, "They promised us they'd bring the officers from New York to Saudi Arabia, but what happened? They moved them here, but gave them no authority. The final authority was vested in an executive committee of the four parents in New York." [6] Particularly in the marketing of Middle East oil are local oil company managements without voice. Tariki tells the story of a Saudi merchant

[6] Wanda M. Jablonski, "Is Arabia Moving to a New 50-50 Oil Pattern?" *Petroleum Week*, February 22, 1957, p. 23.

who came to him wanting to export 20,000 tons of heating oil to Germany; Tariki sent the merchant to Aramco, but Aramco told him to contact New York![7]

The Arabs and Iranians are certain to press continuously for larger governmental participation in management. The young, educated people are socialists and very much inclined to believe in government controls, if not ownership, in all basic industry. Reinforcing their socialistic inclinations is the desire to provide a counterweight to the influence of the far-away parent oil companies.

Again and again as Arabs and Iranians seek ways of attaining their objectives, whether they are higher profits, a larger participation in management, or the ultimate goal of nationalization, they must be struck by the power of the international majors, power which rests on major-company control of world markets outside the United States. A dedicated Arab or Iranian petroleum economist must be obsessed with thoughts of how to check or counter this power. In succeeding sections of the chapter we will review three methods, three strategic devices, by which people, at least some people, in the Middle East hope to deal with the market power of the majors: vertical integration, the gaining of independent routes to market, and governmental control of output.

5. Vertical Integration

Abdulla Tariki insists that the parent companies of the Arabian American Oil Company should agree to develop it into a "fully integrated" company, one which produces, refines, transports, and markets petroleum products. As a first step toward this vertical integration, Tariki wants Aramco to post its own prices and begin making f.o.b. export sales of crude and products to nonowner purchasers.

Tariki and many others in the Middle East apparently believe that the profits of refining and marketing are very great, and

[7] *Ibid.,* p. 24.

he and others think that the Arabs should share in these profits. At one time he estimated that "our profits from these added activities would be almost double." [8] Dr. Omar Haliq estimated that the Arab half-share of the profits of refining, transport, and marketing would amount to about 73 cents per barrel, which would be added to an estimated 80 cents a barrel currently being received by the Arab governments on production.[9] We have already seen evidence that the international majors have kept posted prices high and have, as a consequence, left small profits in refining and marketing. (See Chapter III, Section 3.) When one looks at the profit situation alone, it is difficult to understand why Tariki is so intent on vertical integration. In the writer's opinion, profits have very little to do with his urge in this direction. Whether or not he really believes that the refining and marketing stages of the oil industry are very profitable is difficult to say. Certainly emphasis on profitability will generate governmental and popular support for Arab insistence on vertical integration. But it seems likely that Tariki is really interested in vertical integration as a device for checking the power of the international majors, the power arising out of their control of markets. He wants Aramco, the oil company whose facilities Saudi Arabia will one day own, to have *direct access to markets.* He is said to believe that an integrated Aramco would leave Saudi Arabia with a world-wide marketing organization of its own at the expiration of the Aramco concession. The companies deny this and contend that under the terms of the concession no Aramco facilities outside of Saudi Arabia would revert to Arabia.[10] Whether Tariki is right or not, it is clear that he is interested in vertical integration as a means of breaking the international majors' hold over markets. Perhaps he is indeed

[8] Quoted by Wanda M. Jablonski, "How Could Aramco Compete against Its Owners?" *Petroleum Week,* October 18, 1957, p. 20.

[9] Omar Haliq, "The Problem of Arabian Oil: An Arab Appraisal" (a paper read at the Seventh Annual Arab Students' Convention, Urbana, Ill., 1958), p. 7.

[10] Jablonski, "How Could Aramco Compete against Its Owners?" p. 22.

thinking of the time when the Aramco concessions expire in the years 1999 and 2005. More probably he is thinking of an earlier date, a date when, if Aramco had direct and secure access to markets, nationalization might be successfully accomplished.

What of vertical integration as Arab strategy? Is it a feasible approach? Will the oil companies accept it?

Oil men have argued that the proposed initial step of f.o.b. export sales by Aramco to nonowners would not produce substantial results because there are so few independent outlets; independents represent less than 10 percent of the total market for Middle East oil. A serious difficulty would arise out of the fact that Aramco as seller would have only a single source of supply. Buyers would prefer to buy from a major company which could supply a customer from an alternative source should Arabian oil be interrupted. Lacking geographical diversity in its holdings, Aramco probably would have to sell at a discount in order to find purchasers. Of course the parent companies find the thought of competing with their own progeny most objectionable. It is scarcely to be imagined that they would agree to competition (between Aramco and themselves) which undermined the sale price of Arabian oil. Nor would this be in the interest of the Saudi government.

It has been suggested that the parent firms might keep their old business but cease bidding on new, allow Aramco to represent them, and let Aramco build up a position in marketing. Were Aramco to be as vigorous and effective in selling oil as the parents had been as a group, the total share of the market held by the group would remain unchanged, though particular owners, the more energetic ones, might collect less in dividends from Aramco than they would have earned had they gone out to sell the oil themselves. The U.S. Department of Justice would be very unhappy to observe the parents of Aramco step out of the market in favor of Aramco, whether it involved turning old customers over to this producing subsidiary or ceasing to bid on new business. Four sellers would be replaced by one, and competition would be less. Tariki has said that the U.S. anti-trust laws have nothing to do with Saudi Arabia, and he has suggested that if the Department of Justice will not let Aramco become a marketing company, Saudi Arabia may ask that the concession be split up among the four owners, each of the resultant four firms, presumably, then to be vertically integrated.[11]

The parent companies can be expected to oppose any efforts to break up the concession and to resist bitterly all moves which threaten to deprive them of their marketing facilities. They will not agree to any proposals which would put the non-Saudi assets of Aramco in the hands of the Saudis at the expiration of the concession or at the time of a nationalization. Nor would they agree to proposals which would put in the hands of Saudis the non-Saudi assets of producing companies which replaced Aramco in a splitting up of the concession. The international majors would lose too much of their power if they gave up control of their marketing properties. Should the international majors vest in their Middle East producing subsidiaries title to marketing facilities which are located outside the Middle East, foreign courts, in the event of nationalization, might award the installations to the nationalized producing company, thus enabling it to succeed in marketing its oil. It is most doubtful, then, that Tariki's strategy of insisting on vertical integration can surmount the opposition of the oil companies.

Actually, it is difficult to see how the Arabs, without an investment of capital in the later stages of the oil business, can claim a "right" to participation in the profits which most of these activities yield. They can claim a share in the return on production and land transport without a corresponding investment because they are the owners of the natural resources, the oil and the land route, and can, as the "landlord" customarily does, collect the economic rent. (It would scarcely be fair for Americans or Europeans, dwelling as they do in lands rich in

[11] Jablonski, "Is Arabia Moving to a New 50-50 Oil Pattern?" p. 23.

natural resources and inherited technology, to invoke Henry George at this point and allege that the Arabs did not create the oil or the land and have no right to the unearned economic rent which it yields.) Although the Arabs can claim a share in the return on production and land transport without having invested in it, they have little basis for claiming a share in the profits of the later stages of an oil operation. The returns of sea transport, refining, and marketing reflect mostly the investment of capital by the oil companies, and the Arabs can point to no contribution which they have made.

Further participation in oil is a legitimate aspiration; but it would mean supplying a commensurate share of the huge capital requirements of this industry, as against enjoying the fruits of the most profitable part of it without supplying any capital at all.[12]

If an Arab or Iranian country were to offer to buy into the operations through which the international majors market Middle Eastern oil, it would be more difficult to say that it had no rights in the matter. But a general scarcity of capital in the Middle East probably will save the companies from being required to deal with such an offer.

One other point may be made concerning Arab participation in the profits of transportation, refining, and marketing. The Arabs might consider the *taxing power* of their governments rather than point to the resources which their governments own. It is doubtful, however, that a government can claim to tax income earned in another jurisdiction. Middle Eastern governments, along with governments in consuming countries, might properly tax value added at sea, but a claim to tax value added in foreign manufacture or distribution seems dubious. The United States could scarcely tax the profits of a British textile mill which was processing U.S. cotton.

All in all, Tariki's interest in the vertical integration of Aramco and his desire for Saudi participation in the majors' transport,

[12] *Economist*, April 18, 1959, p. 254.

227

refining, and marketing profits do not appear to be warranted—either by the gains in income or in power which the Arabs might hope to make or by the claims of justice. More promising are the efforts of the Arab and Iranian governments to have a part of their oil developed and marketed independently of the majors.

6. Independent Routes to Market

We have already discussed (in Chapter II, Section 6) the nonaffiliated, independent companies which have been invited into the Middle East—Ente Nazionale Idrocarburi and Indiana Standard in Iran and the Arabian Oil Company, Ltd., offshore from the Neutral Zone. If these independents find oil and sell it to firms or individuals other than the international majors, if the National Iranian Oil Company, the Iranian government oil firm, markets its share of the oil produced under these new agreements to firms or individuals other than the international majors, then Iran, Saudi Arabia, and Kuwait will have gained a certain measure of independence from the international oil companies. (The Arabian Oil Company has found oil.) By reducing their dependence on the international majors for oil revenues, the Arabs and Iranians improve their chances of winning future disputes over the division of oil income, or even over nationalization—for in the event of disrupted major production part of their income would probably continue.

If the Middle Eastern governments were to insist upon marketing their own royalty oil—in the old concessions, where possible, and in the new ones—rather than sell it to the majors, they would gain an additional measure of independence and thereby further improve their bargaining position with the oil companies.

In the next few years each of the countries of the Middle East is likely to form a national petroleum company which will engage in exploration on its own account, purchase tankers, perhaps build a refinery and develop its own distinct marketing outlets,

228

and possibly join in an Arab (or Arab-Iranian) pipeline to the eastern Mediterranean. The Middle Eastern governments from time to time will put pressure on the international majors to relinquish acreage, which their national oil companies can then explore (or which can be granted as concessions to independents). The National Iranian Oil Company has already found some oil and purchased tankers, and in April, 1959, Kuwait's first tanker was chartered for five years to BP Tanker Company and Gulf Oil Corporation.

Though the Arabs and Iranians can check the power of the international majors by developing independent routes to market in these various ways, they will find it a slow process. In the first place, there will be a constant temptation for the independents and the governments to sell their oil to the majors at attractive prices, as Iraq now sells its royalty oil and Iran its oil in lieu of stated payments. And while the large companies cannot purchase unlimited quantities of this outside oil (even if it is "distress oil"), they will do what they can in the interest of orderly markets and maintenance of their market control. Only if the Arabs and Iranians demonstrate an uncommon austerity and forgo the easy way—perhaps in the short run the more profitable way—of selling to the majors, and only if they insist that their new independents do the same, will they succeed in developing independent routes to market and reducing the power of the majors. In any case, it will take time. The international majors will continue to grow, and the Arabs and Iranians will only gradually see an increase in the proportion of their oil which is being marketed independently of the major companies. Slow and gradual it must be, but it is probably more certain than anything else the Arabs and Iranians can do to gain for themselves an independent position in world oil.

Perhaps in part because independent routes to market can be obtained only slowly, Arabs and Iranians have interested themselves in governmental control of production.

7. Government Control of Production in the Middle East

The present serious interest in controlling production arises almost entirely out of commercial considerations. A world oil surplus, leading to Caribbean and Middle Eastern price reductions in the winter and spring of 1959, generated a strong interest in output control in Venezuela and the Middle East. A Venezuelan delegation arrived at the first Arab Oil Congress in April, 1959, with an informal proposal that the Arabs join Venezuela in arrangements to stabilize production and prices. There was a good deal of discussion of the idea; Abdulla Tariki expressed enthusiasm for it but recognized many obstacles in the way of its realization. In effect the Venezuelans proposed a system of world-wide "prorationing," similar to the arrangements already established in Texas, Louisiana, Oklahoma, and a number of other states. (There is something disingenuous in the way oil companies describe Venezuelan and Arab proposals along these lines as artificial, unsound, and improper when these same companies have remained silent for so many years about production controls in the American Southwest.) In September, 1960, Venezuela along with Iran, Iraq, Saudi Arabia, and Kuwait established the Organization of Petroleum Exporting Countries; its members propose, among other things, to stabilize prices through regulation of output.

An agreement to control production in Venezuela and the Middle East would be most difficult to obtain. Each country would want the others to cease expanding output or to cut back. Iran would be a big problem. During her drive for nationalization under Mossadegh she fell from first place in Middle East output to last place, and she has been striving for some years to recover the first position. Iran is a non-Arab country and is said to resent the fact that Arab oil was so freely supplied to former purchasers of Iranian oil when Iran was struggling to nationalize. So it would be difficult to get Iran to stop expanding her output.

It would also be hard to persuade the North African countries with newly discovered oil to check its development.

But it is possible to exaggerate the problems of obtaining a world-wide control of oil production. Substantial price declines, or the threat of these, will intensify interest in controls and increase the inclination to come to agreement on quotas. Texas oil men sometimes become restive under tight production controls, but a threatened price cut finds them demanding that the authorities order a reduction in output. Tariki has observed:

The entire oil surplus supply comes from the Middle East and Venezuela, all from countries which depend on petroleum for some 90% of their revenues. Therefore, these governments have a big stake in seeing that prices for their oil are not weakened by excessive exports.[13]

One Arab oil director suggested to the writer that he would be willing to see the Arabs make considerable concessions to Iran to get it into an agreement; he said that he would acquiesce in Iran's regaining its historic, pre-Mossadegh share of the market for Middle East oil, provided that it not try to obtain this position overnight but only over a period of years. (It is not certain, of course, that his government would back him in this.) Along with making a place for an increased Iranian output, the oil countries with a large established production may check their output enough to make room for North African oil.

The long-run goal of many people in the Middle East who are interested in seeing the Arabs and Iranians together control production is probably that of checking the power of the international majors or even of wresting control from them. Should the Middle Eastern governments as a group obtain a tight control on output, they would be in a strong position to impose their will on the majors, whether it was a question of managerial participation, prices, profits, or nationalization. Certainly this

[13] *Petroleum Week*, June 5, 1959, p. 13.

would be true if Libya, Algeria, and Venezuela joined them. Although a measure of agreement on output control in the interest of price stabilization is conceivable, during the oil surplus, it is very doubtful that the Arabs, Iranians, and Venezuelans could agree on the strategy and timing of a major drive to break the power of the international oil companies by withholding supplies from the West. Indeed, such a politico-economic weapon would be hard to forge, and very dangerous to use, for a collective effort to withhold oil from the oil companies and the West might very well be taken as an act of war. To be sure, as the oil companies find oil fields in new locations and as the West develops substitutes for oil, the weapon of collective output control may become less dangerous to wield, but at the same time it will have been blunted and made less effective.

8. The Economic Response of the West

The oil companies themselves have responded to the rise of nationalism in several ways. They have developed programs of "integration" in the hope of making their operations more acceptable to Arab and Iranian opinion. In addition to the development of more Arab and Iranian nationals for senior positions in the companies, these programs attempt to integrate the companies into local economies through increased local purchases, creating thereby a group of national businessmen who, it is hoped, will support them. And the companies are trying to promote social integration, trying to break down the social barriers between their expatriate employees and the Arabs and Iranians. Probably integration is looked at as a holding action, designed to take a certain amount of pressure off the companies but not expected to reconcile the intellectuals or the people generally to an indefinite tenure for the international majors. At least this would be a realistic appraisal of the program. A similar view probably should be taken of the various home-ownership schemes set up to assist nationals in purchasing their own homes.

The international majors are preparing a more effective defense when they develop reserve productive capacity in each of the several concession areas. In the late fifties, for example, despite a temporary surplus in world oil, the majors went ahead with huge programs to increase capacity in Kuwait and Iran. Of course these programs can be explained partially by an expected long-run growth in demand and by a desire to obtain the economies of large-scale operation through the construction of installations which are initially too big. Nevertheless, one motive for these large increases in capacity has undoubtedly been the desire to augment the bargaining power of the companies in any one area by having reserve productive capacity in another. In July, 1958, after the revolution in Iraq, *Petroleum Week* ran an article entitled, "West Would Not Feel Iraq Oil Shutdown," [14] which pointed out that "Iraq's exports could readily be made up by neighboring Kuwait and Saudi Arabia" and that there was surplus capacity in Iran, Venezuela, the United States, and Canada.

Various oil companies are building supertankers which can go around the African Cape almost as cheaply as through the Suez Canal. These tankers might carry Iranian oil or Kuwait oil if Iraq or Saudi oil were withheld from the market or its transit through pipelines or through the Canal not permitted.

The international majors are seeking oil all over the world, and to the extent that they are successful they reduce western dependence on supplies from the Middle East.

We have already discussed European programs to increase reserve stocks of oil (Chapter VII, Section 3). Some countries require oil companies to hold certain minimum stocks; at least one provides state funds for an additional stockpile. The bargaining power of the West with respect to the Middle East is naturally increased by stocks which can be used to tide consumers over a period during which new sources of supply are being developed to replace interrupted Middle Eastern supplies.

European governments have also given more attention in recent years to the development of alternative sources of energy,

[14] July 25, 1958, p. 13.

particularly nuclear energy, which could reduce western dependence on Middle East oil.

In Europe there has been little interest in state trading as a device for protecting western consumers against high prices induced by Arab-Iranian control of supply or, for that matter, by oil company control of supply. Serious interest in state trading is mostly to be found in Argentina, Brazil, and perhaps India. Of course the governments of Britain, France, and the Netherlands, being so closely associated with British Petroleum, Compagnie Française, and the Royal Dutch–Shell group, probably identify themselves with the international majors and possess the producer's point of view. The rest of the European governments may stand aside from state trading because they doubt the ability of Middle Eastern governments to agree on a program of production control, because they do not want to drive them into such a program, because they recognize that the oil companies themselves have only a limited oligopoly power, or because they have concluded that the majors do a great deal more to protect the West against Arab and Iranian ambitions than they do to hurt Europeans as consumers.

The efforts of the West to reduce its dependence on Middle East oil and Middle East transit routes, or on any particular country in the Middle East, cannot be criticized. Buyers must be free to protect themselves against situations which are potentially monopolistic. A turn to state trading would be questionable, and even a continued reliance on the existing market power of the international majors to protect the interests of western consumers is dubious, since the creation or use of a buyers' monopoly or oligopoly (monopsony or oligopsony) encourages, almost requires, the Arabs and Iranians to seek market control themselves through control of production. The prospect of bilateral monopoly or oligopoly in Middle East oil leaves much to be desired.

But beyond a dubious western reliance on the market power of the international oil companies to protect their interests in

Middle Eastern oil, there are some extremely questionable western political and military policies in the Middle East.

9. The Political-military Response of the West

Part of the difficulty arises out of a tendency in the West
to confuse nationalism with Communism. Particularly in the
United States are people inclined to view all world events, including the acts of nationalists, as part of the conflict between
the North Atlantic powers and Russia and China. A nationalist
rising against a semifeudal ruler is assumed to be Moscow-
inspired and thought to threaten western interests. Preoccupied
with the East-West conflict, Americans and Europeans often do
not understand that people in the Middle East are mostly concerned with quite other matters—elimination of the remains of
foreign rule, unification of the Arab world, and social reform.
To see Arab and Iranian activities exclusively through the glasses
of the cold war is indeed to view the Middle East darkly.

In addition to confusing nationalism with Communism, Americans and Europeans tend to fear change in the Middle East.
Changes are thought, in a vague way, to threaten western oil
supplies. No one knows for sure what a revolutionary Arab government will do or what to expect of a united Arab world. So
the tendency is to cling to the known present and oppose the
emerging future—which is, of course, a formula almost guaranteed to produce sudden, violent changes, when bottled-up forces
explode.

Following a policy which is very nearly one of divide and rule,
the West, perhaps Britain especially, inclines toward a military
defense of the independence of oil-producing states. The movement for Arab unity is believed to threaten western oil supplies,
and it is thought by many that the oil-producing states must be
kept out of a unified Arab nation, by force if necessary. These
attitudes came to light very clearly at the time of the turmoil in
the Middle East caused by the revolution in Iraq during the
summer of 1958. What, it was asked, should be the policy of the

West if the Iraq rising spread to Kuwait, a British protectorate, or to Saudi Arabia? What if efforts were made to attach these states to a larger Arab grouping, perhaps to the United Arab Republic headed by President Nasser? The British sought from America a commitment to join them in using force, if required, to keep the Persian Gulf oil states separate and distinct. Diplomatic activities in London and Washington were revealed in a series of newspaper dispatches:

One of the most important results of Mr. Lloyd's visit to the United States was said to be the United States and British agreement on the paramount importance of retaining present connections with Kuwait and other oil states of the Persian Gulf, such as Qatar [London dispatch, *New York Times*, July 23, 1958, p. 10].

The British believe they received an assurance from Dulles in his talks here last week with Foreign Secretary Lloyd that the United States is prepared to back them in the defense of the western oil resources of the Persian Gulf. But this has not been stated publicly by the administration [James Reston, Washington dispatch for the New York Times News Service, in the *Milwaukee Journal*, July 24, 1958, p. 4].

The United States and British Governments . . . are in agreement that the *status quo* in Kuwait must be preserved [*Economist*, July 26, 1958, p. 274].

Britain wants only political stability in the Middle East and unrestricted communication with the oil fields, but in the Government's view these are impossible to obtain while President Nasser, the head of the United Arab Republic, with Soviet support is undermining the remaining independent states of the area. . . .
    The view of the British is that they can live with Arab nationalism and continue to have access to oil supplies. They draw the line —and they intend to make this clear to Mr. Khrushchev—at an Arab imperialism that seeks to overthrow small existing governments—Kuwait is an example—and grab control of the Middle East and the oil supplies [Drew Middleton in a London dispatch, *New York Times*, July 25, 1958, p. 1, quoted by permission].

[Dulles] is willing neither to make common cause with President Nasser's movement nor to make a military stand with the British, if necessary, to keep the oil of Kuwait and Saudi Arabia from going to President Nasser. . . . Washington will issue warnings and offer [economic] aid as an alternative, but if this combination does not work, then these additional power moves will be considered [James Reston in a Washington dispatch, *New York Times,* August 13, 1958, p. 4].

So the United States, apparently, did not commit itself to a military defense of the Persian Gulf oil states if their absorption by an Arab union or federation were threatened, but it agreed to consider such a defense. A military action of this sort, in the writer's opinion, would be extremely unwise. Middle East oil should be treated purely as a commercial, or trading, proposition. Americans and Europeans should go to the Middle East as purchasers of oil, nothing more; they should expect to dictate neither the social patterns nor the political configuration of the area. The president of Continental Oil Company in the United States spoke very wisely when he said:

Governments of consuming countries should recognize that their nationals have no inherent "right" to the oil in the areas from which they draw their supplies. Their positions are essentially those of large buyers, seeking adequate, dependable sources of supply, and they should conduct their relationships with producing countries from that standpoint.[15]

Military intervention to prevent Arab union or federation is clearly a policy of divide and rule and can quite accurately be labeled "imperialism." Such action is out of date in the twentieth century. As the *Observer* of London has stated, "The time has passed when, even in the Middle East, we can do business at the point of a gun." [16]

[15] L. F. McCollum, "Oil's Contribution, Past and Future," *Proceedings of the Fifth World Petroleum Congress* (New York, June 1, 1959), p. 9.
[16] April 27, 1958, p. 12.

X

Middle East Oil from Several Points of View

MIDDLE EAST oil looks strikingly different in the various parts of the world. The Atlantic divides Americans and Europeans in point of view most surprisingly, and western arithmetic in profit maximization is a long way from Arab and Iranian tendencies to view oil as a weapon in their national struggles. An attempt to look at Middle East oil from several different viewpoints may assist us in reaching conclusions about future policy with respect to oil in the Middle East.

1. The Case for the International Majors

The first and most obvious contribution which the majors have made is their provision of administrators and engineers to find, extract, transport, and in part refine oil. Working in the desert under tremendous physical difficulties, the men of oil have constructed entire cities, developed a large network for the distribution of supplies, provided water, and built roads, schools, and hospitals. These desert enterprises certainly constitute one of the most remarkable accomplishments in engineering and organization which our age has known. Now that the oil has been found in vast quantities, it is easy to forget the risks which the oil companies took when they entered the area; they ventured millions; they were entrepreneurs on the grand scale.

Having found the oil, the majors developed large and diversified markets for it, risking additional capital. In recent years, the majors have squeezed Middle East oil through potential barriers arising out of protectionist sentiments in Europe and America, probably in larger quantity than the Arabs and Iranians without western partners could have done. Perhaps we are witnessing a slow shift in the role of the large oil companies in world oil. As governments interest themselves more and more in exploration and production, and in domestic distribution, the companies increasingly may find themselves to be simply "international traders," uniting buyers and sellers in the world market for oil. Trade in oil internationally is a function which the oil companies can perform better, in most cases, than can any single government or group of governments. Along with diversified markets, the majors possess diversified sources of supply, both in and out of the Middle East, and this diversity provides producing countries and consuming countries with considerable security. (Even so, we may expect to see frequent governmental efforts to by-pass the oil companies through bilateral trade agreements and the like.)

The international majors as they produce and trade in oil act to promote stability in price. They are large, they control much of the supply of oil outside the United States, they have long pocketbooks and need not incautiously dump oil in world markets to meet a note at the bank, and in conjunction with state conservation authorities in the United States they perform, it can be argued, the function of "eveners,"[1] adjusting supply to the requirements of the market.

[1] Frankel, *Essentials of Petroleum*, p. 113.

2. The American Point of View

The large American companies would not care to admit their role in controlling supply and stabilizing prices; they have always wanted to appear as ordinary businesses operating in a normally competitive market. Nor is this surprising in the land of the Sherman Antitrust Act, where competition is so greatly admired and so vigorously sought.

Although many Americans admire the enterprise of the international oil companies and have no doubts about their operations in the Middle East, others believe that Middle East oil looks like something of a monopoly or even a cartel. (The writer has labeled it "oligopoly.") Constantly under surveillance, frequently attacked in Congress, from time to time hauled before the courts, the international majors have a hard time of it; their prices are often thought to be too high, too closely tied to the U.S. Gulf Coast price, too rigid. Those in the United States who are unhappy about the market for Middle East oil are inclined to believe that what it needs is more competition.

While being attacked as monopolistic in the United States, the oil companies up to now have been able to count on little U.S. diplomatic support in the Middle East. It is the American noncolonial, even anticolonial, tradition that American enterprises abroad are pretty much on their own. Recent U.S. preoccupation with the cold war, the tendency to confuse nationalism with Communism, perhaps the persuasiveness of the British, have inclined the United States, regrettably, toward military intervention in situations which in the past would have been left alone.

3. The European Point of View

Perhaps more than Americans, Europeans see a degree of monopoly in Middle East oil. But their reaction to monopoly is quite different from that of people in the United States. Competition is not greatly admired in Europe; order, stability, and large-scale organization are. A dash of competition in a market such as that of oil is all that is thought desirable, or feasible. A larger measure of competition is feared as a source of extreme instability. Large fixed costs, increasing returns, irregular discoveries, it is believed, threaten serious instability in an oil market of numerous small producers. (See Chapter VIII, Section 3.) Europeans, far from viewing the structure of world oil prices as too rigid, seem to think that it is very precariously stable; they appear to imagine that should an independent oil man stamp his foot, the whole price structure would tumble down. "It is difficult to see where prices will come to rest once they start to move." [2]

In America quite a different view prevails: increasing returns are thought, in the long run, to promote natural oligopoly, or monopoly, and sticky, rigid prices. Americans tend to feel that, were it possible, increased competition would be desirable in order to make such markets more flexible. The writer has already shown that he is an American in outlook, believing that while long-run increasing returns may temporarily cause instability in price, as emerging oligopolists struggle for position, over a period of time they are more significant as a source of price rigidity. (See pp. 205–206.)

Because Europeans feel that market control by the international majors is necessary in order to avoid extreme instability in price, they seldom propose an increase in competition even when they become concerned about the monopoly power of the majors. Rather they think in terms of an increase in government regulation, or state trading, or of a price negotiated by the governments of consuming and producing nations. Read the hesitant but unmistakable call for intervention by European governments as expressed in the ECE Report:

In the Middle East there is direct and continuous contact between the Governments holding title to the oil resources in the region and the major companies entrusted with their exploitation. There has,

[2] ECE Report, p. 38.

however, been no corresponding development of Government influence on the consuming side in Europe to serve as a counterweight to these governmental and private interests on the producing side.

While the working out of acceptable compromises between public and private interests always presents difficult problems, more effective consumer representation in solving the problem of oil pricing might well be regarded as to the long-run advantage of the industry itself. . . .[3]

The European, or at least the British, approach to Middle East oil definitely has a larger political component than the American and includes more positively the notion of military action.

An additional influence on events in the Middle East is a British suspicion of American intentions. For many Britons the United States is by no means as politically innocent as it likes to make out. Its anti-imperialism is thought to be pure hypocrisy; it is believed to be using its power to move into Middle East oil and edge Britain out. The writer is skeptical, inclined to the view that U.S. policy in the Middle East can best be understood as a combination of the simple commercial instinct and a fumbling anticommunism, rather than as a calculated imperialism. In any case, British suspicion of American oil policy exists and must be taken into account.

4. In Arab and Iranian Eyes

Arabs and Iranians are inclined to be vague about the kind of market structure they consider desirable. Many of them follow the lead of numerous western critics and speak of a world oil cartel, inferring that the Middle Eastern countries would do better in a more competitive market. But a few people in the Middle East are beginning to think that their governments may obtain larger incomes by sharing in the profits of oligopoly,

[3] Ibid., pp. 37–38.

either an oligopoly of oil companies or, better, an oligopoly of Middle Eastern governments controlling supply.

While current interest is thus in control of supply, the long-run goal is still nationalization. Even if the Arabs and Iranians were shown that nationalization would not release them from the dominance of the international majors, as long as the latter controlled world markets outside the United States, they probably would remain attached to this goal. Indeed, they would gain in dignity through operation of their own industry, even if the financial gains were nil or even if they lost income by the change. An African leader has said, "It is far better to be free to govern, or misgovern yourself, than to be governed by anybody else." Most Arabs and many Iranians would say that it is far better to manage, even mismanage, your own oil industry than to have it managed by others.

In general, Arabs and Iranians approach the problem of oil with deep-seated suspicions, suspicions of the oil companies and of western governments. The bitterness, the distrust, and the fear of the oil companies—hatred is scarcely too strong a word —among the younger, educated Arabs and Iranians has to be experienced by direct contact to be believed. It is, of course, a legacy of western imperialism, particularly a legacy of the division and apportionment of much of the Middle East between Britain and France after the First World War; memories of past oppressions and humiliations are long. There is a feeling that the oil companies tend to support the *status quo,* tend to support reactionary governments and governments with vested interests in a divided Arab world—though it is not made clear how the companies can do anything but work with the constituted political authorities, whether they be modern progressive governments, ancient feudal regimes, tribal sheikhs, or British political residents.

Fundamentally, the Arabs look at oil as a weapon in their national struggle for independence and unity, and many Iranians possess the same outlook. Oil men miss the point when they sit in New York and London and calculate in commercial terms alone the gains which the Arabs or the Iranians can hope to make from an unorthodox agreement with an Italian oil company or a Japanese independent. Pecuniary returns are often of far less importance than the desire to become independent of the international majors, and money will be sacrificed for national pride. Considerable risks may even be taken: "If driven to despair in the West's correct understanding of their planning and aspirations, the Arabs can handle their oil in a technically and economically hazardous way." [4] The blocking of the Suez Canal by the Egyptians and the blowing up of the Iraq Petroleum Company pipeline pumping stations by the Syrian army, both during the Suez affair in 1956, are evidences of an Arabian willingness to make economic sacrifices for national independence. Americans and Europeans whose ancestors revolted in the name of liberty should hesitate to call these activities irrational.

[4] Haliq, *op. cit.*, p. 16.

XI

Guidelines to the Future

THE market for Middle East oil is an oligopoly, but there is little evidence to support the view that the international majors are in a cartel. The large oil companies are aware of the actions of one another, hesitate to lower prices (knowing that reductions will be matched), and elect policies that seem most likely to bring stability. But, in the period following the Second World War, it is extremely doubtful that they have entered into formal agreements to limit output, raise prices, or divide up markets. Major company actions may be consciously parallel; they have not, it appears, been concerted by agreement.

Because the market for Middle East oil is a *natural* oligopoly, reflecting the economics of large-scale exploration, production, and transportation in the Middle East, independents, with their smaller volumes and higher costs, find it difficult to gain entry and difficult to compete effectively. The advantages of the majors, however, are not exceedingly great, and good luck plus good management could eventually enable a number of low-cost independents to enter, enough, perhaps, to change the character of the market.

What can the large oil companies and the various governments do, over the years to come, to live with the market as it is and to encourage in it and in the environment at large those tendencies which seem most desirable for the future?

1. Policies for the International Majors

Great businesses should make sure that all projects for expansion are sound and economic; bigness must not become an end in itself. Expansion should take place only when it will bring economies of larger-scale operation. Above all, oil companies wanting to limit governmental intervention in the oil trade will hesitate before they expand for the purpose of promoting stability; they will hesitate before they try to win a concession or a sale which will not give them additional economies of scale but which may assist in checking the entry of other, perhaps unstabilizing firms. Stability is of value and is a generally valid objective, but in Middle East oil the tendency has been to serve it too well, at the expense of progressive change.

A policy of avoiding uneconomic expansion will include a policy of forgoing the purchase of sound and economic independent operations, perhaps even a policy of forgoing the purchase of oil which is for sale by independents and threatening to unsettle markets. The "ventilation" provided by the sales of nonaffiliated firms is most desirable in the rather rigidly structured market for Middle East oil, and the existence of numerous healthy independents is in the long-run interest of the majors.

In order to make easier the successful entry of additional independents, the international majors ought also to give serious thought to relinquishing some acreage when, under the terms of their concessions, they hold very large tracts. Independents would have a chance of picking up some of the relinquished acreage as governments offered it in new concessions. Relinquishment would make the Middle East a little more like areas such as western Canada where concessions are granted on a checkerboard pattern and part of the squares are reauctioned by the governments concerned after oil has been discovered. It is true that provisions for relinquishment are not in most of the Middle Eastern concessions, whereas such provisions were a part of the checkerboard concessions when granted, enabling the companies, who knew in advance that they would have to give up part of their acreage, to plan accordingly. But more experienced and freer governments might have insisted upon a checkerboard pattern in the earlier days of Middle East oil. Moreover, concessions in the Middle East are unusually large and often cover entire countries, and the international majors have made extraordinarily high profits on their Middle Eastern properties. It would seem reasonable, then, that concessions be renegotiated with respect to the surrender of acreage. Actually, the Iraq Petroleum Company has relinquished its offshore holdings and has agreed in principle to relinquish part of its acreage ashore. The Kuwait Oil Company, on the other hand, holds all the land of Kuwait in its concession and so far has revealed no plans for relinquishing any of it. (It is possible that the Kuwait government has not asked for relinquishment.)

In order to promote a more competitive market, the international oil companies also should encourage the open-market sale of Middle Eastern government oil. With a larger number of suppliers, the market probably would be more competitive, and the companies would be less vulnerable to criticism. To get Middle Eastern governments to sell their own royalty oil, the majors would have to stop taking it from them at posted prices; they might negotiate with the Arabs and Iranians an agreement to reduce by 5 percent a year the price at which they acquire this oil, these annual reductions to continue until adequate incentives were given the governments to market their own oil. At first the Arabs and Iranians probably would oppose elimination of oil company obligations to purchase royalty oil at attractive prices, but it seems likely that in time they would recognize their interest in becoming less dependent on the international majors. And the oil companies would be in a stronger position to face their critics when they were no longer buying what might be thought of as Arab and Iranian "distress oil."

Although it is not feasible to contemplate the breaking up of existing ventures in joint production, the international majors would be wise to avoid new joint ventures which interlock them more tightly in world oil markets. The majors are large enough so that each can spread its risks around the world in a series of distinct, solo projects; there is no need for such giants to divide up the risks of a single venture by calling in a number of companies. One suspects that present-day joint exploration is usually undertaken by large oil companies to check stockholder criticism of a failure to discover oil. The officers of corporation A can point out that corporations X, Y, and Z also invested in an unsuccessful project and lost large sums of money. It does not seem unreasonable, however, to ask a large corporation, capable of obtaining diversification through numerous ventures in different parts of the world, to educate its shareholders on the necessity of experiencing losses in particular undertakings and the undesirability of moderating competition by the establishment of unnecessary joint operations.

Still, no matter to what extent the international majors restrain themselves from uneconomic growth, from the purchase of sound independent firms, from the purchase of government oil, and from unnecessary joint enterprises, they are likely to find themselves in the position of oligopolists for an indefinite period in the future. As oligopolists hoping to minimize government intervention, the majors should behave in large measure, over the long run, as though they were in a market of numerous competitors. Behavior of this sort would make their policies concerning price and output more defensible, for though short-run restraints on competition are desirable, the competitive model in the long run provides a close approximation to optimum price and output.[1]

[1] The reader at this point may want to review Chapter II, Section 1, "Competition or Monopoly: Quest for a Norm." It might be noted that

How, specifically, should oligopolists who want to follow the competitive pattern behave? They must act *unnaturally*, act as though a price reduction would not be matched immediately by their few rivals. They should study the competitive model, lower their prices over a period of time to long-run average costs (including necessary profits in costs), and ignore the fact that their price cuts, being matched by rivals, do not bring compensatory increases in output. They should over time eliminate geographical price discrimination, withdrawing supplies from distant, low-netback areas and increasing shipments to nearby, high-netback markets until the same netbacks are realized on deliveries to all destinations. In other words, we are suggesting that oligopolists should forgo the comforts of oligopolistic stability and enter upon the uneasy life of more competitive behavior. (Of course, the Arabs and Iranians, who will gain more influence in Middle East oil in the years to come, may not agree to such competitive conduct.)

Oil men sometimes claim that the enlightened and progressive large companies in international oil already behave in the manner suggested, that they do not charge all the traffic will bear, that they do not exercise the market power which their commanding position gives them. But there is reason to doubt that even the best companies practice the degree of restraint which is desirable. It is very difficult for a businessman to act contrary to his commercial inclinations, to ask himself new questions: not whether a price cut will be matched by his rivals or whether a price cut will produce a larger volume of sales, but whether a price decline would occur in a market of numerous competitors. Too many oil men have used the language of "oligopolistic rationality" in speaking to the writer for him to believe that the international majors do not behave as oligopolists. "Price cutting does not

---

advocates of market socialism model their systems on a classical, competitive capitalism; a good statement of this position is found in Oskar Lange, *On the Economic Theory of Socialism* (Minneapolis: University of Minnesota Press, 1938).

pay," they reply to suggestions that oil prices might be reduced. "Demand is inelastic, with a standard product competitors must meet the cut, and after prices are reduced, everyone ends up in the same market position as he held before the price cutting began." Moreover, it is very difficult for a businessman to be detached about the level of necessary profits. Most men are able to persuade themselves that they or their companies are worth whatever they can get. Oil men in the Middle East observe the extraordinary political risks of the area and conclude that all the profits they earn are necessary; they conclude that they are not exploiting their oligopolistic positions at existing prices. The writer is doubtful that profits need be so high, and he inclines to the belief that oil prices in the Middle East possess the rigidity of oligopoly.

But how large ought price reductions to be? We will find it useful to consider separately a reduction in prices to the costs (including necessary profits) of an average or representative Middle East holding and a reduction in prices to the costs of an exceptionally profitable operation such as the one in Kuwait.

It might be argued that should the oil companies reduce their prices to the costs of an average Middle East concession, the sales of Middle East oil relative to the sales of oil produced in other areas of the world would expand; sales would grow at the expense of Indonesia perhaps, or at the expense of North Africa, Western Canada, South America. Then it might be suggested that the attraction of low-cost, low-priced Middle East oil would lead consumers to become too dependent upon this one region for their supplies and undesirably check the economic development of other areas in possession of oil. The student of international oil can understand that consumers ought not become unduly dependent on a single source of foreign oil, and he can see that people in an underdeveloped country outside the Middle East would be unhappy to lose their best, quite possibly their only, hope of rapid economic development. But many areas which are well located or prolific in oil—probably Libya in

North Africa and Venezuela, perhaps others—could survive more vigorous competition from Middle East oil. Production would continue in these other regions, a considerable diversity of supply sources would be maintained—and world oil prices would be lower. To be sure, lower prices would hurt underdeveloped countries in possession of oil: lower prices might put countries with very poor fields out of the oil business and would probably force many of the others to reduce royalty and tax collections on oil, that is, force them to reduce their "rents," in order to keep their oil competitive. It does not seem right, however, that consumers of oil should carry a large part of the burden of assisting underdeveloped areas which possess high-cost oil. One is inclined to think that the burdens of foreign aid should be apportioned on some basis other than oil consumption.

The same conclusions follow when one considers the possibility of reducing Middle East prices to the long-run average costs of an exceptionally profitable concession such as the one in Kuwait. Some would argue that should the companies in Kuwait (Gulf Oil and British Petroleum) really take advantage of their low costs and cut prices accordingly, they would gain volume at the expense of other Middle East concessions, possibly put some of them out of business (Qatar, perhaps, or Bahrein Island), make consumers excessively dependent on this one source of supply, and force some governments in the Middle East other than Kuwait to reduce their royalty and tax collections in order to keep their oil competitive. (And it might be argued that Kuwait expansion would give the Kuwait government additional revenues which it does not need.) Yet the major concessions in the Middle East—Saudi Arabia, Iraq, and Iran—could survive the most vigorous competition from Kuwait, so that a diversity of supply sources in the Middle East would be maintained in the face of such competition. At the same time, with lower prices some excess, oligopolistic, profits would be eliminated. Consumers of Middle East oil should not be asked to forgo the lower prices at which they might buy Kuwait oil in order to assist people dwelling in Middle East countries with high-cost oil. Assistance to Middle Eastern countries which might be put out of the oil business by competition from Kuwait oil or assistance to countries which would receive smaller royalties and tax revenues as a consequence of this competition ought to be provided by a larger group than the consumers of oil.

Admittedly the thought of a marked increase in Kuwait oil revenues at the expense of other Middle Eastern countries is disturbing when this tiny state of 200,000 people already has so large an income from oil. Perhaps the ideal solution would expand Kuwait output, give lower prices to consumers, and then redistribute oil revenues from the wealthier to the poorer countries. The distribution of oil revenues generally in the Middle East leaves much to be desired, and a good deal can be said in any case for their redistribution. Being, however, largely a problem for Middle Eastern governments, the possibility of redistributing oil income will be discussed in the next section.

The writer concludes that insofar as Middle East oil is low-cost oil he would hope to see it expand steadily relative to production in other regions and steadily put pressure on world oil prices. To the degree that Kuwait oil, or other oil in the Middle East, is exceptionally low in cost, he would like to see it expand relative to production elsewhere in the Middle East, exerting pressure on the price of Middle East oil as well as on the world price of oil. Some oil men believe that when quality differences are taken into account Kuwait oil is already priced 10 to 15 cents per barrel below other Middle Eastern crudes; certainly Kuwait production has grown rapidly relative to production elsewhere in the Middle East. (See Appendix Table, pp. 269–270.)

Though it is in the long-run interest of the international majors to seek more competition in Middle East oil and to behave more competitively themselves, the writer does not really expect them to act in this manner. Members of an oligopoly generally behave as oligopolists.

2. Policies for Middle Eastern Governments

When they recognize that nationalization will not change their basic position vis-à-vis the international majors, as long as the latter control world markets outside the United States, the Arabs and Iranians might advantageously concentrate on developing independent routes to market. They might bring in sound independent companies and insist that these firms integrate vertically and avoid sales to the international majors. (At the same time the Arabs and Iranians would be wise to avoid driving unduly hard bargains with the new entrants; otherwise they might be forced to let them produce large quantities and disorganize world markets in order to give them an early return on the funds they have invested in large bonuses.) Middle Eastern governments can also develop an independence from the major oil companies by insisting that their own oil be sold in the open market rather than to the international majors. They will have to wean themselves from the attractive prices the majors are willing to pay them, prices which keep them in a state of dependence and which assist in preserving the market control of the majors. Although the development of independent routes to market is a slow process, and not as spectacular as nationalization, it will ultimately bring to the Arabs and Iranians very considerable benefits.

In the opinion of the writer, the Middle Eastern governments, as they gain a measure of control over output, would be wise to avoid oligopolistic or monopolistic behavior—except as a reaction to substantial state trading in the West, should that occur. And they would be wise to avoid putting pressure on the major companies to act as oligopolists, would be wise to avoid, for example, insisting that the companies engage in geographical price discrimination. Middle Eastern governments are bound to become increasingly involved in oil, but as governments they can forgo oligopolistic behavior, they can forgo limiting output in order to collect higher, oligopolistic prices. And as the Arab states become unified into an Arab nation, they would be wise not to place control of oil output in the hands of a central government; a dispersion of control over output can minimize the danger that monopolistic actions will be taken. Market control in the Middle East, whether by companies or governments, amounts to an open invitation for the governments of consuming countries to engage in state trading. Oligopoly or monopoly in the Middle East may lead to oligopsony, conceivably even monopsony, in the West. The Arabs and Iranians will not find western European consumers so acquiescent in market control as the authorities of Texas, Louisiana, and Oklahoma find consumers on the eastern seaboard of the United States, for the Arabs and Iranians are foreigners, not in the family, and their actions will arouse more quickly the anxieties of purchasers.

Now we come to the question of the distribution of oil revenues among governments. One finds two views on this subject. One view is that these gains are unearned incomes, economic rents, and that the Arabs and Iranians have no more right to collect them than any of the other peoples who dwell on the earth. Land, the economist's term for all natural resources, is the free gift of nature, say most of the classical economists and, of course, Henry George. The Arabs and Iranians did not put the oil there, they did not produce it, and so, some critics assert, they have no particular right to the income which they collect from it. The other view is that the Arabs and Iranians who control an area with oil are entitled to take, and to keep for themselves, all of the money which the oil companies, and indirectly the consumers, will pay them for the oil. The 200,000 Kuwaiti, according to this view, have a right to all of the riches of Kuwait oil. (It follows, according to some, that the West should use its military forces to defend them in their wealth.) Let us look into the subject of land and land rent.

Though the notion of land rent as an unearned income is

usually associated with the name of Henry George, classical economists long before he wrote had recognized, rightly, that there is something peculiar in land (natural resources) and the income from land. Adam Smith said that "the landlord demands a rent even for unimproved land" and "he sometimes demands rent for what is altogether incapable of human improvement." [2] David Ricardo wrote that "the interest of the landlord is always opposed to the interest of every other class in the community." [3] John Stuart Mill asserted that "the essential principle of property being to assure to all persons what they have produced by their labour and accumulated by their abstinence, this principle cannot apply to what is not the produce of labour, the raw material of the earth." [4]

Economists today generally observe that wages are the reward for labor, interest the reward for waiting, and profit the reward for bearing risk. Many economists go on to say that land rent is received by men who perform no service at all. The landowner, the owner of natural resources, simply gets there first and puts up a fence. Indeed, the basic truth that land rent is an unearned income has never been effectively refuted (though it has often been ignored).

Ideally the economic rents of the world would be collected in taxes by a world government and distributed in some manner to people generally, perhaps equally, or in accordance with need. (Should this be done, the West—rich in natural resources and a similarly unearned inherited technology—might expect to see collected in its territories more than was spent there.) In the absence of world government, the detached economist can advocate that all economic rents be as widely distributed as polit-

[2] *Wealth of Nations*, 5th ed. (1789), Book I, chap xi.

[3] *An Essay on the Influence of a Low Price of Corn on the Profits of Stock* (1815), in *The Works and Correspondence of David Ricardo*, Vol. IV, ed. Piero Sraffa (Cambridge: The University Press, 1951), p. 21.

[4] *Principles of Political Economy* (London: Longmans, Green, 1871), Book II, chap. ii, para. 5.

ically feasible. (Foreign aid to underdeveloped countries might be viewed, accordingly, as a matter of simple justice, an international redistribution of economic rents.)

A wider distribution of oil revenues in the Middle East might be accomplished through a Middle East development fund or bank or through an Arab development fund or bank. Proposals for an Arab development bank and an Arab development fund are not new; it has often been suggested that the Arab governments and the oil companies should turn over a certain percentage of their oil incomes to one or the other of these proposed institutions. But a scheme in which larger sums were paid by governments and companies benefiting from unusually fortunate discoveries—a scheme, that is, which varied contributions according to the value of the different oil fields found in the Middle East—would conform to the knowledge that surpluses associated with natural resources, and available for public use, vary with the location and the quality of the resources under consideration.

A wider distribution of economic rents in oil might be promoted by the political unification of Arab countries. Unification could lead to a co-ordinated, regionally planned expenditure of oil revenues. (But the Arabs would want to learn a lesson from Indonesia, and move cautiously. One factor which contributed to the disintegration of central government authority in Indonesia, and to civil war there, was the dissatisfaction of the people on the island of Sumatra, who felt that too small a share of the revenues from their island's oil was being spent on their behalf.)

Although very serious political difficulties stand in the way of a redistribution of economic rents in Middle East oil, it should be understood that an Arab state such as Kuwait, fortunately situated in an oil-rich area and surrounded by less fortunate Arabs living in extreme poverty, has a very weak moral claim to all of its oil revenues. The notion that the Kuwaiti did not produce the oil over which they live strikes one with great force when one contrasts their wealth with the plight of the Arabs in surrounding countries, who live on the edge of starvation. With the tiny state of Kuwait receiving its vast income, large possibilities of *regional* development remain unrealized. Outlets for investment of oil revenues in Kuwait itself, with its barren soil and its 200,000 people, are very limited. After the hospitals, schools, homes, roads, and sea-water distillation plants have been built, the possibilities of productive outlays are few. A large part of Kuwait's income goes to London where it is invested in the City. In western eyes this appears to be very sensible; the funds will be at the disposal of Kuwait later, perhaps when the oil is depleted, and meanwhile the City of London seems to be a good place to put it. But the arrangement looks quite different to an Arab who feels deeply the plight of his region. Arabs are hungry, he says, and in rags while an Arab land is *exporting* capital to a developed nation. Actually, it is doubtful that the Kuwaiti themselves, in exclusive receipt of large revenues, are as well off as they might be. Were Kuwait part of a larger Arab union, its oil revenues would be invested in regional development, mostly in the Fertile Crescent, in Iraq, Syria, and perhaps Lebanon, and the Arabs of Kuwait would follow the capital north, moving in the traditional pattern of Arab migration out of the peninsula into the more productive Crescent.

The writer finds it difficult to believe that the Arabs of Kuwait can be happy living, however luxuriously, in lax, undignified, and weak dependence on a foreign power to protect them in their wealth (Kuwait is dependent on British protection) when they might be participating actively in the development of a united Arab nation. Indeed, Arab nationalism finds a great deal of support in the Sheikhdom, particularly among younger people.

3. Policies for Western Governments

However much U.S. authorities may dislike joint production in the Middle East, believing it a check on competition, an attempt to break up these joint enterprises would be undesirable. Division of the assets of any jointly owned company would be extremely difficult. Division of the assets of the Arabian American Oil

Company, which with its entirely American ownership is the most likely candidate for a Department of Justice offensive, would be pointless. Aramco's giant Ghawar field (140 miles long) must be treated as a unity. If Aramco were broken up and no longer able to control the output of the Ghawar field, the Saudi government, in the interest of conservation and following the model of the Texas Railroad Commission, would have to step in, establish output, and prorate it among the several owners. Competition in the oil of the Ghawar field would be checked through the actions of Saudi authorities, and the breaking up of Aramco would have done little to make Middle East oil more competitive. Indeed, in all of the producing countries of the Middle East the growing interest of governments in controlling production probably would defeat the purpose of breaking up the jointly held concessions. The likelihood that a Middle Eastern government would permit the several parts of a dismembered operating company to produce so free of control as seriously to compete with one another is small, so small that it would not be worth while to undertake the exceedingly difficult and painful task of breaking up an existing joint enterprise.

At the same time, however, western governments might discourage new joint endeavors on the part of the international majors. Each of these companies is large enough to spread its risks over a series of distinct projects and need not divide the risks of a single venture with other firms. By discouraging new joint enterprises, western governments could see a small measure of competition added to world oil markets unless future control of production by the Arabs and Iranians turns out to be so tight as to prevent all competition between different producers in a country, no matter how carefully separated.

Western governments should be careful not to discourage, through exchange controls or import licensing, new entrants into the marketing of Middle East oil. Independents or Middle Eastern governments bringing oil to market can increase the degree of competition in the oil of the Middle East.

Western authorities will have to move against geographical price discrimination very cautiously. To repeat an earlier conclusion: The experience of ECA appears to indicate that a governmental agency which chooses to attack geographical price discrimination may hope to eliminate only major and prolonged discrimination of this sort. Difficulties in comparing f.o.b. and c.i.f. prices may arise, and it would have to recognize some value in stability and not expect frequent shifts in supply patterns or very frequent price adjustments. But even if an agency was very self-denying and sought only to eliminate large and enduring geographical price discrimination, it would run into many difficulties. The companies might withdraw small supplies from distant markets rather than reduce prices in those nearby; this could check competition at a distance without helping purchasers nearer the center of production. The companies, if they had alternative markets, might simply refuse to sell at scheduled or official prices in nearby markets, and an interruption of supply might cause trouble. Potential reformers who are unhappy about geographical price discrimination in oil markets may console themselves with the knowledge that such discrimination is ubiquitous in the imperfect markets of a modern economy and that, apparently, little can be done about it. A grocer, for example, who does not charge for delivery is discriminating against his nearby "cash and carry" customers.

While avoiding attempts to break up existing joint enterprises and while moving cautiously against geographical price discrimination, western authorities should do all that they can to encourage competition. Except as a reaction to the most serious and unyielding market imperfections in the production of oil, maintained by the international majors or by Middle Eastern governments, it would be very unwise for western governments to engage in state trading (or in limitation of imports for the purpose of obtaining lower prices). Efforts by consumers to obtain market control would force the Arabs and Iranians into counteraction, into efforts to control production—and the resulting bilateral oligopoly would be an unhappy state of affairs. The closer the oil industry remains to competition, the smaller the range of indetermination within which prices will have to be negotiated by buyers and sellers.

We have already said that western governments should think of Middle East oil purely as a commercial proposition. Whether it ends up a competitive market of private enterprises or a bilateral oligopoly of regulated production and state trading, the authorities in western countries should treat the oil of the Middle East simply as a matter of trade, as an economic question. Admittedly the politico-military approach will be increasingly hard to forgo if regulation of production and state trading become prevalent. This is an argument both for a competitive economy in Middle East oil and for uncommon restraint on the part of governments should such an economy prove impossible or undesired.

The writer believes that the West can accept the goal of Arab unity without fear that political unity will bring with it an oil monopoly. (An *oligopoly* of Arab governments regulating production is likely whether or not political unity comes.) Because of their diversity, Arabs who seek to unite a large area are likely to set up a federation rather than a unitary state. Each of the oil countries probably will insist on a large measure of control over its own oil policy, and the possibility that the various regions will disagree on matters of output and price is very real. It is not at all certain that the united Arabs could agree to restrict output in order to raise prices. Moreover, in all likelihood a united Arab world would face the competition of oil from Iran and Venezuela, the competition of coal and natural gas, and in time the competition of nuclear energy, shale oil, and oil from tar sands. Then, should an Arab oil monopoly seriously threaten, a western defense that would be more suitable than opposition to Arab political unity would be state trading, along with, perhaps, an appeal to international agencies in which both consuming countries and producing countries were represented.

Finally, officials in western governments should recognize that there is a great deal to be said for a redistribution of oil revenues among the people of the Middle East. Governmental oil revenues are economic rents, and the more widely they are distributed the better. Certainly the moral claim which the people of Kuwait have on their revenues is not great enough to warrant a western military defense of their position; it would not justify a western military effort to keep Kuwait, its oil, and its oil revenues from becoming part of a larger Arab union.

4. The Future Structure of the Market

Schumpeter in his *Capitalism, Socialism, and Democracy* expressed great admiration for capitalism—and forecast socialism. The present writer has expressed his belief that a more competitive market, largely but not entirely capitalistic (he would have governments market their own royalty oil), would be the most satisfactory institutional pattern for Middle East petroleum. But he is inclined to forecast a market which is not very competitive, and less and less capitalistic. It is fairly easy to foresee increasing state intervention in Middle East oil on both sides of the market —control of production by Middle East governments and state trading or control of imports by governments in consuming countries. The tendency is toward bilateral oligopoly, an oligopoly of sellers facing an oligopoly of buyers.

Should change in this direction continue, prices may increasingly be negotiated by governments. A wide range would exist within which they would be indeterminate (though not so wide a range as economists find in bilateral *monopoly*). Within the range of indetermination, in a terrain devoid of landmarks, prices would have to be set by bargaining; the outcome would be a reflection of the skill of the negotiators, their abilities to bluff, outmaneuver, and intimidate. One could anticipate long periods of extreme rigidity broken by intervals of intense struggle. Those who earlier feared the instability of a competitive market might learn to dislike a great deal more the alternating rigidity and extreme instability of a market dominated by governments. A certain nostalgia for competition might develop when it was seen that often, because it was thought equitable, an imagined competitive model was used as a basis for compromises between the contending state oligopolists and oligopsonists.

Why may we expect a large measure of state intervention in Middle East oil? In the first place, Middle East oil is a natural oligopoly and it is doubtful that the international majors will restrain themselves from acting as oligopolists. We have already (pp. 249–250) pointed to the compelling power of a businessman's commercial inclinations, to the attractive plausibility of "oligopolistic rationality," and to the difficulty of remaining detached about the level of necessary profits. The governments of consuming countries as a reaction to the prices of oil company oligopoly may interest themselves in state trading. These governments are even more likely to react to production control and an emergent oligopoly of Middle Eastern governments. Just as oil companies probably cannot follow a policy of restraint, so Middle Eastern governments, as they acquire the power to control production, are likely to use it and to act as oligopolists. Men exercise the power they possess and persuade themselves that they are entitled to what they can get.

Another factor tending to induce governmental intervention in Middle East oil, intervention by governments of both consuming and producing countries, is the inadequate moral authority of the international majors. These large companies are, as Dr. Frankel has observed, "international institutions"; [5] at least one oil man has described them as public utilities. But they lack the moral authority to fill a role so elevated; they cannot command the deep respect of the various parties whose conflicting interests they try to adjudicate. This is partly because their basic goal is profit, albeit profit in the long run. Commercial principles tend to rule their conduct in a market which is inadequately competitive (so that commercial conduct does not produce a socially optimum price and output) and in a milieu in which noneconomic

[5] P. H. Frankel, "Oil Supplies during the Suez Crisis," *Journal of Industrial Economics*, VI (1958), 97.

considerations are of extreme importance. Moreover, the profit motive itself is not accepted as a proper guide to human action by many people outside the United States and, indeed, is rejected by most intellectuals in the Middle East. The international majors can expect to find little support among the socialists.

There is little formal apparatus for governmental regulation of the oil companies such as exists for most public utilities in sectors of limited competition,[6] though a great deal of informal supervision is exercised by governmental agencies in the various countries. With widely dispersed stock ownership, managements are self-perpetuating as long as they keep their stockholders happy; their ultimate responsibility is to shareholders who represent only one interest in Middle East oil and not the most important, and who are concerned only with dividends.

Finally, the international majors lack moral authority to perform the role of international institutions effectively because their directors and upper-level executives are almost entirely western. They are unrepresentative and cannot be expected to recognize the interests of, and to serve equally well, all the nations who are concerned with Middle East oil.

One of the problems with which the world at large is faced is that . . . the world-wide activities of the U.S.A., including those of the American oil companies, are subject to domestic, nay parochial, political and economic interests. This creates difficulties at the best of times, in an emergency it may be fatal. By taking first place in world oil in normal times, the American oil companies have become responsible to the world and not only to Senate Committees.[7]

Dr. Frankel might have mentioned that the activities of European oil companies also are subject to the pressures of domestic interests.

---

[6] The British Government owns a majority of the stock in the British Petroleum Company and appoints 2 of its 12 directors. The French Government has a 35 percent interest in Compagnie Française des Pétroles and 40 percent of the voting rights.

[7] Frankel, "Oil Supplies during the Suez Crisis," p. 99.

It is, in the writer's opinion, no reflection on the ability or the dedication of world oil men to say that the companies they direct—motivated by profit, operated in accordance with commercial principles, responsible to shareholders, led by westerners —cannot adequately perform the role of international institutions. Under these circumstances and with the general drift of the world toward socialism along with the inclination of the Arabs and Iranians to control production, a general increase in intervention by governments becomes almost inevitable.

5. An International Oil Authority?

As governments in consuming countries and producing countries intervene more and more in the production and distribution of oil, new international institutions are likely to develop. Thought has been given to a European oil community, which, it is hoped, might improve the bargaining position of Europe with respect to the oil-producing countries of the Middle East. On the other side of the market, the Arab League petroleum department has long sought to co-ordinate oil policy in various countries, and recent interest in a unified control of Persian Gulf oil production, Iranian as well as Arab, could lead to the development of new regional bodies in the area. Eventually an international oil authority might be created, in which consuming countries and producing countries would both be represented. Such an organization might collect information, prepare plans, and act as an institution through which conflicting interests could be reconciled in an orderly manner.

But the advocates of an international body for oil probably will have to wait a long time for it to materialize. The Arabs are very suspicious of a proposal of this sort. They fear that an international organization would support the *status quo* in oil and "freeze the march of Arab economic progress." [8] People in the United States are likely to oppose an international oil authority as vigorously as the Arabs, though for different reasons;

[8] Haliq, *op. cit.*, p. 18.

they would oppose it in the name of free enterprise. It was resistance in the United States that defeated attempts to establish a world oil authority in 1944 and 1945.

On August 8, 1944, the governments of the United States and Great Britain signed an Agreement on Petroleum; it was an agreement to establish an International Petroleum Commission composed of eight members, four members to be appointed immediately by each government. The commission, among other things, was

To prepare long-term estimates of world demand for petroleum, having due regard for the interests of consuming countries and expanding consumption requirements;

To suggest the manner in which, over the long term, this estimated demand may best be satisfied by production equitably distributed among the various producing countries. . . .

To recommend to both Governments broad policies for adoption by operating companies. . . .[9]

The two governments also proposed the creation of a larger international organization to deal with oil:

With a view to the wider adoption and effectuation of the principles embodied in this Agreement they agree that as soon as practicable they will propose to the Governments of other interested producing and consuming countries an International Petroleum Agreement which, *inter alia*, would establish a permanent International Petroleum Council composed of representatives of all signatory countries.[10]

The agreement clearly was directed toward a unified and agreed control of production by interested governments. As such it was anathema to the American industry and contrary to prevailing American ideology. It was never ratified by Congress. A second, watered-down agreement was signed on Sep-

[9] Agreement on Petroleum between the Government of the United States of America and the Government of the United Kingdom of Great Britain and Northern Ireland, August 8, 1944, Article III.
[10] *Ibid.*, Article II.

tember 24, 1945. According to this agreement, the proposed commission was not "to suggest the manner in which . . . estimated demand may best be satisfied by production equitably distributed among the various producing countries. . . ." (the wording of the first agreement), but it was "to report as to means by which . . . demands and supplies may be correlated so as to further the efficient and orderly conduct of the international petroleum trade. . . ." [11]

The second agreement also stated "that no provision in this agreement shall be construed to require either Government to act upon any report or proposal made by the Commission, or to require the nationals of either Government to comply with any report or proposal made by the Commission." [12] But even the second, diluted agreement was never put into effect. The time for new international institutions in oil was not yet ripe.

Nevertheless, given the difficulty—very nearly the impossibility—of obtaining in Middle East oil a competitive market of numerous producers, given the multiplicity of political jurisdictions involved and the growing inclination of national governments in producing countries and consuming countries to intervene in oil production and distribution, given these circumstances, the development of international institutions devoted to oil becomes highly probable. For a time, perhaps for a very long time, conflicts will be settled in bilateral negotiations, in *ad hoc* conferences, or in existing international organizations. Eventually advantages may be seen in a continuing, specialized body, an international oil authority. It would be useless, however, to establish an organization of this sort ahead of world public opinion, since it would have to be a voluntary association and could be effective only as its resolutions were voluntarily accepted and implemented by the various countries concerned. Rather

[11] An Agreement on Petroleum between the Government of the United States of America and the Government of the United Kingdom of Great Britain and Northern Ireland, September 24, 1945, Article IV.

[12] *Ibid.*, Article VI. For an interesting discussion of the two agreements see Frankel, *Essentials of Petroleum*, pp. 120–125.

than become attached to this particular dream, the dream of an international oil authority, those who have doubts about existing institutions should keep their minds open to a variety of possibilities.

Indeed, the free mind is the great hope of Middle East oil. There must be a willingness to experiment with new forms— mixed companies, unorthodox exploration contracts (such as Argentina negotiated with numerous oil companies in 1958 and 1959), new international bodies. Americans must avoid a doctrinaire adherence to capitalism, Arabs and Iranians avoid a dogmatic socialism. With knowledge, unfettered minds, and mutual respect, with genuine desires to discover the interests which they have in common and a determination peacefully to reconcile their interests which conflict, men can find satisfactory solutions to the problems of Middle East oil.

Appendix Table

Crude Oil Production in the Major Producing States of the
Middle East, in the Entire Middle East, in the Entire World
(thousands of barrels per day)

	Iran	Iraq	Saudi Arabia	Kuwait	Middle East total	World total
1937	213	87	0.2	—	321	5,590
1945	359	96	58	—	532	7,100
1946	403	98	164	16	701	7,540
1947	425	98	246	44	839	8,270
1948	521	72	392	127	1,140	9,400
1949	562	85	477	246	1,400	9,320
1950	665	128	547	344	1,747	10,400
1951	342	167	762	561	1,911	11,730
1952	30	374	825	747	2,075	12,320
1953	57	565	845	862	2,444	13,120
1954	62	615	953	952	2,729	13,710
1955	328	691	965	1,092	3,245	15,450
1956	542	638	986	1,093	3,451	16,670
1957	716	448	992	1,140	3,539	17,890
1958	826	729	1,015	1,396	4,270	17,990
1959	925	837	1,095	1,390	4,587	19,460

Sources: *World Oil*, August 15, 1958, pp. 128–130, February 15, 1960,
p. 95; Economics Division, Arabian American Oil Company, *Middle East
Petroleum Data* (n.p., 1957), p. 5.

Selected Bibliography

Arabian American Oil Company. *Middle East Oil Development.* New York: The Company, 1956.

Burck, Gilbert. "World Oil: The Game Gets Rough," *Fortune*, May, 1958.

Economic Commission for Europe, Secretariat. *The Price of Oil in Western Europe.* Geneva: United Nations, 1955.

Evans, William S. *Petroleum in the Eastern Hemisphere.* New York: First National City Bank of New York, 1959.

Frankel, P. H. "American Oil in a Changing World," *Oil Forum*, November, 1950.

——. *Essentials of Petroleum: A Key to Oil Economics.* London: Chapman & Hall, 1946.

——. "Oil Supplies during the Suez Crisis," *Journal of Industrial Economics*, 1958.

——. "The State of the American Oil Industry." Reprint of a series of articles published in the *Petroleum Times*, May–August, 1946.

——. "A Turning Point," *International Oilman*, 1957, American Petroleum Institute issue.

Grigg, Vernon Herbert. "The International Price Structure of Crude Oil." Ph.D. dissertation, Massachusetts Institute of Technology, Boston, June, 1954.

Haliq, Omar. "The Problem of Arabian Oil: An Arab Appraisal." A paper read at the Seventh Annual Arab Students' Convention, Urbana, Ill., 1958.

Jablonski, Wanda M. "How Could Aramco Compete against Its Owners?" *Petroleum Week*, October 18, 1957.

Jablonski, Wanda M. "Is Arabia Moving to a New 50-50 Oil Pattern?" *Petroleum Week,* February 22, 1957.

——. "Terms for New Saudi Concessions Spelled Out," *Petroleum Week,* June 20, 1958.

Laudrain, Michel. *Le Prix du Pétrole Brut: Structures d'un Marché.* Paris: Éditions Génin, n.d.

Laurence M. Marks & Co., Research Department. *Middle East Field Report.* New York: The Company, 1957.

Lenczowski, George. *Oil and State in the Middle East.* Ithaca, N.Y.: Cornell University Press, 1960.

Levy, Walter J. "The Past, Present and Likely Future Price Structure for the International Oil Trade," *Proceedings Third World Petroleum Congress* (Leiden, 1951), Sec. X, Preprint 16, 1951.

Longrigg, Stephen Henry. *Oil in the Middle East: Its Discovery and Development.* Rev. ed. London: Oxford University Press, 1961.

Organization for European Economic Co-operation. *Europe's Growing Needs of Energy: How Can They Be Met?* Paris: The Organization, 1956.

Penrose, Edith Tilton. "Profit Sharing between Producing Countries and Oil Companies in the Middle East," *Economic Journal,* June, 1959.

Shwadran, Benjamin. *The Middle East, Oil and the Great Powers.* 2d ed., rev. New York: Council for Middle Eastern Affairs Press, 1959.

United States, Federal Trade Commission. *The International Petroleum Cartel.* Washington, D.C., 1952.

United States, Mutual Security Agency, Industry Division, Petroleum Branch. *Statement on ECA/MSA Petroleum Price History.* Submitted to Monopoly Subcommittee, Senate Small Business Committee, August 15, 1952.

United States, Senate, Subcommittees of the Committee on the Judiciary and Committee on Interior and Insular Affairs. *Emergency Oil Lift Program and Related Oil Problems,* Hearings, 85th Congress, February, 1957.

United States vs. Standard Oil Company of California, the Texas Company, and several ("Caltex") affiliates. 155 F.Supp. 121.

Index

273